WALKING
WITH JESUS

WALKING WITH JESUS

DAILY INSPIRATION FROM THE GOSPEL OF JOHN

GREG LAURIE

BakerBooks

Grand Rapids, Michigan

© 2007 by Greg Laurie

Published by Baker Books
a division of Baker Publishing Group
P.O. Box 6287, Grand Rapids, MI 49516-6287

Printed in the United States of America

Library of Congress Cataloging-in-Publication Data
Laurie, Greg.
    Walking with Jesus : daily inspiration from the Gospel of John / Greg Laurie.
        p.   cm.
    Includes bibliographical references.
    ISBN 10: 0-8010-6815-0 (pbk.)
    ISBN 978-0-8010-6815-7 (pbk.)
    1. Bible. N. T. John—Meditations. 2. Devotional calendars. I. Title.
BS2615.54.L38 2007
242'.2—dc22   2007026745

CONTENTS

INTRODUCTION

A BACKSTAGE PASS

Sometimes the Bible can be seen as an overwhelming read. Though most of us own one, many of us have never fully understood its primary message. Needless to say, that is a huge mistake, as it is God's very message to humanity. The Bible is God's very message to you.

When I talk to people who want to read the Bible but aren't sure where to start or what to make of what they've read so far, I point them to one place: the Gospel of John. John wrote his version of the life of Jesus so that unbelievers might believe, making it the perfect introduction to Jesus, to his mission here on earth, and to God's extraordinary love for his people. I believe John's Gospel has the power to transform lives. I believe anyone who says, "God, if you are real, reveal yourself to me," will find God in the words of this Gospel. I believe it because I've seen it happen.

Yet John wrote his Gospel not only to convince the skeptic but to encourage believers in the commitment we have already made. John 20:31 sums up John's hopes for his work: "But these are written that you may believe that Jesus is the Christ, the Son of God, and that believing you may have life in his name." John was saying that the more we believe, the more life we will experience.

John brought a unique perspective to his Gospel. In fact, 90 percent of the material found in John's Gospel is not found in any of the other three. It is in John's Gospel that we find the great "I am" statements of Christ: "I am the bread of life" (6:48); "I am the light of the world" (8:12; 9:5); "I am the good shepherd" (10:11, 14); "I am the resurrection and the life" (11:25); and of course, "I am the way and the truth and the life" (14:6).

Perhaps the reason we find so much new insight in John's story is that he was particularly close to Jesus. His view of Jesus is that of an insider. Following John through these events is like having a backstage pass, so to speak, to the ministry of Jesus. Peter, James, and John went with the Lord on a number of occasions when the other disciples did not. They were there when Jesus was transfigured. They were there when he raised Jairus's daughter from the dead. They were there when Jesus experienced a night of agony in the Garden of Gethsemane.

Interestingly, John refers to himself as "the disciple whom Jesus loved." At first, this almost sounds boastful, as if to say, "Jesus loved me more than the rest." But that wasn't it at all. It was simply an acknowledgment of God's love for him. So often, we struggle to believe God can love us as much as we hope he will. Yet John assures us, over and over, that God loves us far more than we can imagine.

In the days ahead, you'll read about the earliest days of Jesus's ministry and how he responded to people in need, people looking for answers, people who were hurting and empty, people who were alone and without hope. As you spend time with these devotional readings, my prayer is that you "may have power, together with all the saints, to grasp how wide and long and high and deep is the love of Christ, and to know this love that surpasses knowledge—that you may be filled to the measure of all the fullness of God" (Eph. 3:18–19), and that along with John, you will be able to say, without a doubt, that you are a disciple whom Jesus loves.

WHEN HEAVEN CAME DOWN

> We know also that the Son of God has come and has given us
> understanding, so that we may know him who is true.
> And we are in him who is true—even in his Son Jesus Christ.
> He is the true God and eternal life.
>
> 1 John 5:20

In December 1956, a television game show called *To Tell the Truth* made its debut on CBS. The show featured three contestants who all claimed to be the same person. It was the job of a four-member celebrity panel to determine which contestant was telling the truth. The show always ended with that now-famous question, "Will the real _____ please stand up?" The outcome was always a big surprise.

Now imagine you're one of those panelists. There are three contestants on the show claiming to be Jesus, and it's your job to determine which one is the real thing. The first contestant stands up. He has brownish-blond hair and a short, well-trimmed beard. You notice his piercing blue eyes and the otherworldly expression on his face. He is holding a staff in one hand and has a lamb draped around his neck for good measure. So you think, "Hey! He looks a lot like those pictures I've seen. That's Jesus for sure!"

The next contestant stands up and says, "I am Jesus." When he glances your way, he seems to have this look of approval regarding who and what you are. He looks completely nonjudgmental, and more to the point, rather benign. This Jesus seems like a guy who would make you feel better about yourself. So you think, "Maybe that's the real Jesus."

Then the third contestant stands up. Right away, you notice a stark contrast to the other two. He appears to be strong and masculine. At the same time, there seems to be a tender quality about him. As you look closer, you notice he radiates goodness, even holiness. And suddenly you start feeling a little uncomfortable. You realize you're not the person you ought to be. There is something that needs to change. But when you make eye contact with him, instead of seeing rejection and condemnation, you see love—not a watered-down love like the other guy but a sense of someone who loves with genuine affection and care. He makes you want to be a better person. He makes you want to change.

So which Jesus will you choose? Will you choose the stained-glass-window Jesus? The benign Jesus? Or, will you choose the real Jesus of the Bible who loves you and yet challenges you to change? That is the Jesus before us in the Gospel of John. That is the Jesus who became flesh and walked among us.

Recognizing Jesus

Now, I don't know what Jesus looked like physically. It would appear that Jesus had a rather ordinary appearance. In speaking of the Messiah to come, the prophet Isaiah wrote, "He had no beauty or majesty to attract us to him, nothing in his appearance that we should desire him" (Isa. 53:2). After the resurrection, Mary thought he was the gardener (see John 20:11–16). The two disciples on the road to Emmaus took him to be an ordinary man (see Luke 24:13–27).

Jesus's physical appearance was so unimportant that John doesn't even give us a hint about what Jesus looked like. But he tells us more than enough about Jesus for us to recognize that the Lord was no ordinary man.

Believing the Witness

What a thrill it would have been to walk and talk with Jesus, to hear his voice with our own ears, and to see his face with our own eyes. How many of us have wished we could have been one of the twelve disciples who had the privilege of listening to him, speaking with him, hearing the timbre of his voice, and looking into his eyes? Yet those days are long gone. Or are they?

According to John, who personally walked and talked with Jesus during the Lord's earthly ministry, we can. In his epistle, 1 John, he wrote:

> That which was from the beginning, which we have heard, which we have seen with our eyes, which we have looked at and our hands have touched—this we proclaim concerning the Word of life. The life appeared; we have seen it and testify to it, and we proclaim to you the eternal life, which was with the Father and has appeared to us. We proclaim to you what we have seen and heard, so that you also may have fellowship with us. And our fellowship is with the Father and with his Son, Jesus Christ.
>
> 1 John 1:1–3

John was saying that we can have a relationship with God as significant as the one he had. "We walked with him," John was saying. "We talked with him. We had that privilege. We spent practically every waking hour in his presence." The phrase John used, "which we have heard," also could be translated, "still ringing in our ears." John was saying, "I can still hear the tone of his voice, the inflections he used. I hear it still." Jesus made an impact on John, one John never forgot, one John shares with us.

LIVING WITH JESUS

Have you ever had someone stare at you—and keep staring? I'm sure Jesus experienced this on a regular basis. He would probably look down for a moment, look up, and find everyone staring at him. To those who loved him, he was indeed a spectacle—the very Son of God among them! They scrutinized Jesus's every move.

The apostles, and certainly John, understood this wasn't just a good man, this wasn't even a great prophet, as much as this was

God in human form. John was saying, "We were there. We saw him. We heard him. But our fellowship is with the Father, and you can enter into this fellowship with God as well."

Although we have not seen Jesus with our eyes, we believe we are invited into the fellowship of John and the disciples. We are invited to understand the living God with the same intimate knowledge experienced by those who shared meals and conversations with him. No longer do we need to ask the real Jesus to stand up. Instead, it's our turn to stand up and get real with Jesus. Are you ready?

2

GOD WITH SKIN ON

I live by faith in the Son of God,
who loved me and gave himself for me.

Galatians 2:20

We live in a world filled with gods. So we need to understand what makes Jesus so unique. He wasn't a man *becoming* a god; that's impossible. He was God who became a man. Sometimes we view God as distant and unapproachable, but our God is the one who loved us so much he wanted to live among us.

It reminds me of a story I heard about a little boy who was frightened one night during a great thunderstorm. He called out to his father from his bedroom and said, "Daddy, I'm scared. Come in here."

His dad, who had settled in for the night and wanted to go to sleep, told the little boy, "Son, it's all right. God is with you in that room right now. You're okay."

There was a moment of silence. Then the little boy shot back, "Dad, right now I need someone with skin on."

That's exactly who Jesus was. He was God with skin on. So if you've wondered what God is like, then take a look at Jesus. If you've wondered what God thinks about a sinner who repents and wants to be forgiven, look at how Jesus responded to the woman who was caught in the act of adultery (John 8:3–11), or Zacchaeus (Luke 19:1–9), or the woman at the well (John 4:5–26). If you've wondered how Jesus feels about hypocrisy, look at his attitude toward the Pharisees, for whom he saved his most scathing words (Matt. 3:7).

THE GOD-MAN

The deity of Jesus Christ is one of the primary themes of John's Gospel. John shows us that to know Jesus is to know God. Other religions either ignore Jesus altogether or mischaracterize him. For example, Jehovah's Witnesses don't believe Jesus was God. Buddhists believe Jesus Christ was a good teacher, but less important than Buddha. Hindus believe Jesus was just one of many incarnations, or sons of God. Muslims believe Jesus Christ was only a man, a prophet equal to Adam, Noah, or Abraham, all of whom are believed to be below Muhammad in importance.

The Bible is clear in pointing out that Jesus Christ was and is God himself. What sets John's Gospel apart from the others is that he doesn't start with the birth of John the Baptist or even the birth of Jesus. He goes back to the time before there was a little town called Bethlehem, and even before there was a garden called Eden. He even goes back to a time before there was a planet called Earth. John 1:1 tells us, "In the beginning was the Word, and the Word was with God, and the Word was God." John is pointing out the fact that, even before the creation of the universe, Jesus was always there. John isn't suggesting that Jesus had a beginning, because Jesus, being God, is eternal. Rather, Jesus has no beginning. He has no end.

ONE WITH GOD

There is another twist in the original language regarding the phrase, "the Word was with God." This could be translated, "the Word was continually toward God. God the Father and God the Son were face-to-face continually." The preposition "with" bears the idea of nearness, along with the sense of movement toward God. That is to say, there has always existed the deepest equality and intimacy in the Trinity. It is hard for us to grasp the Trinity, the fact that God is a triune being. How can God be Father, Son, and Holy Spirit, and yet be one?

It's a question that many of us have struggled with, sometimes passionately. I heard about a couple who went to a film about the life of Jesus Christ. Somehow, they got into a heated argument afterward about the Trinity. The argument escalated, and by the time they reached their home, it had turned violent. The police had to be called. Upon their arrival, the police arrested both husband and wife. The woman had suffered injuries on her arms and her face, while her husband had a scissors stab wound in his hand. The sheriff, commenting on the incident, said, "It is kind of a pitiful thing to go to a movie like that and fight about it. I think they kind of missed the point."

So let's put our scissors down when we discuss the Trinity. It is hard for us to understand a triune being: Father, Son, and Holy Spirit. But this triune being, this Almighty God, created the heavens and the earth. Many times, we read in the Bible that Jesus was the Creator. According to Colossians 1:16, "For by him all things were created: things in heaven and on earth, visible and invisible, whether thrones or powers or rulers or authorities; all things were created by him and for him." He is the hands-on Creator, bringing about all of the things that we see, bringing about our galaxies and our solar system.

THE LOVING DEITY

That God and Jesus are one is not just a theological issue. It is the heart of our faith. As Christians, we believe that our Almighty Creator, the one who created the whole universe, is more than a distant, powerful God. Our God put on skin and lived with us. God did this because he is passionate about us and wants to be in a relationship with us.

The Word became flesh. The Word lived among us. Ever since humanity's creation, God has sought to connect with us in love. We see this from the first book of the Bible to the last. In Genesis 2:18, we see God caring for Adam by giving him a partner. In Revelation, we see God issuing an invitation: "To him who is thirsty I will give to drink without cost from the spring of the water of life" (21:6). God is longing for fellowship with humanity. Why is that? Some would say it is because God is lonely. But God isn't lonely. God doesn't need fellowship with you or me. Yet at the same time, he does desire it. The Almighty God is among us. Isn't that amazing?

3

GOD IN OUR MIDST

When Jesus spoke again to the people, he said,
"I am the light of the world. Whoever follows me
will never walk in darkness, but will have the light of life."

John 8:12

God became a man. Jesus Christ, who has neither beginning nor end, who has always existed, came to this earth as a living, breathing human being. He walked this earth being fully God and fully man. The birth of Jesus was the union of the infinite with the finite. The one who is larger than life became the smallest form of human life. Jesus went from the throne of heaven to a feeding trough. He went from the presence of angels to a cave filled with animals. The one who sustains the world with his breath became dependent on a young girl.

So often, we focus on the deity of Jesus and forget just how deeply human he was. While it's true Jesus didn't have a sinful nature, he was exposed to the pressure and the presence of temptation. He experienced thirst, hunger, loneliness, and all of the other emotions we go through as men and women. A good example of this is the story of Jesus crossing the Sea of Galilee. The Lord was tired from the day's work and fell asleep. Then a radical storm hit. The disciples woke Jesus, saying, "Master, Master, we're going to drown!" (Luke 8:24a). What could be more *human* than falling asleep in the boat? But the Bible tells us, "He got up and rebuked the wind and the raging waters; the storm subsided, and all was calm" (verse 24b). What could be more *divine* than calming a storm? His own disciples were blown away, figuratively speaking, by this incredible display of power on the part of Jesus. They said, "Who is this? He commands even the winds and the water, and they obey him" (verse 25).

At the cross, we see the same. Nothing could be more human than Christ's crucifixion and death. Nothing could be more divine than the sky darkening, the veil in the temple ripping from top to bottom, and Jesus rising from the dead. God, who became a man, shone his light on humanity. John tells us, "In him was life, and that life was the light of all men" (John 1:4). This shows God's desire to shed his light, righteousness, and goodness into the world, and indeed, into every crevice of our lives.

A LIGHT IN THE DARK

We like to believe we are enlightened. As a human race, we are proud of our achievements and our social, technological, and scientific progress. We may point to our advances in computers, communication technology, space travel, and medical science as marks of our greatness. Yet with all of our progress, we haven't been able to overcome the basic ills of the human condition. In 1948, General Omar Bradley observed, "We are technological giants and moral midgets. We have discovered the mystery of the atom, but we have forgotten the Sermon on the Mount." Well said. And how true.

Yes, we live in darkness, a kind of darkness that permeates every level of our society and culture. It's impossible to turn on the news without seeing humanity at its worst: senseless violence, international turmoil, sexual perversion. It seems that everywhere we look, we see more and more darkness.

The Bible tells us that the love of God turns us from darkness to light (see Acts 26:18). In fact, the first thing God did in creation was to separate the light from the darkness: "And God said, 'Let there be light,' and there was light. God saw that the light was good, and he separated the light from the darkness" (Gen. 1:3–4). We aren't meant to live in the darkness, but to be people of the light.

Shining that light in the darkness around us is what being a Christian is all about. Matthew 5:16 says, "In the same way, let your light shine before men, that they may see your good deeds and praise your Father in heaven." Sometimes our efforts at bringing light to the world will be met with ridicule or resistance. But think about it: When you're sound asleep in your nice, dark room, you usually don't like it when someone flips on the light and announces it's time to wake up. It's this very process of being uncomfortable by the blinding love of God that can help to spiritually awaken us.

A LIGHT ALONG THE WAY

We are born with an innate sense that there is more to life than what we know. God designed every man and every woman with a homing instinct, if you will, for something more. That is why, from the moment we are born, we are on a quest to find that something that will give us a sense of purpose, of meaning.

Sometimes we think, "It is right around the corner . . . that next relationship . . . that next job . . . that next possession . . . that next experience. Once I have that, I know I will be happy." But none of this leads to fulfillment, because what we long for is something else altogether. This homing instinct is driving us toward God.

And God is waiting for us.

We are drawn to God's radiant light. It is a light that exposes all of our spiritual and moral deficiencies, but it is not only there to reveal our shortcomings. It is also there to light the way to our salvation. God's light is there so we can see our way through the darkness and come into his light.

4

How Not to Become a Christian

We did not follow cleverly invented stories when we
told you about the power and coming of our Lord Jesus Christ,
but we were eyewitnesses of his majesty.

2 Peter 1:16

So how do you come into his light? How do you become a
Christian? First, let's look at three ways you *cannot* become a
child of God, according to John 1:

Yet to all who received him, to those who believed in his name,
he gave the right to become children of God—children born not
of natural descent, nor of human decision or a husband's will,
but born of God.

verses 12–13

You cannot be a Christian simply by being born into a Christian family. I'm amazed at how some people, when asked how
they know they are Christians, will answer, "Because I think my
grandfather was," or, "Because my mother is a Christian." It's
as though they believe their family has Christian genes. Having
Christian parents is a great privilege. But you still must personally believe in Jesus. You cannot live off the faith of family.

You cannot make yourself a Christian by your own will. Not
only does faith have nothing to do with your family background,
it has nothing to do with desire. You can't just say, "From this
moment on, I am a Christian." Becoming a Christian involves
putting one's faith in God. Commitment. It involves turning
away from sin, and trusting Jesus for your salvation. It involves
saying yes to God's invitation to change your heart.

You cannot become a Christian by sheer determination. No one in the world can make you a Christian. No minister or priest can make you a Christian by baptism or a sacrament. You cannot be reborn through a ceremony, or by reading a creed, or by standing up or sitting down, or by going forward, or by kneeling at a bench. None of these things, in and of themselves, will make you a Christian.

SO HOW DO YOU BECOME A CHRISTIAN?

Now that we've covered how *not* to become a Christian, let's look at how to become one. We find the answer in verse 12: "Yet to all who received him, to those who believed in his name, he gave the right to become children of God." Being a Christian is not merely following a creed, though it would include that. It is not merely believing certain truths, though it is that, too. It is receiving Christ into your life as Savior and Lord. There has to be a point when you are awakened to your spiritual need and say, "God, I know I'm a sinner. I know I don't measure up. Your light has crept into the crevices of my life, and you have exposed my spiritual nakedness. You have shown me my vulnerability and my need. At the same time, I know I can't become a Christian in my own strength. So I am coming to you on your terms. I am turning from my sin. I believe that your Son, Jesus, the Word who created all things, became a man and walked among us. I believe that he died on a cross for my sin. I put my faith in you. I choose to follow you."

GOD'S GIFT

Becoming a Christian is not unlike having a gift offered to you. God is offering you a gift, but you need to accept and open the gift.

People are funny about opening gifts. People who know me know that they don't need to spend much time on wrapping a gift they give me. To me, wrapping is merely an obstacle. It's just keeping me from the thing I really want, which is what's in the box. That's all I care about.

My wife, on the other hand, enjoys—and will often prolong—the unwrapping process. I don't understand it, but when someone gives Cathe a gift, she'll say, "Thank you so much!" Then she'll set the gift aside for a while. I can't do that. If someone gives me a gift, I want to open it immediately. I want her to do the same, so I ask, "Cathe, are you going to open your gift?"

"I'm going to do it later," she'll tell me. "I'm going to eat dinner first."

"The gift?" I remind her when dinner is over.

"I am going to have dessert."

"The gift?" I will ask, halfway through dessert.

"I am going to have my coffee."

"Open the gift!" I say, unable to stand it any longer. "How can you just sit there in the presence of an unopened gift?"

WHY WAIT?

In the same way, God has given each of us a gift, but it's not any good until we open it. The gift is just sitting there. Maybe you're thinking, "I'll get to it later. I know it's there. It gives me a good feeling to know it is there. I just love the fact that it is there." But wait a second. You need to receive it. You need to open this gift. Until you have done so, you are not experiencing what God has in store for you.

You can say, "I know Jesus is the Lord. I know he is the Creator of all things. I know he died on the cross. I know he has the answer to all my questions. I know he can forgive me of my sins. He is there knocking. It's nice to know he's right there." But that's not enough. A gift is only good once it's being used. So reach out and receive the gift.

Your Christian family can't do it for you. You can't do it for yourself just by saying, "I believe in my own way." You have to say, "Lord, I receive your gift of eternal life, happily and gladly. I choose to follow Jesus."

Have you done that yet?

"I haven't done it, but I am so close," you say.

I am glad you are close. But consider this: Until you believe, you are not really any closer to becoming a Christian than an avowed atheist. Even though you may intend to believe, my point is that until you have acted on it, nothing concerning your eternal destiny has changed. It is not enough to be close. You also have to believe. You have to receive. You have to say yes. You have to open your gift.

5

WHAT DO YOU WANT?

Come to me, all you who are weary and burdened,
and I will give you rest.

Matthew 11:28

"What do you want?" This was the first question to come from
the lips of Jesus during his earthly ministry. He asks that same
question of us today: "What do you want? What are you looking for in life?"

How will you answer?

Deep in our hearts, most of us know what the answer should
be. Yet our lives tell a different story. We seek out power, possessions, recognition, not a meaningful relationship with Jesus.
But Jesus knows that's what we need most. And he asks the
question so that we will acknowledge that need. This is why
Jesus said to the sick man, "Do you want to get well?" (John
5:6). We may wonder, "What kind of question is that? Of course
he would." Not necessarily. For instance, not every person who
has an alcohol or substance abuse problem wants to be free. Not
every person who is living a sinful lifestyle wants to leave that
life behind. Not every person, no matter how miserable his or
her life is, wants to change. But when we are ready for God's
help, God is there.

COME AND SEE

The day Jesus met the two men in the following story, he
asked them what they were looking for. They ended up getting
more than they bargained for because Jesus got to the real need
in their lives. And he will do the same for you. His words to

them were "Come and see," and he is still saying the same today. Let's read about it:

> The next day John was there again with two of his disciples. When he saw Jesus passing by, he said, "Look, the Lamb of God!" When the two disciples heard him say this, they followed Jesus. Turning around, Jesus saw them following and asked, "What do you want?" They said, "Rabbi" (which means Teacher), "where are you staying?" "Come," he replied, "and you will see." So they went and saw where he was staying, and spent that day with him. It was about the tenth hour. Andrew, Simon Peter's brother, was one of the two who heard what John had said and who had followed Jesus. The first thing Andrew did was to find his brother Simon and tell him, "We have found the Messiah" (that is, the Christ). And he brought him to Jesus. Jesus looked at him and said, "You are Simon son of John. You will be called Cephas" (which, when translated, is Peter).
>
> John 1:35–42

This is a classic example of how various people come to faith in Jesus Christ, as well as an illustration of how differently Jesus dealt with each of these people. The first two men, John and Andrew, heard John the Baptist proclaim Jesus as the "Lamb of God," and as a result, sought out Jesus for themselves. Then Andrew, who had begun to follow Jesus the day before, brought his brother Simon Peter to Jesus.

CONVERSIONS THAT COUNT

The story goes on to include Philip, who apparently did not have any believer to really help him, but Jesus himself sought this person out: "The next day Jesus decided to leave for Galilee. Finding Philip, he said to him, 'Follow me.' Philip, like Andrew and Peter, was from the town of Bethsaida" (John 1:43–44).

Then, the newly converted Philip sought out Nathanael and invited him to come and see for himself:

Philip found Nathanael and told him, "We have found the one Moses wrote about in the Law, and about whom the prophets also wrote—Jesus of Nazareth, the son of Joseph." "Nazareth! Can anything good come from there?" Nathanael asked. "Come and see," said Philip.

John 1:45–46

Everyone is different. Perhaps you have heard the testimonies of people who have tragic backgrounds. Maybe they were involved in gangs, prostitution, or spent time in prison. Then, after coming to faith in Christ, their lifestyle changed dramatically— almost overnight. After hearing testimonies like these, you start to feel as though your conversion may not be as significant as theirs. You think, "Nothing quite that dramatic has ever happened to me!" But this doesn't mean these believers had a better conversion than you. It is just a different one.

We need to keep one simple thing in mind: God gives us all the same gift. We all receive the same grace. We all have sin in our lives. We were all on the road to eternal separation from God. We were all saved by the love of Christ. So you see, every one of us has a testimony that is worth sharing.

FAITH AND FEELINGS

Just as people have different kinds of personalities and temperaments, people come to faith in different ways. Some may have a tremendous emotional experience at the moment they decide to follow Christ, while others may not. I didn't. When I prayed and asked the Lord to come into my life, I didn't feel a thing. So I wrongly concluded that perhaps I wasn't even converted. But God wants us to live not just by feelings but by faith. As Romans 1:17 reminds us, "The righteous will live by faith." Emotions are not bad; you may experience God in a very real and profoundly emotional way. But this doesn't happen for everyone.

We all come to Christ differently. Andrew and John found Jesus through a preacher's message. Simon Peter and Nathanael came to Jesus as the result of the personal efforts of another believer. In the case of Philip, there was no human instrument used by God. He literally met Jesus in the middle of a regular day. It didn't matter what these men were looking for. What they found was Jesus.

6

THE INVESTIGATOR

*I too was convinced that I ought to do all that was possible
to oppose the name of Jesus of Nazareth.*

Acts 26:9

The Bible is filled with great characters. Some are the center of attention, others sit on the sidelines. But all of them have stories to tell. For example, we don't know as much about Andrew as we do about many of the other apostles. He seems to have been an inquisitive person, someone who wanted to know something for himself. John the Baptist, whom Andrew was following, pointed him to Christ.

Understand that at this point, John the Baptist was the greatest prophet of all time. Jesus said, "Among those born of women there is no one greater than John" (Luke 7:28). He was the last of a long line of great prophets God had raised up to speak to his people. He was a major figure and was followed and respected by many. It is worth noting that the ancient Jewish historian, Josephus, wrote more about John than he did about Jesus Christ himself.

So, it was a major event when one day John pointed to Jesus and said, "Look, the Lamb of God!" (John 1:36). Any Jew would have readily understood the significance of that statement. In the system of sacrifices used at that time, a lamb was offered to atone for the sins of the people. They would understand that John was saying, "There is the one who will take away our sins. There is the Messiah we have been longing for. That's the One. Follow him!"

GETTING THE DETAILS

You'd think that statement alone would be enough to convince a person. So great was John's position as a prophet and spokesman for God that if John the Baptist said to follow Jesus, you followed Jesus.

In fact, Andrew had such great respect for John that he turned to go with Jesus, but he also wanted to know more about this new leader. Our Lord turned around to find John and Andrew following him. So he asked them, "What do you seek?"

Ever have one of those moments when you were asked a question by a person for whom you have tremendous respect, and you're not quite sure how to answer? John and Andrew were probably feeling awkward at this moment, unsure of what to say. So they asked Jesus where he lived.

Jesus responded, "Come and see." They may have assumed Jesus would take them to a palatial estate somewhere, complete with servants waiting on him hand and foot. But it's more likely Jesus took them to some little place he liked to hang out. Jesus didn't really have a home to speak of, as one of the most telling passages of the New Testament reveals: "Then each went to his own home. But Jesus went to the Mount of Olives" (John 7:53–8:1). While everyone went to the comfort and safety of a home, Jesus lived in the open air. He himself said, "Foxes have holes and birds of the air have nests, but the Son of Man has no place to lay his head" (Matt. 8:20).

CONVINCED AT LAST

John and Andrew stayed with Jesus most of the day. They were discovering that this was indeed the Lamb of God. This was the Messiah. Caution and inquisitiveness were now turning to conviction and belief. Now they knew he was the one they were looking for. This was the very Messiah of Israel, standing before them in flesh and blood.

When it comes to the question of belief, certain people just need to see for themselves. I'm the kind of person who will basically come to my own conclusions. I don't like it when people pressure me. If someone wants to sell me something, the worst thing they can do is try to put the pressure on so they can close the deal. If I decide I want to buy something, like a camera for example, I will do all kinds of research. I will read everything there is to read about that particular camera, and then I will check around and find the best deal possible. Then I will go out and purchase it. In most cases, I will know more about the item I am buying than the person who is selling it.

Some people need a little time to investigate things for themselves. After all, if someone can be pressured into a decision for Christ, he or she can be pressured out of it. If they can be pushed in, they can be pulled out. We need to remember that conversion is the work of the Holy Spirit and that God will do what it takes to draw that person to himself, even if that takes some time.

7

A FRIEND INDEED

Your Father, who sees what is done in secret, will reward you.

Matthew 6:18

We read a lot about Peter in the Bible. He even gets a couple of books all to himself. But Andrew, Peter's brother? Well, let's just say he did not get as much attention as his brother. Yet Andrew seemed to find a niche for himself among Jesus's friends. It may not have been a glamorous role, but you can bet it was an invaluable one.

Once Andrew was convinced Jesus was the Messiah, he brought his friends to meet Jesus. In John 1:41, Andrew brings his brother, Simon Peter, to meet Jesus. In John 6:8–9, we read of Andrew bringing a little boy with loaves and fishes to meet Jesus in the midst of a hungry crowd. In John 12, we read of some Greek men who were looking for Christ, and Andrew helped them meet Jesus. That was his *modus operandi*. Andrew was always bringing people to Jesus!

UNSELFISH FAITH

Now Andrew's efforts to help others meet Jesus might not sound all that exceptional to you, but I think a more selfish person would have kept all this Jesus business to himself; in particular, he would have certainly kept it from Peter. Peter was the kind of guy who was a little bit larger than life. He was a natural leader, evidenced by his influence on the other disciples. Basically whatever Peter did, the others did too.

Andrew could have thought to himself, "I'm tired of living in Peter's shadow. It's always 'Peter this' and 'Peter that.' If I bring him to Jesus, he'll probably try to take this whole thing over. I'd like to get a little attention for once. I found the Messiah. Maybe this time I'll be the one who gets noticed."

But Andrew didn't do anything of the kind. He immediately went out and sought to bring his brother to the Lord. That's often the case with new believers. Many times, those who are new in the faith are the most zealous evangelists, while those who have known the Lord for years grow complacent in their evangelistic endeavors. It should be the very opposite.

A Modern-Day Andrew

What it comes down to is this: most people are brought to Christ by someone else. I need to look no further than the staff of Harvest Christian Fellowship, the church where I pastor, to find a modern-day version of Andrew.

Mike had been a Christian for about three years when he felt it was time to be more open about his relationship with Jesus. He was working at a bottled water company and realized there were opportunities around him to share his faith. He just needed the boldness to do so.

Jeff, who worked at the same company as Mike, had believed in God for most of his life, but he tended to judge Christians based on their behavior and he saw a lot of hypocrisy. Although he also saw a lot of authenticity, he used the hypocrisy as an excuse for not becoming a Christian. Still, the authenticity he saw in Mike intrigued him.

Jeff knew Mike was a committed Christian, not so much by the things Mike said, but by how Mike lived. He could see that Mike was very sincere. He was humble, kind, gentle, and stood out from the other guys at work. But his admiration of Mike didn't make him any more interested in Christianity. Or so he thought.

Mike had recently taken over Jeff's route at the company, so one day, Jeff found himself riding along in the truck with Mike.

Jeff had already decided ahead of time that if Mike attempted to talk to him about Christianity, he would tell him in no uncertain terms that he didn't want to discuss it.

BEHIND THE SCENES

But something strange happened that day. Mike says, "Jeff was about three feet from me all day long. Late in the day, he finally asked me if I was going to church somewhere."

"As it turned out," Jeff says, "it was the Holy Spirit who opened my mouth—maybe like Balaam's donkey—and I was the one who spoke to Mike."

Mike answered Jeff's questions and shared the gospel with him. And when they got back to the office, Mike noticed that Jeff was unusually quiet. He knew something was going on.

"I was really under heavy conviction for the next several days," Jeff says. "God was after me. One night, I just couldn't run anymore. I went into my bedroom, got on my knees, and invited Jesus Christ to be my Lord and Savior. The next day at work, I told Mike about my decision. I am not sure he believed me at first. It took a little convincing, but then he saw it was genuine."

The following Sunday, Jeff attended Harvest Christian Fellowship for the first time with Mike. Now, more than twenty years later, Mike and Jeff are both pastors and are serving God faithfully and being used by him to bring others to Jesus.

A story like this one reminds us that there wouldn't be any Peters if there weren't any Andrews. We celebrate the Peters of the world, but we often forget the Andrews. Andrew serves as the model for all Christians who labor quietly where God has called them. We may not know their names very well, but they are known and greatly loved by the Lord. Andrew is the patron saint, so to speak, of all relatively unknown but faithful followers of Jesus.

8

THE PERFECT GUEST

Humble yourselves, therefore, under God's mighty hand,
that he may lift you up in due time.

1 Peter 5:6

In Jesus's day a Jewish wedding ceremony was a big deal. It could last up to a week, sort of like a bridal shower, bachelor party, family reunion, and honeymoon all rolled into one. But there was one wedding that outdid all the others before or since.

Jesus attended a wedding in a town called Cana. His mother, Mary, was there, along with the disciples. While they were there, the host of the wedding ran out of wine. So Mary spoke to her son about it. "They have no more wine," she told Jesus. Jesus replied, "Dear woman, why do you involve me? My time has not yet come." Mary then turned to the servants and said, "Do whatever he tells you" (see John 2:1–5).

This seems to be an odd exchange, doesn't it? Jesus seems almost rude to his mother and Mary seems to think Jesus should use his divinity to solve a rather earthly problem. But I believe there is something important happening beneath the surface.

MARY'S REQUEST

In addition to sparing their hosts some embarrassment, Mary perhaps had another motive behind her request: an opportunity to redeem her tarnished reputation. Through no fault of her own, Mary, a godly and morally pure woman, had lived her life under the shadow of suspicion. She had been immoral, the gossipers would say. She had become pregnant out of wedlock.

On one occasion when Jesus rebuked the Pharisees for their hypocrisy, he told them, "You are doing the things your own father does" (John 8:41a).

They shot back, "We are not illegitimate children. . . . The only Father we have is God himself" (verse 41b). The implication was clear.

For thirty years, Mary had lived with the humiliation of having her character questioned. In asking Jesus to perform this miracle, perhaps she not only was looking for the supply of wine to be replenished but for vindication as well.

JESUS'S RESPONSE

But Jesus doesn't respond the way we might think he should. Notice the verbiage Jesus used here. The Greek word used here for "woman" implies respect, but not necessarily warmth. It would be like addressing Mary as "Ma'am" or "Lady"—a somewhat curious term for someone to use for his own mother. It seemed unnecessarily formal under the circumstances. And that's precisely why Jesus used it. He was changing the dynamic of his relationship with her. It may seem rather cold on the part of Jesus to address his loving mother this way. But what he said was as much for his mother's good as it was for his Father's good: "Ma'am, this is not the way it will be done, because my time has not yet come."

"My time has not yet come. . . ." It's a phrase Jesus uses seven times in the Gospel of John. But what does it mean? Jesus was referring to the days of his crucifixion, resurrection, and ascension. He was speaking of the time when all the sin of the world would be poured upon him and he would be tortured, humiliated, and crucified on a Roman cross. That was the time—the time of the completion of his earthly ministry—to which he was referring. Ultimately, in the final hours before his arrest, Jesus prayed, "Father, the time has come" (John 17:1). So he was saying to his mother, "Lady, I understand what you're trying to do. I appreciate it, but the time isn't right. It will happen when it is supposed to happen."

Like Mary, we sometimes come to God and say, "I need you to do this right now. I need you to come through for me in this situation." Maybe we see someone getting away with their sin or we hear someone saying unkind things about us. We pray, "Lord, intervene. Do something about this." Sometimes God's timing is such that the situation changes. But sometimes God says, "My time has not yet come. This is not the time for this to happen. Be patient. Wait on me."

THE FIRST MIRACLE

I think Jesus probably enjoyed himself as a guest at this wedding. And shortly after his conversation with his mother, Jesus did, in fact, do something about the wine shortage. (The Bible doesn't tell us why Jesus decided to do so after the conversation he'd just had with Mary.) As I mentioned, running out of wine seems like a rather mundane problem for the Son of God to tackle. This would be Jesus's first miracle, and it might seem like an odd choice. After all, he could have done something a bit more dramatic, like restoring sight to a blind person, healing the sick, or raising someone from the dead. Instead, he chose to turn water into wine. In John 2:6–10 we read:

> Nearby stood six stone water jars, the kind used by the Jews for ceremonial washing, each holding from twenty to thirty gallons. Jesus said to the servants, "Fill the jars with water"; so they filled them to the brim. Then he told them, "Now draw some out and take it to the master of the banquet." They did so, and the master of the banquet tasted the water that had been turned into wine. He did not realize where it had come from, though the servants who had drawn the water knew. Then he called the bridegroom aside and said, "Everyone brings out the choice wine first and then the cheaper wine after the guests have had too much to drink; but you have saved the best till now."

Jesus performed a miracle that would bring happiness and joy to those who were celebrating. That is not to say it was frivolous in any way. If anything, Jesus demonstrated the unlimited power at his immediate disposal. At a moment's notice, Jesus Christ can meet the needs of humanity. He can always provide what is lacking in earthly resources.

This is important to remember when we face what seems to be an impossible situation. Whether it is the loss of a job, an unexpected illness, or a failed relationship, none of these things take God by surprise. And none of them are beyond God's reach. Nothing is too small—or too big—for God to care about.

9

DOING OUR PART

Trust in the LORD with all your heart and lean not on your
own understanding; in all your ways acknowledge him,
and he will make your paths straight.

Proverbs 3:5–6

Jesus was at a wedding when the host ran out of wine. But rather
than make a big scene about turning ordinary water into fine
wine, Jesus performs his first miracle in a subtle, quiet way. So
subtle, in fact, that he doesn't get much credit for it.

In the midst of a busy celebration, Jesus pulls a few servants
aside and says, "Fill the jars with water" (John 2:7). As the servants carry the jars toward the host, the water turns to wine.
The host tastes it, then compliments the bridegroom for his
generosity (John 2:10). No one but the servants knew what Jesus
had done. Soon the disciples who were with Jesus figured out
what had happened and the Bible tells us they "put their faith
in him" (John 2:11).

FIRST COMES TRUST

This story offers us two important lessons:

First, God wants us to trust him, even when we don't understand his ways. Notice Jesus didn't say, "Fill the jars with
water, and it will turn to wine." Rather, he gave a simple though
somewhat puzzling command. The servants did what they were
told, and only later discovered what Jesus was doing.

Often, we expect God to reveal his will to us, to show us what
he's doing. But just as often, God asks us to trust him. We say,
"Lord, I need to know what you're up to here."

"All right," he says. "Then take this first step of faith."

"What? But I want to know what will happen after that."

"You don't need the blueprints," the Lord might say. "Just take this first step."

We want to know God's will *before* we decide to submit to it. But God wants us to submit to him first. We find this principle in Romans 12:1–2, where the apostle Paul wrote:

> Therefore, I urge you, brothers, in view of God's mercy, to offer your bodies as living sacrifices, holy and pleasing to God—this is your spiritual act of worship. Do not conform any longer to the pattern of this world, but be transformed by the renewing of your mind. Then you will be able to test and approve what God's will is—his good, pleasing and perfect will.

THEN COMES KNOWLEDGE

This passage offers us a conditional promise: You will know what God's will is. But the conditions are (1) that you present yourself to God, (2) that you do not conform to this world, and (3) that you renew your mind, resulting in a change of attitudes, beliefs, and behavior. If you want your mind to be enlightened—that is, to know the will of God—then you must surrender your heart.

The second lesson is that there is God's part and there is ours. "Fill the jars with water," Jesus said. He was asking them to step out in faith. With a simple word, Jesus could have spoken the wine into existence. But he told the servants to fill the containers with water.

This brings to mind the miracle of Jesus feeding the crowd (see Matt. 14:15–21; Mark 6:35–44; Luke 9:12–17; John 6:5–13). Jesus took the loaves and fish, blessed them, and handed them to his disciples to give to the people. They had to take a step of faith and distribute what was there, not knowing that their supply would be continuously replenished.

A Step of Faith

Maybe God is asking you to step out in faith right now, even though you don't know what will happen next. Maybe God is asking you to start that conversation with an unbelieving co-worker. Maybe the Lord is leading you to adopt a child or go into the mission field. Whatever the call, God asks you to move forward in faith. That is what the servants at this wedding did, and others were blessed as a result.

At this wedding in Cana, Jesus was saying, "The best is yet to be." And that's what he continues to say to all those who have put their trust in him. We know that whatever happens, whatever ailments we have, whatever suffering we go through, ultimately for the Christian, that is not the end of the story. We will see the Lord one day. We will spend all eternity with him. Talk about your happy endings!

10

QUESTIONS IN THE DARK

My soul finds rest in God alone; my salvation comes from him.

Psalm 62:1

There are certain things in life we all know. For instance, we know you don't tug on Superman's cape. You don't spit into the wind. You don't pull the mask off the old Lone Ranger, and you don't . . .

If you know how to complete that sentence, then you're probably over the age of forty-five. And you've probably heard Jim Croce's song "You Don't Mess Around with Jim" more than a time or two.

We all know certain things, but sometimes we don't know as much as we think we know. We are about to look at a very familiar passage of Scripture, the conversation between Nicodemus and Jesus. This story is so familiar that I think we often skim over it. To do so, however, is to miss an essential truth of life. What's more, to miss this truth is to miss everything.

LOOKING FOR CHANGE

Nicodemus was a highly intelligent, cultured, and moral individual. He was as close to fitting the description of a "good person" as anyone could hope for. But despite the fact that he was a leader in his country and in his faith, Nicodemus was dissatisfied. So he came to Jesus, looking for answers. Jesus revealed to him essential truths for living, as well as the meaning and purpose of life. The words Jesus gave him have unlocked the mystery of life for countless millions throughout the centuries.

> Now there was a man of the Pharisees named Nicodemus, a member of the Jewish ruling council. He came to Jesus at night and said, "Rabbi, we know you are a teacher who has come from God. For no one could perform the miraculous signs you are doing if God were not with him." In reply Jesus declared, "I tell you the truth, no one can see the kingdom of God unless he is born again."
>
> John 3:1–3

Nicodemus knew something in his life needed to change. We are not much different. And no wonder. We live in a culture obsessed with change. We need to look no further than our weekly TV schedules to see that. We have all seen those before-and-after shows, ranging from cosmetic surgery to home makeovers. That's why this story matters so much. It tells of the kind of change that hits much deeper than new clothes or a new house. It is about soul change.

KNOWING ISN'T ENOUGH

We often think of Pharisees in a negative light, and understandably so. Jesus saved his most scathing words for the scribes and the Pharisees, calling them "whitewashed tombs" (see Matt. 23:27). We tend to think of all Pharisees as hypocrites, but that's not necessarily the case in every situation.

Actually, it was somewhat commendable to be a Pharisee. This was a select group of men, never numbering more than six thousand. Each had taken a solemn vow before three witnesses that he would devote every moment of his entire life to obeying the Ten Commandments. The Pharisees took the law of God very seriously and sought to apply the Ten Commandments to every area of life.

However, the Pharisees weren't satisfied with Scripture alone, which is always a problem. They wanted things spelled out more specifically. So a group of people called scribes arose from within the Pharisees. Their job was to spell out how the Ten Commandments were to be applied to every area of life.

Not only was Nicodemus from this order, but he was also one of their primary leaders. To arrive at his position would mean that Nicodemus was a careful student of the sacred books of the Jews and must have studied them for many years. In addition to this, Nicodemus was well-known. In John 3:10, Jesus refers to him as "Israel's teacher," which means Nicodemus was likely a popular and prominent teacher in Israel—a household name, if you will.

Even with all this going for him, Nicodemus sensed there was something missing in his life. And that brought him to Jesus. With great humility, Nicodemus begins by saying, "Rabbi, we know who you are." For a man like Nicodemus to call Jesus "Rabbi" was an important acknowledgment. Nicodemus would have been familiar with the prophets and their words concerning the Messiah. He continues with the phrase, "We know." Yet he had come to Jesus alone. He wasn't ready to say, "*I* know." In a sense, he was probably hiding behind this phrase, just as people say, "I have a friend who wants to know. . . ." But Jesus immediately got to the point because he knew exactly what Nicodemus needed. With a single, sharp, and penetrating phrase, Jesus sliced through all the layers of rules and legalistic attitudes that had accumulated in the mind of Nicodemus, saying, "I tell you the truth, no one can see the kingdom of God unless he is born again" (verse 3).

CUTTING TO THE HEART

It's as though Jesus was saying, "I am about to reveal a fundamental reality of life to you, Nicodemus. Listen very carefully!" Like a sword, these words pierced this Pharisee's heart. Jesus was saying, "Nicodemus, your religious beliefs are not enough. In spite of the fact that you are at the top of the heap in your religion, it means nothing. It has not brought you any closer to heaven." This is not optional. This is essential. This is absolute. It is the life-changing truth that I was speaking of at the beginning of this chapter: You must be born again.

11

"Born Again" Defined

The Spirit of God has made me;
the breath of the Almighty gives me life.

Job 33:4

There is a lot of confusion today regarding what the term *born again* means. In the story of Nicodemus, Jesus is helping us see what it really means, which is, "to be born from above." Some people will say, "I'm a Christian, but I am not one of those 'Born Agains.'" That is impossible. There is simply no such thing as a Christian who is not born again.

Spiritual Rebirth

But *why* must we be born again? Why do we need a spiritual rebirth? We find the answer in John 3:3: "No one can see the kingdom of God unless he is born again." So what exactly did Jesus mean by "the kingdom of God"? Well, the kingdom of God has past, present, and future applications.

The past application of the kingdom of God was when Jesus walked this earth. He gave us a glimpse, a sneak preview, of what is to come. On one occasion Jesus said, "The kingdom of God has come to you" (Luke 11:20). He was referring to his presence among the people. He was saying, "I am walking among you. The kingdom of God is here." That was the past application.

The present application of the kingdom of God is when we personally live under the rule and reign of Jesus Christ. The Bible tells us, "For the kingdom of God is not a matter of eating and drinking, but of righteousness, peace and joy in the Holy Spirit" (Rom. 14:17). The idea is that of Christ ruling and reigning in your life. This is what Jesus was referring to when he said, "But seek first his kingdom and his righteousness, and all these things will be given to you as well" (Matt. 6:33).

The future application of the kingdom of God will be when Christ comes back to establish his kingdom on Earth. This will be when the wolf will lie down with the lamb (see Isa. 11:6–7) and the earth will be filled with the knowledge of the Lord (see Isa. 11:9).

SEEING THE KINGDOM OF GOD

So here's what Jesus was saying to Nicodemus:

- "You will not see the kingdom of God *presently* unless you realize who I am."
- "You will not experience the kingdom of God *internally* until you open your heart to my rule and reign."
- "You will not live in the kingdom of God *externally* until you are born again."

So when we pray, "Your kingdom come, your will be done," we are praying for the rule of Christ in our lives and for the day of his return.

THE NATURE OF CHANGE

Jesus had the Pharisee's attention. Nicodemus asked, "How can a man be born when he is old? Surely he cannot enter a second time into his mother's womb to be born!" (John 3:4). Nicodemus was essentially saying, "Lord, I accept what you say in theory, but how can I start over again? Is it really possible to be born all over again?"

It's a good question. Can people really become different than what they are? After all, how many times have we tried to change ourselves? We make resolutions to lose weight, exercise more, watch less TV, and read the Bible more often. We try new clothes or maybe a new job. Yet we fail at these and return to our old habits. Can we really change?

Years ago, my oldest son Christopher had a little pet rat, ironically named Nicodemus. He was a really cute little rat, and we all grew to like him. He was like a member of the Laurie family. But Christopher began to feel sorry for Nicodemus and the fact that he lived in a bare cage. Christopher was convinced that his little rodent friend needed a shelter of some kind, so he decided to build one for him. He constructed a very clever little house out of balsa wood, complete with a little roof, little windows, and a tiny front door that opened and closed. Over the door, Christopher hung a little sign that read "Nicodemus." He then lowered Nicodemus's new home into his cage. I think it gave us all a good feeling when we went to bed that night, knowing Nicodemus had his own little house to sleep in. The next morning, we got up to find the house missing and Nicodemus looking a little plumper. He had eaten his house! Nicodemus didn't get it. He didn't understand that it was his *house*. He simply thought, "This looks appetizing. I think I'll eat it." Why? Because he was a rat, that's why. We may have attached human attributes to this little rodent and given him his own house to sleep in, but the fact is, a rat is still a rat. We couldn't change his nature.

But is it possible to change the nature of a human being? Can we really become different than who we are? That is the question Nicodemus was asking. And that's the question we're still asking today. Jesus's answer was yes—but only when that change comes through the Spirit of God.

12

LIFE IN THE SPIRIT

For the message of the cross is foolishness to those who are perishing, but to us who are being saved it is the power of God.

1 Corinthians 1:18

It is not always easy to understand the person of the Holy Spirit. There are times in the Bible when there is a visible symbol of God's spirit, such as a dove (Luke 3:22) or a flame (Acts 2:3). But most often, it is more difficult to understand what it means to be filled with the Holy Spirit. As he talks with Nicodemus, Jesus offers us a beautiful example of how God's Spirit flows around us.

Maybe Jesus and Nicodemus felt a warm breeze blowing, which prompted an illustration: "The wind blows wherever it pleases. You hear its sound, but you cannot tell where it comes from or where it is going. So it is with everyone born of the Spirit" (John 3:8).

In other words, Jesus was asking, "Can you see the wind, Nicodemus?"

"No."

"But do you see its effect?"

"Yes."

"So is everyone who is born of the Spirit," Jesus replied. "You can't see this with your eyes, but you can see the work of God that takes place in the human heart."

I read an article about a town that had been hit hard by a storm all night long. In the morning, the residents of the town were amazed to find a common, plastic drinking straw driven deep into a telephone pole by the powerful winds of the night before.

We may not see the wind, but we can see its effect. The same is true when you have been born from above by the Holy Spirit.

REMAINING QUESTIONS

As Jesus and Nicodemus get to the end of their conversation, I imagine Nicodemus may have begun to feel a bit desperate. "How can these things be?" he asks Jesus in John 3:9 (NKJV). "I'm still not sure I get all of this." "Are you the teacher of Israel and do not know these things?" (verse 10 NKJV). Jesus asked. The implication is that Nicodemus was famous. He was respected. He was well-studied. Yet he didn't understand.

As a student of Scripture, Nicodemus certainly should have known there were passages in the Old Testament that even alluded to what Jesus was speaking of when he said, "You must be born again." One such verse is Ezekiel 11:19, where God said, "I will give them an undivided heart and put a new spirit in them; I will remove from them their heart of stone and give them a heart of flesh." This was pointing to the born-again experience. "Nicodemus, it can happen," Jesus was saying. "You should know this from studying the Word."

THE ABCS OF THE GOSPEL

Apparently, Nicodemus's religion had not prepared him for what he really needed. So Jesus laid out to Nicodemus the ABCs of the gospel: "Just as Moses lifted up the snake in the desert, so the Son of Man must be lifted up, that everyone who believes in him may have eternal life" (John 3:14–15).

Jesus was sending Nicodemus back to familiar territory: the Scriptures, specifically Numbers 21. Nicodemus would have known this story from Israel's wilderness wanderings. The Israelites were complaining that God had abandoned them. They accused Moses and God of failing them and of bringing them to the wilderness to die. They were sick of what God had provided for them. So the Lord sent venomous snakes to bite them. They quickly came to their senses and sought Moses's help. God instructed Moses to erect a pole with a serpent of brass wrapped around it. Whoever looked at that serpent on the pole was healed of his or her snakebite.

God did everything he could do. The Israelites simply had to look at that pole. They could have known of the pole's existence, yet chosen not to look. But if they wanted to be healed, then they only needed to look at the pole.

LOOKING AT THE CROSS

That was a picture of what Christ would do on the cross. We all have been bitten by the serpent, Satan. We have his deadly venom in our system. We must quickly find the antidote, and it is provided through Christ and his blood shed on the cross. If we will look to Jesus for salvation, we will be forgiven. In fact, on the day that Jesus hung on the cross, some looked and believed (Matt. 27:54; Luke 23:42–43). Others looked and turned away (Matt. 27:39–44; Luke 23:35–39). And that is what it ultimately comes down to. Either you will look and live, or you will look and leave. As Isaiah 45:21–22 says, "And there is no God apart from me, a righteous God and a Savior; there is none but me. Turn to me and be saved, all you ends of the earth; for I am God, and there is no other."

Jesus pointed Nicodemus to this simple truth. Then the whole story comes together in the most well-known verse of the New Testament, John 3:16: "For God so loved the world that he gave his one and only Son, that whoever believes in him shall not perish but have eternal life." Some people picture God as some kind of cosmic killjoy who is out to ruin their lives. But the truth is that God loves you. He wants to have a relationship with you. We can talk about love all day long, but God showed his love for us in a tangible way: "But God demonstrates his own love for us in this: While we were still sinners, Christ died for us" (Rom. 5:8).

13

TWO SIDES OF A COIN

The earth is the LORD's, and everything in it,
the world, and all who live in it.

Psalm 24:1

The story of Nicodemus brings us to a reassuring, yet often overlooked passage: "For God did not send his Son into the world to condemn the world, but to save the world through him" (John 3:17). Jesus came to this world not to come down on people but to reach out to people. While religion tells us what we must do to reach up to heaven, God reached down from heaven by sending his Son, Jesus. We are not reaching out to God, trying to earn his approval. Rather, it is God reaching out to us. That is the message of the gospel. It is the message that, through Christ—who lived a perfect life, who died on the cross in our place, and who shed his blood for us—we have the gift of eternal life.

BELIEVING WHAT?

But what does it mean to believe? So many people say they believe. But *what* do they believe? The Bible says, "You believe that there is one God. Good! Even the demons believe that—and shudder" (James 2:19). To believe does not simply mean intellectually accepting something to be true. To believe means to adhere to, commit to, have faith in, rely upon, trust in. It comes back to the issue of being born again. To be a believer means not only embracing Christ and Christ alone for salvation but also turning from your sin and starting life again. Repentance is a part of belief, like two sides of a coin.

I fear for those who say they believe but have never repented. There is a lot of confusion regarding the definition of the terms "Christian" and "born again." But how can someone claim to be a Christian and not believe that the Bible is the Word of God? How can someone claim to be born again and believe that Jesus is anything other than the Messiah? How can someone claim to be a real follower of Jesus and yet reject what the Bible clearly teaches? Answer: They can't.

CHOOSING OR CHOSEN?

How about you? Do you know that you have eternal life? Do you have the assurance of salvation? The choice is yours as to what you will do with this wonderful gift of God. You can gladly accept it or reject it. When someone offers you a gift, you either take it or reject it. You can't say, "I'm neutral on this. I can't decide." Some people may say that they have no choice in the matter, that God does the choosing and not us. They believe that you are either predestined to heaven or to hell. Those of the Reformed persuasion would lean perhaps toward overstressing the sovereignty of God, and for all practical purposes, do away with the personal choice of humanity in the matter. On the other hand, those of the Arminian point of view might tend to dismiss the sovereignty of God and instead emphasize the free will of humanity.

I don't subscribe to either point of view wholeheartedly. I do believe in the sovereignty of God and predestination. However, I reject the idea of irresistible grace and limited atonement, because I believe the grace of God is resistible, though not easily. I also believe that Jesus Christ died for all the world, not just the "elect." Otherwise, why would the Bible say, "Today, if you hear his voice, do not harden your hearts" (Ps. 95:7–8)? This, along with other countless passages, implies that the heart can be hardened and grace can be resisted. As evangelist D. L. Moody once said, "Lord, save the elect, and then elect some more!"

GOD'S LOVE FOR ALL

Christ did not die for the elect, but for the world: "For God so loved *the world* that he gave his one and only Son" (John 3:16, emphasis mine). And, "While we were *still sinners*, Christ died for us" (Rom. 5:8, emphasis mine).

On the other hand, there is free will. We must personally choose whether we will put our trust in Jesus Christ for our salvation. It's an undeniable fact that Jesus said, "You did not choose me, but I chose you" (John 15:16).

So how do I reconcile these two approaches? I don't. And thankfully, I don't have to. You don't have to reconcile friends. I simply follow the scriptural emphasis, recognizing that God's sovereignty and humanity's responsibility are taught side by side in the same Bible.

Jesus will receive and reveal himself to any person who will come to him honestly and heart to heart, just as he did with Nicodemus. So don't give up on the unbeliever you have been praying for. And don't give up on yourself. Jesus said, "Whoever comes to me I will never drive away" (John 6:37).

14

OSCAR AND NICODEMUS

If you confess with your mouth, "Jesus is Lord,"
and believe in your heart that God raised him
from the dead, you will be saved.

Romans 10:9

Do you know a Nicodemus? A religious person? A moral person? I'd like to tell you about one I knew. His name was Oscar Laurie, and he was an attorney who lived in New Jersey. My mother, who was married and divorced many times, married him while I was still a young child, and he adopted me. Oscar Laurie was the only man during my childhood who actually treated me as a father should treat a son. When I messed up, he would discipline me. When I did well, he would commend me. He taught me respect, and he taught me manners. Because he treated me as his son, I respected him and loved him, which is why it was hard when I came home from school one day and the car was loaded up. When I asked my mom where we were going, she told me we were going to Hawaii.

"Where's Dad?" I asked.

"He's not coming," she told me.

My mother left him and married another guy, and on it went.

FINDING THE FATHER

After I became an adult, I really wanted to see Oscar Laurie again. I had become a Christian at the age of seventeen and I wanted to tell him about what Christ had done for me. With the help of someone from our church who worked for a bar association, I was able to get in touch with him. He told me he wanted to see me. I mentioned I was coming to New York soon for a speaking engagement and suggested we have lunch.

He said, "No, come stay at our house." Because he had remarried and had a family, I didn't want to impose. But he insisted. So I went to my speaking engagement and when it was over, I got on a train to Oscar's house. When I got off the train and saw him, I recognized him immediately. As we spent a little time together, I found out he had recently had a heart attack and almost died.

One night, after his wife had made a wonderful Italian meal, we were sitting around the table, talking. His wife said, "Well, Greg, tell me about how you became a Christian and a pastor." As I shared my story, Oscar's wife was very responsive. My dad, on the other hand, sat at the other end of the table, listening quietly, like an attorney in a court of law. I thought, *This is not going well.* But he reminded me a little bit of Nicodemus. He was a moral man. He was an educated man. He was a good man, a man of integrity. But he didn't have Christ living in him.

At the end of the evening, he said, "Well Greg, do you want to go walking with me in the morning?" (The doctor had advised him to get exercise because of his heart condition.)

"Sure, Dad," I said. "What time?"

He said, "I'll knock on your door at 6:00."

A VERY SPECIAL WALK

Well, that meant 3:00 A.M. California time, but when the knock on the door came the next morning, I got up. As we started to walk along, he said, "Greg, I listened very carefully to what you said last night, . . ." (Suddenly I was wide awake!) "and I want to become a Christian right now."

I was shocked.

So he said, "I . . . I want Jesus to come into my life."

I couldn't believe it. I didn't even think he'd been doing anything more than being polite while I talked about my faith and here he was, wanting to be part of it.

"Well, we should pray," I told him.

He said, "Let's pray right now." So he got down on his knees, right there in the park. As we prayed, tears flowed down the cheeks of this not-so-emotional man. When we finished, he said to me, "I know the Lord has come in." Then he added, "Let's pray for my heart condition. God can heal me too."

So we prayed a little more. When we were done, he said, "I know I'm saved. And I think the Lord has healed me. Let's go tell my doctor."

"Now wait, Dad," I said. "I don't know if God has healed you."

"Well, I think he has." So we went to his doctor's office. We walked in, and my dad told his Jewish doctor, "I just got saved. Christ is in my life and I'm healed."

It was hard for me to leave New Jersey and to return home to California. But I located a church for him to attend and told him, "Dad, just start reading the Bible and I will be back."

A LIFE CHANGED

Three weeks later, I returned. I was afraid he wouldn't be doing well. So I said, "Well, let's read something from the Bible. . . ."

I read a verse, and he said, "Oh, right. That is Paul in Ephesians, right?"

"Yes it is. That's right."

As we went on, I discovered he had read the entire Bible while I'd been away. And it started changing his life. He got involved in his church and eventually became an elder. He got involved with The Gideons International and helped distribute Bibles. He served the Lord for the rest of his life. Now he is in heaven, and I am looking forward to seeing him again someday.

Maybe you know people like Oscar Laurie. You know they aren't caught up in intentional sin. They are not drug users, alcoholics, or party animals. They work hard. They pay their taxes. They are trustworthy. They are dependable. They are admirable. You have told them about Christ, but nothing has happened. You think it is never going to work.

Remember Nicodemus. And remember my dad. While they didn't know Christ, they saw their need and came to faith in him. So keep praying, and don't give up.

God can change each one of us—if we will come to him on his terms. We can experience a true "extreme makeover," not on the outside, but on the inside.

15

CHARLENE'S STORY

To him who is thirsty I will give to drink without cost
from the spring of the water of life.

Revelation 21:6

Charlene McDaniel was a beautiful young woman. Some even compared her to Marilyn Monroe, which was pretty heady stuff for someone from Friendship, Arkansas. Although she had been raised in a Bible-teaching Baptist church, she bristled at the idea of following God's Word and not being free to do what she wanted to.

During her first marriage (it would be one of seven), Charlene gave birth to a son. But feeling her husband was not the man she was looking for, she divorced him. She married again, and after the anguish of giving birth to a stillborn child, she returned to the party scene, looking for something more exciting than married life. She had a fling, then found out she was pregnant. Not wanting to have her child out of wedlock, she married again and had her second son. Charlene's extended family nicknamed this son Pogo, because, according to his aunt, "He was always so cute and mischievous, like the little opossum character in the cartoon strip."

Charlene's first son lived with his grandmother, but Pogo lived with his mom off and on as she made her way from one dead-end relationship to another, marrying and divorcing again and again. While Pogo was with his mother, all he saw was partying and violence. One night, he watched as her latest husband nearly killed her.

These were frightening times for a young boy. Some nights he didn't know where his mother was. Some nights she'd return home at four o'clock in the morning and pass out, drunk. Pogo felt his mother had no one to care for her but him, so he did his best. He was a ten-year-old boy playing the parent to his self-destructive mother.

I know that for certain, because I was the mischievous Pogo, and Charlene was my mother.

BACK TO HER ROOTS

As the years passed by, my mother's once-legendary beauty began to fade. All the drinking, smoking, and hard living began to take its toll, and one night, while driving under the influence, she had an accident that horribly disfigured her face. Her beauty, the one thing she had counted on throughout her life, was now greatly diminished.

I saw my mom begin to soften. She would wait for a prayer before a meal. She always seemed proud of me and was glad to tell everyone I was her son. And although I didn't know it at the time, she saved every newspaper clipping about our ministry.

After she discovered she had kidney failure and would need dialysis three times per week, she began returning to her spiritual roots. One month before her death, I had a very direct conversation with her. I asked her if she believed in Jesus Christ as her Savior and Lord. She said she did. I then told her that she ought to be coming to church. And the next Sunday, she came.

Her search brought her back to what she knew as a young girl. Like the prodigal son, she returned. But sadly, she spent almost all her life looking to men and to romance for fulfillment. Yet all along, that fulfillment could have been found in a relationship with Jesus Christ.

AN APPOINTMENT WITH GOD

We are about to look at another story of a woman who was a lot like my mother. Or, perhaps I should say that my mother was a lot like her. We know her as the woman at the well, an empty person who thought romance and sex would fill the void in her life. She went from husband to husband, hoping to find her prince. But after five husbands, she simply gave up. She was disillusioned, scorned, and ignored. That is, until Jesus came along.

As we will see, Jesus had an appointment with her. Of course, she didn't know anything about it, but he did. And Jesus always keeps his appointments.

Our story opens in John 4:

> [The Lord] left Judea and went back once more to Galilee. Now he had to go through Samaria. So he came to a town in Samaria called Sychar, near the plot of ground Jacob had given to his son Joseph. Jacob's well was there, and Jesus, tired as he was from the journey, sat down by the well. It was about the sixth hour. When a Samaritan woman came to draw water, Jesus said to her, "Will you give me a drink?" (His disciples had gone into the town to buy food.)
>
> verses 3–8

A little historical background will help us understand some important things about this passage. No Orthodox Jew would ever travel through Samaria to Galilee. In fact, an Orthodox Jew would go out of his way—literally choosing a much longer route—to avoid Samaria altogether. The reason most Jews chose the longer route was prejudice, pure and simple. The Jews did not want to associate with the Samaritan people, preferring to endure the long, uncomfortable road rather than to let go of their bigotry.

But Jesus chose the shortcut, not because it was easier, but because there was a hurting, lonely, and searching woman in Samaria. In spite of the strong, deeply rooted prejudice between these two groups of people, Jesus had to go.

This shows us that the love of God knows no racial, economic, or sinful boundaries. Long before the creation of the world, it had been settled in eternity that Jesus was to meet a burned-out, immoral Samaritan woman that day.

THIRSTY AGAIN

This woman had searched but never found her heart's desire. What she (and people like my mom) did not understand is that she was trying to fill a void in her life that was created by God. That void is loneliness for God. Jesus told this woman, "Everyone who drinks this water will be thirsty again" (verse 13). In fact, this statement could be written over all the wells of life.

We could write it over the well of success: *Everyone who drinks this water will be thirsty again.*

We could write it over the well of pleasure: *Everyone who drinks this water will be thirsty again.*

We could write it over the well of materialism: *Everyone who drinks this water will be thirsty again.*

No matter how much we have, if we don't have Christ, we will always be thirsty. But when Jesus quenches that thirst, we will be satisfied.

16

OUT OF THE COMFORT ZONE

The LORD is gracious and righteous;
our God is full of compassion.
Psalm 116:5

The story of Jesus talking with the woman at the well isn't just a story about a desperate woman who found the love of Jesus. It is a story about the compassion and tenderness we all need to show when we talk about Christ with others.

Jesus's conversation with this woman offers us five lessons.

LOVING LIKE JESUS

We need to reach out to people who are not like us. Jesus couldn't have chosen a less-likely person to speak to. An ordinary Jew would never accept a cup of water from a Samaritan but Jesus requested one from her. In addition, Jesus was frequently called "Rabbi" by those who approached him. According to Jewish law, rabbis were never to talk to a woman in public, not even to their wives or sisters. Yet Jesus chose to share his great truth with a woman—and an immoral, Samaritan woman at that.

So let's learn from Jesus's example and be willing to reach out to those who may not necessarily be just like us. God may lead you to share your faith with someone you may not be comfortable with. We need to be open to reach the category of people God invites to believe, which is, "whoever." As John 3:16 tells us, "Whoever believes in him shall not perish but have eternal life."

GOING OUT OF OUR WAY

We have to go to where people are. I remember visiting a central California farm, where the owner shared some words of wisdom that his father had passed along to him. "For the fruit to grow," his father said, "the farmer's shadow has to fall on the field." In other words, the farmer needs to be in the field, watching and harvesting his crops.

This is what Jesus was doing. He was going out of his way to be with someone who needed him. After all, the Bible does not say that the whole world should go to church. Rather, it says that the church should go to the whole world. We simply cannot cloister ourselves away from those who are aching to know the good news of Jesus.

PRESSING ON IN OUR WEAKNESS

We need to keep at it, even when we are tired. Jesus rarely had a moment to himself. His ministry was not only physically draining but emotionally and spiritually draining as well. That is why he often spent nights in prayer to recharge.

Often, we guard against burning ourselves out. And that's okay. I have heard some say they are "burned out" in their ministries and they can't go on. But in more than thirty years of having the privilege of serving the Lord, I can honestly say I have never been tired of service. I have been tired *in* it, but not *of* it. And honestly, I can't think of anything more worthy of my time and energy than serving God. It's never a waste. Our greatest recreation and rest will come later, in heaven. Meanwhile, we're told to "press on" (Phil. 3:12), to "not become weary in doing good" (Gal. 6:9), and to "run in such a way as to get the prize" (1 Cor. 9:24). We never will do great things for God until we have learned to minister even when we are tired.

SHARING WITH COMPASSION

We need to care about the people we speak to. Effectively sharing our faith begins with a God-given burden for other people. Jesus spoke to this woman because he hurt for her. He wanted to help her, to release her from her pain and loneliness. Is your spirit stirred when you see people who are lost in lives of sin, when you see men and women (especially young men and women) throwing their lives away as they chase after empty dreams and pursuits? Do you feel genuine compassion for those who are hurting? Every generation needs regeneration, and ours is no exception.

SPEAKING WITH CARE

You must share the truth of God with tact and love. In speaking to the Samaritan woman, Jesus, the Master Evangelist, used something most of us too often lack: tact. Jesus appealed to her curiosity and to her inner spiritual thirst:

> The Samaritan woman said to him, "You are a Jew and I am a Samaritan woman. How can you ask me for a drink?" (For Jews do not associate with Samaritans.) Jesus answered her, "If you knew the gift of God and who it is that asks you for a drink, you would have asked him and he would have given you living water." "Sir," the woman said, "you have nothing to draw with and the well is deep. Where can you get this living water? Are you greater than our father Jacob, who gave us the well and drank from it himself, as did also his sons and his flocks and herds?" Jesus answered, "Everyone who drinks this water will be thirsty again, but whoever drinks the water I give him will never thirst. Indeed, the water I give him will become in him a spring of water welling up to eternal life." The woman said to him, "Sir, give me this water so that I won't get thirsty and have to keep coming here to draw water."
>
> John 4:9–15

Notice that Jesus did not start out with some statement like, "Are you saved?" or "Did you know you are going to hell?" No, this was a dialogue. Jesus spoke, and Jesus listened.

Jesus was genuinely interested in this woman. He didn't have any agenda except to talk to her, to care for her, and to offer her the love of God. Our witness falls flat when we are more interested in the results of our conversation than the person with whom we are conversing.

17

LOOKING FOR LOVE

*We were therefore buried with him through baptism into death
in order that, just as Christ was raised from the dead
through the glory of the Father, we too may live a new life.*

Romans 6:4

If you've ever imagined having a face-to-face conversation with Jesus, it may seem surprising that the woman at the well didn't respond to him the way we might expect. Her initial response was sarcastic, flippant, and cynical. No doubt this woman was cynical about men in general. And why wouldn't she be? She had been used and abused by men. But now the men were gone, her beauty had most likely faded, and she was left with bitter memories of bad relationships.

Many young women today think that if they just could be beautiful, they would be happy and fulfilled. Yet I find it interesting that one of the most beautiful women in Hollywood doesn't seem to agree. She once told an interviewer, "Beauty? Let me tell you something. Being thought of as 'a beautiful woman' has spared me nothing in life. No heartache. No trouble. Love has been difficult. Beauty is essentially meaningless, and it is always transitory."[1]

This Samaritan woman could have said the same thing. She had never found the fulfillment she was looking for in a relationship with a man. As she talked with Jesus, she may have thought, *What is this guy doing? What game is he playing with me? What does he really want?*

WHO IS THIS GUY?

Suspicious, the woman asked, "Are you greater than our father Jacob, who gave us the well and drank from it himself, as did also his sons and his flocks and herds?" (John 4:12). Jesus could have responded, "Am I greater than Jacob? I wrestled with him—he was a wuss! I knew Moses and Abraham too. Am I greater? I'm their Creator! I'm the one *they* worshiped!" Had he said this, she would have thought he was insane. She wasn't ready for this spiritual truth yet.

Instead, Jesus cut to the core of her pain. He told her there was nothing the world had to offer that would quench her spiritual thirst. He said, "Everyone who drinks this water will be thirsty again, but whoever drinks the water I give him will never thirst. Indeed, the water I give him will become in him a spring of water welling up to eternal life" (verses 13–14).

She had come to the well of relationships five different times, hoping to meet the perfect man who would fulfill all her desires. But time and time again, her Prince Charming turned into a frog. Her life was a miserable chain of unfulfilling relationships.

Jesus spoke of a spring of water, water that is always fresh, always clear. Unlike the stagnant water of shallow relationships and broken promises, the water Jesus offered was the kind that would refresh and renew the woman's soul. Jesus was telling the Samaritan woman that her deepest thirst would be completely and permanently satisfied.

WHAT DOES HE WANT?

Naturally, the woman was intrigued. This man had offered her the spiritual refreshment she'd longed for: "The woman said to him, 'Sir, give me this water so that I won't get thirsty and have to keep coming here to draw water'" (verse 15). But Jesus made it clear that something in her life had to be set straight before she could drink of the living water.

He told her, "Go, call your husband and come back."

"I have no husband," she replied.

Jesus said to her, "You are right when you say you have no husband. The fact is, you have had five husbands, and the man you now have is not your husband. What you have just said is quite true."

verses 16–18

Jesus forced her to admit her sin, because there can be no conversion without conviction. There can be no forgiveness without repentance.

But she pushed back, saying, "Sir . . . I can see that you are a prophet. Our fathers worshiped on this mountain, but you Jews claim that the place where we must worship is in Jerusalem" (verses 19–20). She had never met a man like this before. It was as though he could see right through her façade. Although she believed he was a prophet, she still sought to shake her personal conviction and talk about religion instead.

WHAT DID HE DO?

Jesus went to the heart of the matter. He set the record straight and got things back on track. "Believe me," he said, "a time is coming when you will worship the Father neither on this mountain nor in Jerusalem" (verse 21).

So she told him, "I know that Messiah (called Christ) is coming. When he comes, he will explain everything to us" (verse 25).

Jesus dropped the bombshell: "I who speak to you am he" (verse 26). It would appear that, at this moment, instantaneously, despite her hardness, world-weariness, and emptiness, she believed.

How about you? From what "well" are you seeking satisfaction right now? Is it the well of pleasure? Is it the well of possessions? Or, are you seeking satisfaction from the well of some perfect relationship? That was the problem with my mom. She thought what she was looking for could never be found in the faith of her childhood. It had to be found somewhere else. She thought it was in men. She thought it was in all of those empty, shallow things the world offers. And sadly, she found out by experience that this was not the case. As Jesus said, "Everyone who drinks this water will be thirsty again" (John 4:13). But in the end, she came back to the Living Water.

There are many out there today just like these searching women, people who are waiting for someone like you to reach out to them with the life-changing message of the gospel. Will you make yourself available to the Lord to be used in such a way?

It will change our world for the better—one person at a time.

18

THE WORSHIP OF WORSHIP

Ascribe to the LORD the glory due his name.
Bring an offering and come before him;
worship the LORD in the splendor of his holiness.

1 Chronicles 16:29

Have you noticed how popular worship music has become?
It seems as though almost every Christian band is recording a
worship album these days. I think it's great because I am all for
any attempt to honor and glorify God, and worship music is a
fantastic way to do that.

But I also believe it's important to keep worship in its proper
perspective. Not long ago, I saw a television program—an infomercial, if you will—for a worship product. The program
featured the testimonies of people who alleged to have found
new meaning in their lives through worship music. One man
talked about his drug addiction and how he had been delivered
from it because of worship music. A couple whose marriage was
in shambles described how worship music saved their marriage.
Another person who had lost a loved one talked about how worship music helped make it possible to cope with the loss.

WORSHIPING WORSHIP

As I was watching this, I thought, *Now wait a second. We're
getting the cart before the horse here.* Worship music doesn't
free a person from the power of an addiction. God does. Worship music doesn't save a marriage. God does. Worship music
doesn't heal a heart broken by grief. God does. Worship music
is a vehicle whereby we honor and praise God. It's designed to

bring us into the presence of God. It was God who worked in the lives of those people on the infomercial. We want to be sure and give glory to whom the glory is due.

We need to make sure we are worshiping God, not worshiping worship, because when you get down to it, everyone worships someone or something. There is some passion, some god with a small "g," or some belief system that drives us in life. It might be undiluted hedonism. It might be materialism. It might be bowing at the altar of self, but we all worship something or someone.

MADE FOR WORSHIP

Ecclesiastes 3:11 tells us, "He has made everything beautiful in its time. He has also set eternity in the hearts of men; yet they cannot fathom what God has done from beginning to end." God has uniquely wired human beings to worship. It has been built into us. But the idea is to worship the true and living God. In fact, the apostle Paul lists worship as one of the three great distinctives of true belief. In Philippians 3:3, Paul mentions that true believers

- worship by the Spirit of God
- glory in Christ Jesus
- put no confidence in the flesh

And in John 4, we will learn that "God is spirit, and his worshipers must worship in spirit and in truth" (verse 24). But it is important for us to know there is a right and wrong way to worship God. When we watch shows like the Academy Awards and the Grammy Awards, we see certain people suddenly thanking God and referring to their blessings when we normally wouldn't expect them to. Their lives tell a different story, a story of rebellion against God. And we wonder what's going on.

We see this happen with political candidates as well. They are careful to include the phrase "God bless America" in their speeches, and talk about how important faith is in their lives. We see news clips of them attending church services and carrying Bibles. But my question is: How do they live and vote? Do they seek to follow Jesus in their political lives or simply use religion as a way of attracting voters?

WORSHIP GONE WRONG

An amazing story in the Old Testament shows us this is nothing new. As the story opens, Moses has led the Israelites out of the bondage of Egypt. They have seen miracle after miracle as God has intervened on their behalf and provided for them. Now God has instructed Moses to go up to the mountain and receive his commandments. While Moses is away, his brother Aaron is in charge. Let's pick up our story in Exodus 32:1:

> When the people saw that Moses was so long in coming down from the mountain, they gathered around Aaron and said, "Come, make us gods who will go before us. As for this fellow Moses who brought us up out of Egypt, we don't know what has happened to him."

So Aaron told the people to bring all their gold, and he would make a golden calf for them. The people loved this idea.

> When Aaron saw this, he built an altar in front of the calf and announced, "Tomorrow there will be a festival to the LORD." So the next day the people rose early and sacrificed burnt offerings and presented fellowship offerings. Afterward they sat down to eat and drink and got up to indulge in revelry.
>
> verses 5–6

Aaron called this "a festival to the Lord," and the people gladly went along. It is amazing how some people can do something the Bible clearly warns against, and then somehow rationalize it and think it is okay, even good. By doing their "religious stuff," the people felt they were free to do what they wanted. They had given God his worship; now it was time to party.

So here they were, dancing naked before a golden calf in this so-called "festival to the Lord," when Moses came down from the mountain. In an attempt to explain, Aaron offered Moses the lamest excuse ever recorded:

> "Do not be angry, my lord," Aaron answered. "You know how prone these people are to evil. They said to me, 'Make us gods who will go before us. As for this fellow Moses who brought us up out of Egypt, we don't know what has happened to him.' So I told them, 'Whoever has any gold jewelry, take it off.' Then they gave me the gold, and I threw it into the fire, and out came this calf!"
>
> verses 22–24

We might smile at this and even feel a little smug, but is this really any different from going to church, lifting our hands in worship, and then going out and breaking God's commandments left and right? Make no mistake about it: there is a *right way* and a *wrong way* to worship.

19

RIGHT WORSHIP

Therefore, I urge you, brothers, in view of God's mercy,
to offer your bodies as living sacrifices, holy and
pleasing to God—this is your spiritual act of worship.

Romans 12:1

In his conversation with the woman at the well, Jesus gives us a great overview of the purpose of worship. She was a Samaritan, lonely and miserable after five failed marriages. She apparently thought a man was going to meet the deepest needs of her heart, so she had bounced from relationship to relationship.

That's what happens when God is missing in our lives. Someone or something will take his place, as Romans 1:21 tells us: "For although they knew God, they neither glorified him as God nor gave thanks to him, but their thinking became futile and their foolish hearts were darkened." Failing to glorify God, this woman turned to immoral living and tried to fill the void with men.

Yet Jesus sought her out and engaged her in conversation. And in the process, Jesus helped her understand what real faith, real worship really is.

MISSING THE POINT

So first, let's look at what Jesus had to say about *where* we should worship:

> "Sir," the woman said, "I can see that you are a prophet. Our fathers worshiped on this mountain, but you Jews claim that the place where we must worship is in Jerusalem." Jesus declared, "Believe me, woman, a time is coming when you will worship the

Father neither on this mountain nor in Jerusalem. You Samaritans worship what you do not know; we worship what we do know, for salvation is from the Jews."

John 4:19–22

The Samaritan woman was making a big deal about *where* God is worshiped, claiming the Samaritans believe God should be worshiped at Mount Gerizim. But Jesus brushed it off, essentially telling her, "You're completely missing the point."

If Jesus had gone into greater detail with her, no doubt he would have pointed out that the Samaritans' worship was flawed because they used only the first five books of the Bible, thus limiting themselves to an incomplete revelation of who God is. They worshiped in ignorance; you cannot effectively worship a God you know nothing about.

AT ONE WITH WHAT?

I read a newspaper article about a group of clerics, neuroscientists, and architects who had joined efforts to study how the mind reacts to the sensation of entering a house of worship. They asserted that the brain responds to certain styles of architecture, allowing for great worship. One of these experts cited his experiments with Franciscan nuns and Buddhist monks who were deep in meditation and how they attained states in which they felt united with a greater spirit or force. He said, "In deeply religious states they find a sense of oneness with the world."[2]

But that is not worship. That is mysticism. I don't want "a sense of oneness with the world," because the Bible tells me not to love the world or the things in the world (see 1 John 2:15). We don't need ornate buildings to worship God. We can be in a cathedral and worship him. We can be out in an open field and worship him. We can be in a little country church with a few boards missing and worship him. You see, it is not about *where* we worship. It is about *how* we worship and *why* we worship, and, of course, *who* we worship.

WHEREVER WORSHIP

Consider some biblical examples of where people worshiped. Paul and Silas were thrown into a dungeon—and I don't mean a prison cell like there is today. This was a cave, a place with no ventilation or sanitation and no windows. Not only were Paul and Silas thrown into this horrible environment, but their backs had been ripped open by a Roman whip and their feet were fastened in stocks, causing excruciating pain. Yet the Bible says that at midnight, Paul and Silas sang praises to God (see Acts 16:25).

Or how about Jonah? He worshiped in the belly of a very large fish (Jonah 2:1). How's that for a cathedral?

We can seek out the most beautiful churches. We can build the most high-tech worship centers. We can boast about the thousands of people who can fit into our comfortable stadium seats. But unless we are genuine in our efforts to meet God in these places, our buildings and big screens are useless. It's not our buildings that matter to God, it's our hearts and our motives.

20

Worshiping in Truth

Now this is eternal life: that they may know you,
the only true God, and Jesus Christ, whom you have sent.

John 17:3

Jesus was clear with the woman at the well: True worship is not about *where* or *when*. True worship is about *how*. Jesus explained, "God is spirit, and his worshipers must worship in spirit and in truth" (John 4:24). With these words, Jesus indicated the fundamental elements of true worship:

1. God must be worshiped in spirit.
2. God must be worshiped in truth.

Let's start with the latter—God must be worshiped in truth. This comes back to our view of God. The God we worship must be the true God—not a god of our own making. So our worship of God must be based on truth. And what is that truth?

The One True God

First, God can only be approached and known through Jesus Christ. It is through his blood, and his blood alone, that we have access to God. Hebrews 10:19 says, "Therefore, brothers, since we have confidence to enter the Most Holy Place by the blood of Jesus . . ." Jesus is God made flesh. The more we know about Jesus and the life he calls us to, the more clearly we can see God.

Second, God is worthy of our worship, and we should worship him whether or not we feel like it. As Hebrews 13:15 reminds us, "Through Jesus, therefore, let us continually offer to God a sacrifice of praise—the fruit of lips that confess his name." Do you think Paul and Silas were in the mood to worship there in the dungeon? Would you have been?

Or take Job for example. Talk about a bad day. He lost his possessions. He lost his family. He lost his health. He lost everything. Yet what does the Bible say Job did?

> At this, Job got up and tore his robe and shaved his head. Then he fell to the ground in worship and said: "Naked I came from my mother's womb, and naked I will depart. The LORD gave and the LORD has taken away; may the name of the LORD be praised."
>
> Job 1:20–21

You see, it is one thing to come to church and worship when we feel like it, when things are going reasonably well. The bills are paid. The sun is shining. The birds are singing. Everything is good. So we say, "Praise God!"

Then the next Sunday, the sun is not shining. The birds are not singing. There are problems. So we think, *I don't feel like going to church*. But that's when we need to worship more than ever. That is when we need to say, "Lord, I'm helpless. Lord, I need your wisdom. I need your guidance. I need your power. I need your comfort. Lord, I am turning to you." We worship regardless of our circumstances, because God is worthy of our praise. We should worship God not because we are in the mood, but because God has asked us to and has everything in control. That is the sacrifice of praise.

THE WHY OF WORSHIP

Third, God is far more interested in our motives than in our talents. When we worship, we stand before an audience of one. If, in worship, we want people to look at us or we are thinking about something else altogether, that's not worship.

Remember Cain and Abel? Both were raised in a godly home. Both heard the Word of God from their youth. Both were no doubt taught to pray and to worship God. But one was a true worshiper, offering a genuine act of worship. The other was a false worshiper, offering a synthetic act of worship. One was accepted. The other was rejected. Hebrews 11:4 tells us, "By faith Abel offered God a better sacrifice than Cain did. By faith he was commended as a righteous man, when God spoke well of his offerings. And by faith he still speaks, even though he is dead." The same passage goes on to say, "Without faith it is impossible to please God" (verse 6). It all comes down to motive—the *why* of worship.

True worship comes down to what is happening in our hearts. Jesus told the story of the Pharisee and the tax collector who went to pray (or worship):

> The Pharisee stood up and prayed about himself: "God, I thank you that I am not like other men—robbers, evildoers, adulterers—or even like this tax collector. I fast twice a week and give a tenth of all I get." But the tax collector stood at a distance. He would not even look up to heaven, but beat his breast and said, "God, have mercy on me, a sinner." I tell you that this man, rather than the other, went home justified before God. For everyone who exalts himself will be humbled, and he who humbles himself will be exalted.
>
> Luke 18:11–14

Sometimes we pray, but we do not worship. Sometimes we sing, but we do not worship. Sometimes we give, but we do not worship. And sometimes we do none of these things, but we are in our deepest worship. After all, the heart of the matter is the matter of the heart.

A READY HEART

Fourth, we cannot worship God when we knowingly have sin in our lives. The psalmist wrote, "Who may ascend the hill of the LORD? Who may stand in his holy place? He who has clean hands and a pure heart, who does not lift up his soul to an idol or swear by what is false" (Ps. 24:3–4).

That doesn't mean we have to be sinless before we can worship God—that's impossible. Rather, the idea is that when we knowingly, willfully sin against God, our prayers will not be heard and our worship will not be received. For example, if I know I've lied to someone and have no plans to come clean anytime soon, I cannot expect my worship to be meaningful to God. Or if I am holding a grudge against someone and have no intention of trying to work things out with them, then I shouldn't expect God to be honored by my worship. Or if I am living in sexual sin, I shouldn't expect God to want to hear my songs of praise or prayers and petitions.

God wants our lives and our worship to be combined together in an honorable way. God wants us to worship in spirit and in truth. And God wants our hearts more than anything else.

21

The Spirit of Worship

Love the Lord your God with all your heart and
with all your soul and with all your strength.

Deuteronomy 6:5

Not only are we to worship God in truth, but we are also to worship God in spirit: "God is spirit, and his worshipers must worship him in spirit and in truth" (John 4:24). It's not surprising the Bible pairs spirit and truth like this. We can be completely orthodox in our beliefs and still fail to express our praise toward Almighty God in a passionate way. Yes, our worship of God should be based on a true understanding of who God is and the life to which God calls us. And yes, our worship of God should engage the mind and intellect. But our worship of God should engage our affections, our hearts, and our emotions as well.

Think about all the places where we express our emotions: weddings, movie theaters, football games, political rallies, and concerts to name a few. Yet we often bury our emotions in church, for fear of appearing fanatical or weird. What a shame! If we engage our emotions in no other place, we should at least do so when we are with our brothers and sisters in Christ, worshiping our God.

Emotional Worship

One of the ways we can worship God in spirit is by lifting our hands in an expression of praise. We are told in Psalm 63:3–4, "Because your love is better than life, my lips will glorify you. I will praise you as long as I live, and in your name I will lift up my hands."

Now if someone came up to you with a gun and said, "This is a holdup," you would probably raise both hands in surrender. When we lift our hands to God, we are surrendering. We are saying to the Lord that we surrender our lives, our plans, and everything we have to him. It may seem awkward, but it's a simple way to honor God and worship with our spirits.

Notice that in addition to lifted hands, the psalmist also mentions praising lips. Sometimes when believers are worshiping together, a few people will just fold their arms, look around, and not join in. They don't engage. They don't sing or pray out loud. They just look around. I often wonder why that is. Maybe they don't know the words, maybe they don't think they sing well, maybe they don't like to worship in public. I believe these reasons for resisting the emotional side of worship are more about us than about God. We are worried about looking good (or at least not looking bad). We are unwilling to step out of our comfort zones in order to praise God. Remember, it brings joy to God when we praise him. Worship simply isn't about us.

OUR MINDS ON GOD

We can also praise God by *thinking* about him. The psalmist said, "May my meditation be pleasing to him, as I rejoice in the LORD" (Ps. 104:34). And Malachi 3:16 tells us,

> Then those who feared the LORD talked with each other, and the LORD listened and heard. A scroll of remembrance was written in his presence concerning those who feared the LORD and honored his name.

The phrase "the LORD listened and heard" brings to mind a God who cares so much about us that he wants to know what we're thinking. God created our minds and I believe he loves it when we use the gift of our intelligence to deepen our relationships with God and others.

So God wants us to express our worship in spirit and in truth. But it all comes back to this: our entry into God's presence, our access to his throne, is made available because of the death of Jesus Christ on the cross. God can only be approached and known and worshiped through Jesus Christ.

A MADE-UP GOD

Even when we know how to worship God, it is easy for us to fall into the habit of worshiping a god of our own making. In the late 1500s, a Japanese warlord known as Toyotomi Hideyoshi decided that he wanted to create a colossal statue of Buddha to place in the Nanzenji Temple in Kyoto. For five years, 50,000 workers labored to create this statue. Shortly after its completion, the earthquake of 1596 struck, bringing the roof down on the shrine and ruining the statue. In a rage, Hideyoshi shot an arrow at the fallen Buddha and shouted, "I put you here at great expense, and you can't even look after your own temple!"

Our little self-made gods — work, money, pride, self-image — are just as useless. The true God, the living God, not only can take care of a temple, he can take care of you. He sees you. He knows about you. He cares about you. He hears you. He is interested in you.

And that is why we worship God: because he is worthy. In fact, our word *worship* comes from an old English word that could be translated "worth-ship." In other words, we worship a God who is worth it.

22

AN APPOINTMENT AT THE POOL

> May the God of hope fill you with all joy and peace
> as you trust in him, so that you may overflow with hope
> by the power of the Holy Spirit.
>
> Romans 15:13

I think we all have thought of questions we would like to ask God someday. When something happens in our lives that seems inexplicable, we wonder, "Why did God allow this to happen?" I am glad the Bible promises us a day is coming when all of our questions will be answered.

A Sunday school teacher was speaking to her class about this very subject and invited her students to write down their questions for God. Here are some questions the children handed in:

"Did you mean for the giraffe to look like that, or was it an accident?"

"I like the Lord's Prayer best of all. Did you have to write it a lot, or did you get it right the first time? I have to write everything I ever write over again."

There were also some comments and complaints:

"Thank you for the baby brother, but what I prayed for was a puppy!"

"How come you didn't invent any new animals lately? We still just have all the old ones."

"I bet it is very hard for you to love all of everybody in the world. There are only four people in our family and I can never do it."

"We read that Thomas Edison made light. But in Sunday school they said you did it. I bet he stole your idea."

No matter what age we are, it seems we all have some questions for God. But I would like for us to consider some questions God has for us. Our answers to these questions will, quite literally, change the course of our lives.

VERY SUPERSTITIOUS

Many of these questions are found within a story related in John 5. Jesus posed a loaded question some two thousand years ago to a hurting, lonely, and isolated man. And he's still asking underlying questions like this one today. Let's look at the story together:

> Some time later, Jesus went up to Jerusalem for a feast of the Jews. Now there is in Jerusalem near the Sheep Gate a pool, which in Aramaic is called Bethesda and which is surrounded by five covered colonnades. Here a great number of disabled people used to lie—the blind, the lame, the paralyzed. One who was there had been an invalid for thirty-eight years. When Jesus saw him lying there and learned that he had been in this condition for a long time, he asked him, "Do you want to get well?" "Sir," the invalid replied, "I have no one to help me into the pool when the water is stirred. While I am trying to get in, someone else goes down ahead of me." Then Jesus said to him, "Get up! Pick up your mat and walk."
>
> John 5:1–8

I believe Jesus has a number of these divine appointments—with Nicodemus, with the woman at the well, and at this pool. Here, a poor, forgotten man with a disability was waiting for a healing touch from God. In some translations of this passage, the story includes this verse: "For an angel went down at a certain time into the pool and stirred up the water; then whoever stepped in first, after the stirring of the water, was made well of whatever disease he had" (verse 4). Whether this actually happened, we don't know. While this certainly would be within an angel's power, it does cause one to wonder if this was something an angel of the Lord actually would do. Basically, the healing was on a first-come, first-served basis. If you happened to be close enough and fast enough to step into the water first when the angel allegedly stirred it up, then you would be healed. So whether this was true or whether it was a commonly held belief is something at which we can only guess.

What Do You Trust?

We love to believe there is a tangible thing that can somehow make us better or change our lives. Sometimes it's as simple as a rabbit's foot or a good-luck charm. Maybe it is a lucky jacket, color, or number. It might even be a religious object such as a crucifix that seems to provide some measure of comfort. But a child of God should have no need for religious medals, lucky charms, or any other of these things. Luck plays no part whatsoever in the life of the Christian. To feel a need for these things is really a form of idolatry.

The Christian is guided by Divine Providence, not the luck of the draw. The slogan of the believer is not "*Que sera, sera,* whatever will be, will be." Rather, it is "We know that in all things God works for the good of those who love him, who have been called according to his purpose" (Rom. 8:28).

Putting Trust Where It Belongs

Now I am not saying it's wrong to wear a cross. What I am saying is that if you believe there is some kind of mystical, supernatural power in a particular object, then your trust is in the wrong place. If we need a physical object to help us know a spiritual God, then something is wrong with us and our lives before God. True believers should neither need nor depend on these things.

While Jesus didn't ask a direct question about the subject of this man's hope, it's clear that he was giving the man a choice: Trust the story that might not be true, or trust in me, the one true God. Which choice are you making?

23

WHEN BAD THINGS HAPPEN

My comfort in my suffering is this:
Your promise preserves my life.

Psalm 119:50

In John 5:1–8, we meet a man who believed that if an angel troubled the water, and if he could somehow be the first to get into the water, then he would be healed. He had been waiting for thirty-eight years, unable to move. Perhaps he had been paralyzed by an accident. We don't know. But something happened in his life that brought this about.

Sometimes we get sick simply because we live in a sin-sick world. Disease and death were never part of God's original plan. If Adam and Eve had not sinned, there would not be any sickness. There would not be any aging. And most importantly, I would have a full head of hair. But this is all a result of sin in general. We are told in Romans 5:12, "Therefore, just as sin entered the world through one man, and death through sin, and in this way death came to all men, because all sinned."

THE SICKNESS OF SIN

However, sometimes we fall ill because of our own personal sin. Paul wrote that some of the members of the Corinthian church had become ill and had even died because of their sin: "That is why many among you are weak and sick, and a number of you have fallen asleep" (1 Cor. 11:30).

Consider the person who has abused alcohol for his entire life. One day, his liver fails. Is there a connection between the lifestyle he has chosen and what has happened to him physically? Absolutely.

What about someone who goes out on a drunken binge, gets behind the wheel of a car, and is injured in an auto accident? Is there a connection between the way she was living and the horrible thing that happened to her? Of course.

Or how about the person who is sexually immoral? He frequently engages in extramarital sex. Then he discovers he is HIV positive. Is there a connection between his lifestyle and this horrible virus he now has? The answer is yes.

There can be a connection between what we do and what happens to us. I'm not saying every person who has liver damage, has a car accident, or contracts HIV/AIDS came into those circumstances because they sinned. But we do need to accept the fact that when we choose to sin, there will be consequences.

GOD AND SUFFERING

Still, there are other times when God will allow sickness—physical and spiritual sickness—in the life of a believer to teach something. For example, when the apostle Paul experienced his "thorn in the flesh," it wasn't connected to any particular sin that we know of. Yet the Lord allowed this suffering. Paul asked three times for God to take it away. But God's answer was "My grace is sufficient for you, for my power is made perfect in weakness" (2 Cor. 12:9). This would suggest that God allows sickness so he can show his people something we might not be able to see otherwise. Sometimes we are so stubborn and proud we think we don't need God. So the Lord gets our attention. And suddenly we realize maybe we do need God after all.

Out of this crowd of sick and suffering people at the pool called Bethesda, Jesus selected one man. He didn't preach to everyone. He didn't heal everyone. He went to only one individual and asked a poignant, and in some ways unexpected, question: "Do you want to get well?" (John 5:6).

Now what kind of question is that to ask a man like this? It's not like he would have said, "No, I like hanging out here. This is just a lot of fun. You really ought to join me." But Jesus was asking a legitimate question. It was an important question, because not everyone wants to be made well. Not everyone wants his or her life to change.

READY FOR CHANGE?

It reminds me of another question God asked in the Garden of Eden after Adam and Eve sinned. The Lord came walking in the garden in the cool of the day, looking for Adam and Eve. "Where are you?" God called out (Gen. 3:9). Was God totally oblivious to Adam's whereabouts? Of course not. He knew where Adam was. God called out to Adam because, among other things, God wanted Adam to acknowledge his sin. He was not looking for information, he was looking for a confession. God wanted to confront Adam and Eve with their sin so they could set it right and be restored into fellowship with him.

God could ask some of us that question right now: "Where are you?" as in, "Where are you in life? Are you where you ought to be spiritually right now? Are you satisfied with your spiritual condition, or does change need to take place?"

"Do you want to be made well?" Jesus asked this man. In other words, "Do you want to change your life, not just physically, but also spiritually? Are you willing to place yourself, just as you are, in my hands? Are you ready for me to do for you what you are unable to do for yourself?"

As long as we think we can work things out on our own, as long as we think we will figure life out someday, we never will get anywhere. We need to call out to God and say, "Lord, I can't do it on my own, but I am calling out to you and asking you to help me. I am asking you to forgive me." If you will call out to Jesus Christ, then he will forgive you. If you are willing to turn from your sin, make a clean break with the past, and begin to follow him, then you will see things happen in your life that you never thought were possible.

24

The Way of Change

When I was a child, I talked like a child,
I thought like a child, I reasoned like a child.
When I became a man, I put childish ways behind me.

1 Corinthians 13:11

Have you ever walked out of a matinee and started squinting in the afternoon sun because you had grown accustomed to the darkness of the movie theater? That's what it's like for people who don't want to change.

Not every person who drinks too much wants to stop. Not every person who uses drugs wants to change their ways. Not every person who is living immorally wants to give that up. Some people are comfortable in their sinful lifestyles. They like where they are. They have grown accustomed to the darkness.

So Jesus asks, "Do you want to change your life?" For some of us our answer, if we are honest, would be, "No, not really. I like where I am."

Out of Options

When Jesus asked this question of the man at the pool, the man gave him an honest answer: "Sir . . . I have no one to help me into the pool when the water is stirred. While I am trying to get in, someone else goes down ahead of me" (John 5:7). In other words, "I have tried everything and it failed. I can't get there."

I think it was the utter helplessness of this man that drew Jesus to him. Perhaps the night before, this person had called out to God. Maybe, even on this day, he moaned a quiet prayer to heaven, not realizing, in his wildest dreams, that God himself would personally bring him his answer—not what he asked for, but something far better.

He wanted an angel to "stir the waters," but instead God came and stirred up his life, not only physically, but spiritually as well. The Bible tells us that God "is able to do immeasurably more than all we ask or imagine" (Eph. 3:20).

Maybe you identify with this man. Maybe you have been divorced or widowed. Maybe you are out on your own in some way, shape, or form. Maybe you recently moved to a new town, or you are single and don't want to be. You understand what this man was going through.

Or maybe, like this man, you know what it is like to be paralyzed—emotionally, spiritually, or even physically. Maybe you're stuck in some kind of sin or vice that seems to have a stranglehold on your life right now. You've tried to break free, but you can't. You have lost all hope. Thankfully, this story is meant for people just like you—the hopeless and hurting.

STEPPING TOWARD HOPE

So what was Jesus's response to this man, and to all those who have lost hope? First, Jesus asked for the impossible. Jesus told this man to do what he had not been able to do for thirty-eight years: "Get up! Pick up your mat and walk" (John 5:8). This man's bed probably consisted of something like a bedroll, a sleeping bag, or maybe even a simple straw mat. Jesus was saying, "I want you to pick that up, and I want you to walk. And if I tell you to do it, then you can do it." As the Scripture reminds us, "Ah, Sovereign LORD, you have made the heavens and the earth by your great power and outstretched arm. Nothing is too hard for you" (Jer. 32:17). So when God tells us to live this Christian life, when God tells us to resist temptation, when God tells us to go into all the world and preach the gospel, then it can be done.

Now we cannot do these things with our own strength. But we can do them with God's strength. According to Philippians

4:13, "I can do everything through him who gives me strength."
And as I have often said, the calling of God is the enabling of
God.

RESISTING THE RELAPSE

Jesus told this man to pick up his mat and walk. In other
words, Jesus was saying, "There is no backup plan here, buddy.
If this doesn't work out, you won't have your little bed anymore.
That's over with. That's the past. We are moving forward."

When God calls us to do something, he expects us to make a
break from the past. We see this in the Old Testament story of
Elijah and Elisha. When Elijah was looking for a successor, the
Lord told him it would be Elisha. One day Elijah saw Elisha
plowing a field with a team of oxen. Elijah went over and threw
his mantle around Elisha's shoulders, which was a symbolic
gesture that said, "You are my successor. You are to carry on
my ministry."

Elisha's response was "Let me kiss my father and mother
good-by . . . and then I will come with you" (1 Kings 19:20).
Elisha understood immediately that something big was happening. So Elisha made a bonfire out of his plowing rig. Then
the oxen became filet mignon as the two prophets had a nice
barbecue together.

That's called burning your bridges. And that is what some
Christians fail to do. We say, "Yes, I want to follow the Lord,"
but we never remove the possibility of a relapse. We haven't made
a break with our old lifestyle. We haven't made a break with past
relationships. We haven't made a break with our sinful vices. As
a result, these things still have a hold on us and keep us from
moving forward spiritually. But God asks the impossible. He
asks us to have no conditions for a relapse—no backup plan.

One night, during our first evangelistic crusade in Southern
California, a drug dealer came forward during the invitation for
people to make a commitment to follow Jesus Christ. As part of
his repentance, he handed over his pager, because that's how he

conducted his drug deals. The next day, the follow-up counselor called him to see how he was doing.

He told him, "Well, I was out mowing the grass."

"Oh, you're doing a little yard work?" the counselor asked.

He said, "No, I was actually mowing down marijuana plants." This man was burning his bridges—or mowing them down, if you will. He was leaving no room for a relapse.

Whatever you may be struggling with, my question is: Have you burned the bridge? Have you removed the thing you can go back to? That's what Jesus asked this man. And that's what he's asking you.

25

EXPECT SUCCESS

He has showed you, O man, what is good. And
what does the LORD require of you? To act justly and
to love mercy and to walk humbly with your God.

Micah 6:8

Have you ever met someone who says, "I tried Christianity, but it didn't work for me"? But we are not dealing with an "it." We are dealing with God. Christianity is Christ, and he will work in the life of any man, woman, or child who honestly comes to him.

SET UP FOR FAILURE

Imagine a friend came up to me and said, "Well, Greg, I tried the whole health club thing and it didn't work for me."

"Really?" I'd say.

"Oh, yeah. I tried it."

"So you joined a health club?"

"Oh, yeah. Absolutely."

"How long did you go?"

"For a month."

"You went for a month? And you didn't see any improvement?"

"Not one bit of improvement. In fact, I put on weight."

"Really? Well, what did you do at the health club?"

"I just sat around and ate doughnuts."

Although my friend joined a health club, he didn't do what he needed to do. He didn't really do his part. Saying that he tried a health club but that it didn't work for him is not an accurate assessment of what happened. The truth is, he didn't really try.

DOING OUR PART

So when people say, "Oh, I tried the Christian thing and it didn't work," I wonder whether they did their part. I don't mean to suggest we have to do everything right in order to be saved. Rather, I believe we are asked to take part in the life God has to offer us and that we miss out when we don't do so. To those who think Christianity doesn't work, I ask:

1. Did you begin to study the Bible? The Bible says, "Do your best to present yourself to God as one approved, a workman who does not need to be ashamed and who correctly handles the word of truth" (2 Tim. 2:15). The Bible is where we learn of our history as God's people. It is where we find God's promises to us. It is where we discover the person of Jesus. The Bible is our guide to what it means to be a Christian. We simply can't know and live for God without hearing what he has to say.

2. Did you get involved in a church? Hebrews 10:25 says, "Let us not give up meeting together, as some are in the habit of doing, but let us encourage one another—and all the more as you see the Day approaching."

One Sunday morning after our morning service at Harvest Christian Fellowship, I was answering phones for our television program. A woman called to order a CD we were offering, so I took down her name and information. It turned out that she lived in a city near Riverside, where our church is located, so I asked her where she attended church.

"I go to Harvest Christian Fellowship," she told me.

I said, "It's Sunday. Why aren't you here?"

Sounding a little embarrassed, she offered a not-so-convincing explanation.

I said, "Well, you ought to be here. You can still come to the third service. By the way, this is Pastor Greg." She didn't believe me. So we talked a little bit more. Then I said, "Really, this is Greg Laurie, and I would like to see you at church."

"It really *is* you!!" she said. "I recognize your voice now! I can't believe I'm talking to you, telling you I wasn't at church today!"

Although I was having a little fun with this unsuspecting caller, my point was that we, as Christians, need to be in regular, consistent fellowship in a local, Bible-teaching church.

3. Did you get baptized? While baptism is not required for salvation, the Bible does command us to be baptized (see Matt. 3:13–16; 28:19–20; Acts 2:38). So why not obey the Lord in this area? Talk to your pastor to find out what baptism is about and how you take part in this beautiful act of renewal.

4. Did you turn from all known sin? The psalmist said, "If I had cherished sin in my heart, the Lord would not have listened" (Ps. 66:18).

5. Did you develop a prayer life? The Bible tells us to "pray continually; give thanks in all circumstances, for this is God's will for you in Christ Jesus" (1 Thess. 5:17–18).

6. Did you deny yourself, take up the cross, and follow Jesus? Jesus said, "If anyone would come after me, he must deny himself and take up his cross and follow me. For whoever wants to save his life will lose it, but whoever loses his life for me will find it" (Matt. 16:24–25).

WHEN FAITH WORKS

My question to those who say they have tried Christianity is, did you do these things I have just described? If not, then don't say that you have tried Christianity. You need to do your part. You see, Jesus doesn't "work" for some, but not for others. He will change any person who comes to him, just as they are. Our salvation is free—it comes without strings and through no effort of our own. But living as saved people means allowing God to make us new people.

You see, there are some things only God can do, and there are some things only you can do. Only God can convict us of our sin. Only God can forgive us and empower us to live the Christian life.

Having said that, only you can repent of your sin. Only you can ask God for his power and seek to yield to each and every day.

May God help us all to do just that.

26

The Judgment of God

Judgment will again be founded on righteousness,
and all the upright in heart will follow it.

Psalm 94:15

So many people fear death. They are afraid of the pain that might
come with death. They are afraid that their lives will end before
they are ready. And they are afraid of what will happen to them
when they die. But those of us who trust in God don't need to
be afraid because Jesus tells us what to expect in death:

> I tell you the truth, a time is coming and has now come when the
> dead will hear the voice of the Son of God and those who hear
> will live. For as the Father has life in himself, so he has granted
> the Son to have life in himself. And he has given him authority
> to judge because he is the Son of Man. Do not be amazed at this,
> for a time is coming when all who are in their graves will hear his
> voice and come out—those who have done good will rise to live,
> and those who have done evil will rise to be condemned.
>
> John 5:25–29

A True View of Death

We can find great comfort in Jesus's words. He makes it clear
that death is not the end of existence. Human beings are eternal
creatures, meaning our souls live on forever. Some teach that
we simply cease to exist at death. But the Bible teaches that we
live on.

How we live on, however, depends on the state of our souls.
Jesus tells us there will be a final judgment. This is not something

we hear enough about from our pulpits these days. I rarely hear a pastor mention hell or judgment. The apostle Paul, however, was one preacher who was not afraid to bring this up:

> In the past God overlooked such ignorance, but now he commands all people everywhere to repent. For he has set a day when he will judge the world with justice by the man he has appointed. He has given proof of this to all men by raising him from the dead.
>
> Acts 17:30–31

I'm not suggesting that hell and judgment should always be the focus of our sermons. But we would do well to remember they are clearly taught throughout Scripture. In fact, Jesus gave this sobering warning in Matthew 12:36: "But I tell you that men will have to give account on the day of judgment for every careless word they have spoken."

I realize some people don't like to hear this because they don't believe in a God of judgment. "I believe in a God of love, of mercy, and of compassion," they say. I do too. But I also believe in a God who is just. I wouldn't want to believe in a God who merely demonstrates love and compassion, but fails to execute justice and righteousness.

God's Justice

The fact there is a future judgment assures us that ultimately God is fair. The teaching of a future judgment should satisfy our inward sense of a need for justice in this world. We've all seen things that seem appallingly unjust, and we say to God, "How can they get away with that?" The horrific crimes we hear of in the news desperately show the need for justice in the world. But know this: God is in control, and he keeps very accurate records. The Bible says, "Anyone who does wrong will be repaid for his wrong, and there is no favoritism" (Col. 3:25). Some may escape "the long arm of the law," so to speak, but they will never escape from the God who sees and knows everything.

The teaching of a future judgment frees us from the need to hold grudges and seek revenge in our lives. It's not up to us to take vengeance on those who have wronged us, or even to want to do so, because God Almighty has reserved that right for himself. Romans 12:19 reminds us, "Do not take revenge, my friends, but leave room for God's wrath, for it is written: 'It is mine to avenge; I will repay,' says the Lord."

THE GOOD JUDGE

Every wrong ever committed ultimately will be paid for. It will be paid when the offender has repented of his sins and put his faith in Jesus Christ, who died on the cross for our sins. Or, it will be paid for at the final judgment for those who do not trust in Jesus for salvation. God will avenge all wrongs that have been done in this world.

Jesus gave us the example to follow. The Bible tells us: "'He committed no sin, and no deceit was found in his mouth.' When they hurled their insults at him, he did not retaliate; when he suffered, he made no threats. Instead, he entrusted himself to him who judges justly" (1 Peter 2:22–23).

27

Two Resurrections

Now we know that if the earthly tent we live in
is destroyed, we have a building from God,
an eternal house in heaven, not built by human hands.

2 Corinthians 5:1

In John 5, we read of two forms of existence beyond the grave: "Do not be amazed at this, for a time is coming when all who are in their graves will hear his voice and come out—those who have done good will rise to live, and those who have done evil will rise to be condemned" (verses 28–29). According to these verses, there are two resurrections:

1. A resurrection to life, which is for the believer
2. A resurrection to condemnation, which is for the unbeliever

Let's look at another passage that deals with this subject further:

I saw thrones on which were seated those who had been given authority to judge. And I saw the souls of those who had been beheaded because of their testimony for Jesus and because of the word of God. They had not worshiped the beast or his image and had not received his mark on their foreheads or their hands. They came to life and reigned with Christ a thousand years. (The rest of the dead did not come to life until the thousand years were ended.) This is the first resurrection. Blessed and holy are those who have part in the first resurrection. The second death has no power over them, but they will be priests of God and of Christ and will reign with him for a thousand years.

Revelation 20:4–6

The first resurrection is the one all true believers will experience. Believers, meaning those who have put their faith in Jesus Christ, will go immediately into his presence. There will be no layovers. It is a direct flight, so to speak. When a Christian dies, he or she goes straight to heaven. As Jesus said to the thief on the cross, "*Today* you will be with me in paradise" (Luke 23:43, emphasis mine).

A LONGING HEART

The apostle Paul spoke of his longing to be in heaven with Jesus, yet realized there was still work for him to do on Earth. Of this tension he said,

For to me, to live is Christ and to die is gain. If I am to go on living in the body, this will mean fruitful labor for me. Yet what shall I choose? I do not know! I am torn between the two: I desire to depart and be with Christ, which is better by far.

Philippians 1:21–23

Paul spoke of his desire "to depart and be with Christ" (verse 23). Notice that he did not say, "I am torn by my desire to depart for a few thousand years in a state of suspended animation," or "I am torn by my desire to depart for purgatory." Paul was clearly stating that a believer is either at home in the body or is with the Lord.

ANSWERING THE UNANSWERABLE

Many questions are asked about what it will be like in heaven. Do we keep our bodies in heaven? The answer is yes. And no. We will have new bodies in heaven, but they will not be in the same state as they are now. According to 1 Corinthians 15:42–43, "So will it be with the resurrection of the dead. The body that is sown is perishable, it is raised imperishable; it is sown in dishonor, it is raised in glory; it is sown in weakness, it is raised in power. This means that if you were disabled on earth, you won't be in heaven. If your body has cancer, or is simply worn out with age, that won't be the case in heaven.

We often talk about the differences there will be when we make our transition from earth to heaven. But there will be a few similarities too. When we pass over to the other side, our minds will be clearer than ever before. The apostle Paul tells us, "All that I know now is partial and incomplete, but then I will know everything completely, just as God knows me now" (1 Cor. 13:12 NLT).

A FULLER VIEW

After returning home from a trip to England awhile back, my wife Cathe and I were experiencing severe jet lag. We arrived home and decided to go out for a quick dinner, but Cathe wanted to wash some clothes first. So she put some clothes in the washing machine and we left. What she didn't realize was that she had left the faucet running in our laundry room sink. When we came home an hour later, we found three inches of water all over the floor. It totally destroyed our kitchen floor and even went into some other rooms.

I kind of let it go and didn't really say anything to Cathe. But a couple of weeks went by, and one day in conversation, I brought up the subject of our modern-day flood.

Cathe said, "Well, you know what? You left the iron on the other day. You actually had the iron on the pad and left it on, and I found it. You could have burned the house down. Flooding the floor is not nearly as bad as burning down the house."

I said, "You know, maybe we can work together. I'll start the fire upstairs and you can flood the house downstairs. We'll come home, and everything will be just fine."

We both laughed.

In heaven, our minds will be redeemed from the limitations sin has imposed on them. Although we won't know everything (that knowledge only belongs to God), we will know fully, as the Bible promises: "Now we see but a poor reflection as in a mirror; then we shall see face to face. Now I know in part; then I shall know fully, even as I am fully known" (1 Cor. 13:12).

Think of the purest joy on earth, then multiply that one thousand times, and you may get a fleeting glimpse of heaven's euphoria. This is why David wrote, "You will fill me with joy in your presence, with eternal pleasures at your right hand" (Ps. 16:11).

28

Rewards

> The King will reply, "I tell you the truth, whatever you did
> for one of the least of these brothers of mine, you did for me."
>
> Matthew 25:40

One day you and I will arrive home, to heaven. As Christians, we will stand before the judgment seat of Christ. This judgment will be different from the judgment for nonbelievers. At that judgment, there is no reprieve. There is no bargaining. Tragically, for those who end up there, it's too late because this judgment will be final. But there is also a judgment for Christians. However, this judgment is not about whether a person will go to heaven, because the fact is that it takes place *in* heaven. This is a judgment where rewards are given out.

Heavenly Ceremonies

Over the years, many of us have acquired the great awards this world has to offer. Perhaps you've excelled in sports and your shelves are lined with trophies, plaques, and ribbons. (Growing up, I always received Honorable Mention ribbons, which means I basically showed up, but lost.) When we think of a judgment for Christians, we ought to think of the Olympic ceremonies, for example. Just to compete as an Olympic athlete is a great feat. To actually medal is even more incredible. So the idea is that you are in the Olympics, yes, but only some are going to win, in effect, the gold, the silver, and the bronze. And the rewards of heaven are not medals but are often referred to as "crowns" (1 Cor. 9:25; 2 Tim. 4:8).

In heaven, there will be many rewards for those who have been faithful to God over the years. God does not overlook even the smallest, most insignificant gesture on behalf of his kingdom. Jesus said that our service to God, though not seen by people, is seen by God: "Your Father, who sees what is done in secret, will reward you" (Matt. 6:6). Speaking of this day in the future for all believers, the Bible says, "For we must all appear before the judgment seat of Christ, that everyone may receive what is due them for the things done while in the body, whether good or bad" (2 Cor. 5:10 TNIV).

Good Work

This same concept is further developed in 1 Corinthians 3:11–15:

> For no one can lay any foundation other than the one already laid, which is Jesus Christ. If any man builds on this foundation using gold, silver, costly stones, wood, hay or straw, his work will be shown for what it is, because the Day will bring it to light. It will be revealed with fire, and the fire will test the quality of each man's work. If what he has built survives, he will receive his reward. If it is burned up, he will suffer loss; he himself will be saved, but only as one escaping through the flames.

This judgment is known as the Bema seat, or the judgment seat of Christ. The "wood, hay, or straw" to which verse 12 refers is speaking not so much about gross sin as it is of putting more importance on the passing things of this world than on the things of God. It might be a career, sport, hobby, television, or something else that will one day pass away. At the judgment seat of Christ, he will want to know what you did with your time, what you did with your resources, and what you did with your opportunities. He will want to know what you did with the gospel with which you were entrusted.

THE REWARD OF HONOR

According to this and other passages, our presence in the kingdom is guaranteed by the promises of God. But our position in the kingdom will be won or lost by the quality of service we render here and now. God will not hold you accountable for what he has called me to do. And he will not hold me accountable for what he has called you to do. But he will hold you accountable as a Christian who was purchased with his blood at the cross of Calvary.

There is an important distinction to make here. I'm not talking about earning your place in heaven or in making your life about getting the best rewards in eternity. On the contrary, this heavenly reward system is based on humble service given out of the right motive for the Lord. Salvation is a gift through faith in Jesus Christ; honor is a reward for service to Jesus Christ.

29

MAKE IT COUNT

Moses . . . regarded disgrace for the sake of Christ
as of greater value than the treasures of Egypt,
because he was looking ahead to his reward.

Hebrews 11:24, 26

At the end of our lives here on earth, we will meet our heavenly Father face-to-face. And he will ask us, "Well, what did you do with the life I gave you?"

How sad to have to respond, "Honestly, I didn't do much with it, Lord. What can I say? I was a bit on the self-absorbed side. And by the way, I wanted to thank you for purchasing my salvation. I really do appreciate that. But I didn't really do much of anything for you."

How much better to say, "Well, Lord, I didn't do as much as I could have done, but I did some things. And I did them for your glory. I offer them to you as my worship and my praise. There is no way that this even comes close to equaling what you did for me, but it is my way of saying 'thank you' for loving me and forgiving me."

THE FINAL WORD

I've done a lot of funeral services over the years, both for people I knew and people I didn't know, for Christians and non-Christians. The most difficult have been the services for those who did not know the Lord, because I had very little hope to offer. The best I could do was hope and pray that in the last moments of his or her life, that person trusted Christ.

During a funeral service, I try, of course, to talk about some of the deceased person's good qualities. And I have yet to stand up and say, "You know, George made so much money. Do you know how much money is in his bank account right now?" Although that may have been the most important thing to George while he was alive, no one wants to hear that at his memorial service. What people want to hear at memorial services are endearing traits of the person, some sacrificial act, something about his or her character or nature that indicated goodness, compassion, and honor.

It's always so sad when I find nothing of the kind, nothing of substance to point to. As the prophet Daniel said to the irreverent King Belshazzar, "You have been weighed on the scales and found wanting" (Dan. 5:27). In other words, "Belshazzar, you are a spiritual lightweight. You have no substance." What a tragedy to discover that a person has largely wasted his or her life. And it happens far too often.

Your Eulogy

Imagine what would happen if we really told the truth at funerals. What if the pastor said of the deceased, "He wasted his life pursuing a bunch of stuff that his family will now fight over"? Or, "She was selfish, never spent time with her family, and was dishonest too." Of course, we would be horrified to hear something like this at a funeral. But for some people, these would be accurate statements.

One day, someone will conduct your memorial service, your funeral. What would you want people to say? Would you want them to say, "She really lived for the Lord. Her life really touched mine," or "The world is a better place because he lived here. My life is better off because I met him"? How we live our lives is important, because one day our lives will end, the eulogy will be given, and the inscription will be made on the tombstone.

When mob boss John Gotti died, the florists of Queens reportedly delivered floral displays that included a six-foot replica of a martini glass, a racehorse, a royal flush, and a Cuban cigar. These supposedly were the things that Gotti's life was about.

What if your friends and family were to have someone design a few floral representations of your life? What would they be?

Maybe a Bible? A television set? A football? A car? What is your life about? Can you think of a few icons that would symbolize it? What would you want to be remembered for? What *will* you be remembered for?

THE BEST LIFE

How we live matters. But what matters most is not whether we live a good or a bad life. Even if you live the best, most commendable life imaginable, if you live without accepting Christ and his offer of forgiveness, you have nothing. Even if you have made terrible mistakes in your life, God's forgiveness and grace are available to you. What matters is knowing you can be forgiven, and you can have the guaranteed hope that when you die, you will go to heaven. If you don't have that hope, then don't let another day go by without it. The only way that a person gets into heaven is through Jesus Christ. Jesus said, "I am the way and the truth and the life. No one comes to the Father except through me" (John 14:6). There is no other way.

If you want to make sure you are going to heaven, if you are ready to put your trust in Christ and receive his offer to be forgiven of your sins, then will you take a moment to pray this prayer?

Lord Jesus, I know I am a sinner. But I thank you for dying on the cross and shedding your blood for my sin. I turn from that sin, and I choose to follow you. Be my Savior. Be my Lord. Be my God. Be my friend. I want to go to heaven when I die. I want to be ready for your return. In Jesus' name I pray. Amen.

If you prayed that prayer and meant it, then Jesus Christ has come to live in your heart. To help you grow in your newfound faith, be sure to spend time regularly reading the Bible, praying, going to church, and sharing your faith in Christ with others. And welcome to the family of God!

30

THE TEST

May the God who gives endurance and encouragement give you a spirit of unity among yourselves as you follow Christ Jesus.

Romans 15:5

I don't know about you, but I hated tests in school. When it comes to tests, there's always the temptation to cheat. And plenty of students have given in to that temptation, like one little boy named Joshua, who was called to the front of the class by his history teacher.

His teacher said, "Joshua, I have reason to believe you cheated on a test."

"Why would you think that?" Joshua asked.

"Well, you sat by Brittney during the test. And on question number one when it asked, 'Who was the first president of the United States?' Brittney wrote, 'George Washington.' *You* wrote, 'George Washington' also."

"But everyone knows that one!" Joshua said.

"Well, on question number two, it asks, 'Who wrote the Declaration of Independence?' Brittney wrote, 'Thomas Jefferson' as her answer," the teacher said, "and you did too, Josh."

"Everyone knows that one too," Joshua replied. "It doesn't mean I cheated."

His teacher continued, "The last question asked, 'Who was the seventeenth president of the United States?' and Brittney wrote, 'I don't know!'"

"So?"

"Joshua," his teacher said, "you wrote, 'Me either!'"

TESTING TIME

Tests. They're no fun, but they have their purpose, as James 1:2–4 reminds us, "Consider it pure joy, my brothers, whenever you face trials of many kinds, because you know that the testing of your faith develops perseverance. Perseverance must finish its work so that you may be mature and complete, not lacking anything."

In John 6, we find a series of tests, or pop quizzes, if you will, that Jesus sprung on his disciples to see if they were listening, learning, and paying attention. He was preparing them for the future because he wanted them to become what that passage in James describes: mature, complete, not lacking anything.

We see the first of such tests in the feeding of the five thousand, the only miracle that's mentioned in all four Gospels. At this point in his ministry, Jesus was on a roll. His fame was growing by the minute. The crowds swelled wherever he went. In some circles, Jesus's popularity alone would qualify his ministry as a success. In some churches, it doesn't seem to matter why people come, just as long as they come. It is all in the numbers.

But for Jesus, motive was everything. We see this in John 2:23–25:

> Now while he was in Jerusalem at the Passover Feast, many people saw the miraculous signs he was doing and believed in his name. But Jesus would not entrust himself to them, for he knew all men. He did not need man's testimony about man, for he knew what was in a man.

Jesus knew there were those who followed him because he was "the next big thing." He knew those people weren't really paying attention to what he said or to the life he was calling them to. Many of those in the crowd were little more than thrill seekers. John tells us, "A great crowd of people followed [Jesus] because they saw the miraculous signs he had performed on the sick" (John 6:2). According to Matthew's Gospel, as Jesus surveyed the massive crowd, which numbered as high as ten thousand people (including women and children), he knew some of them were there for the spectacle of it all.

THROUGH THE EYES OF JESUS

Yet Jesus didn't scold them or shame them or even ask those who were just gawking to leave. Instead, he had compassion on them (see Matt. 9:36). Jesus was deeply moved as he looked at the crowd. He knew their fickleness. He knew they would soon turn against him. And still his heart burned for them.

Now, if I had been there with these multitudes and had known what Jesus knew, I would have been very tempted to let them starve. After all, if I knew at that moment that some of the very people being fed would, in a short time, join the jeering crowds who would cry out, "Crucify him!" I wouldn't have given these people the time of day, much less a free lunch.

MAKING THE GRADE

In some ways, the very set-up of this story is a kind of test—for us. It causes us to ask ourselves why we follow Jesus. Is it because it feels good or because being a Christian gives us a better standing in our social circles? Is it because we like the music or the preaching at our particular church? Is it because we're hedging our bets that, if there is a God, we'd like to be on his good side? If it were you standing in that crowd on the hillside, what do you think would have brought you there?

God doesn't want us to follow him because we have nothing better to do, or because we need the comfort of a little religion in our lives. God wants us to follow him because we love him and want to know him. Are you passing this test?

31

THE CHALLENGE OF JESUS

He also saw a poor widow put in two very small copper coins. "I tell you the truth," he said, "this poor widow has put in more than all the others. All these people gave their gifts out of their wealth; but she out of her poverty put in all she had to live on."

Luke 21:2–4

Even the most faith-filled among us have our moments of doubt. In the midst of the story of the feeding of the five thousand, we see two of Jesus's disciples show just how little they understand about Jesus and what he came to accomplish. Here were men who knew Jesus, who watched him perform miracles and heal the sick. Yet they couldn't quite let go of their skepticism. Despite all their knowledge of Jesus, they hadn't yet let their hearts fully believe he was who he said he was.

PHILIP

Among the twelve disciples, Philip was the apostolic administrator—the road manager, so to speak. He seemed to possess the classic traits and personality of an administrator. So, surrounded by these massive crowds and seeing they were hungry, Jesus turned to Philip and asked him a question: "Where shall we buy bread for these people to eat?" (John 6:5).

Philip did not really answer the Lord's question but responded with some statistics: "Eight months' wages would not buy enough bread for each one to have a bite!" (verse 7). In other words, "It would take a small fortune to feed them, Lord!" Philip saw the situation only through the eyes of logic. Now, that's not to say logic and faith are incompatible. In fact, I think some people could use a lot more of each. But Philip simply did not see the possibilities. He was responsible, honest, and, at times, lacking in faith. He wasn't able to set aside his pragmatic concerns and learn to lay hold of the supernatural potential of faith.

ANDREW

Next we come to Andrew. Originally introduced to Jesus by John the Baptist, Andrew was a devoted disciple of John's—that is, until the day John saw Jesus walk by and said, "Look, the Lamb of God, who takes away the sin of the world!" (John 1:29). Right away, Andrew found his brother Simon Peter and told him, "We have found the Messiah" (John 1:41).

Andrew had a knack for bringing people to Jesus at just the right moment. Here on the hillside, Andrew turned to Jesus and said, "Here is a boy with five small barley loaves and two small fish, but how far will they go among so many?" (John 6:9). Andrew had the right idea in mentioning this little boy and his lunch. But doubt caught up with him. Though faring better than the doubtful Philip, Andrew, too, missed the point.

THE LITTLE BOY

Then there was the little boy. What do we know about this little guy? Well, we know he was poor. His lunch was largely composed of barley bread, the least expensive of all bread and typically thought of as food for animals, not people. In addition to the loaves of barley bread, the boy had two small fish. The modern equivalent would be something along the lines of sardines and crackers (and stale crackers at that).

Yet this boy did something that set him apart from all other boys who may have been in the crowd that day. This boy gave his lunch, as meager as it was, to Jesus. This little boy, who undoubtedly had very little knowledge about Jesus, had something Philip and Andrew did not: belief. He gave what he had, knowing that Jesus would make something good happen.

The boy was as insignificant as he could be. His lunch was as insignificant as it could be. But that which was *insufficient* in the hands of the *insignificant* became *sufficient* and *significant* when placed in the hands of Jesus.

We see this throughout the pages of Scripture. God takes the insignificant and makes it significant.

What is as insignificant as dust? You can't even plant crops in dust. Yet dust became a human being when molded by the hands of the Creator.

The jawbone of a donkey is pretty insignificant. But God used it in the hands of Samson to defeat the enemies of Israel.

A shepherd's rod is insignificant, yet when God placed it in the hands of Moses, it became a powerful instrument used to deliver the Israelites from centuries of bondage in Egypt.

A sling is unimportant, but God used it in the hands of David to kill the mighty Goliath.

And what is as insignificant as a poor virgin in a distant town of the Roman Empire? Yet God took that young girl named Mary and used her to bring into the world the Savior of all.

It didn't matter that Philip and Andrew were part of Christ's inner circle. They had gifts to bring, but they were stopped by logic, by practicality. They forgot they were living in the upside-down kingdom of God where logic isn't enough. The little boy, however, acted on faith. He gave his ordinary gift and Jesus turned it into something extraordinary.

So bring your fish and loaves (or your stale crackers and sardines), and present them to Jesus. Bring your life, your strengths, and your weaknesses, and see what the touch of the Master's hand can bring about.

32

God of the Impossible

Jesus looked at them and said, "With man this is impossible,
but not with God; all things are possible with God."

Mark 10:27

When Jesus taught the disciples to pray, he told them, "This,
then, is how you should pray: 'Our Father in heaven, hallowed
be your name. . . . Give us today our daily bread'" (Matt. 6:9, 11).
God provides us with everything we need. But there are times
when that provision doesn't come as quickly as we'd like.

Have you ever been in a situation where you had no food
to eat or no money to pay your bills? I have. Maybe you're
in such a situation right now and don't know where to turn.
Having walked with the Lord for more than thirty years, I can
tell you God has always provided for my needs, as Philippians
4:19 promises: "And my God will meet all your needs according
to his glorious riches in Christ Jesus." Notice this doesn't say
God will supply all our *greeds.* But it does say that God will
provide for all our *needs.* Yet so often, we struggle to believe
God will do so.

View Askew

That seemed to be what was happening to the disciples who
were with Jesus on the hillside, looking at the mass of people who
wanted something to eat (see John 6). It doesn't seem to have
occurred to the disciples that Jesus could miraculously feed them.
The lack of belief we often see in the disciples always surprises
me. They had seen a number of dramatic miracles at this point,
from water being turned into wine to a lame man being healed.

So why was it hard for them to consider that Jesus could solve the problem that presented itself?

I believe the disciples had a defective view of Jesus. And I believe we tend to have the same defective view. In the Old Testament, we see a similar problem with the nation of Israel. Years before David became king, Israel departed from God's plan for them (a theocracy under judges) and decided they wanted to be like other nations that were ruled by kings. So they chose Saul, the tallest man in the nation. Had there been such a thing back then, Saul would have won the People's Choice Awards. He just looked like a king, the Israelites thought. So they chose the giant in their nation to be their ruler, only to find themselves cowering before another giant, Goliath, from the enemy army of the Philistines.

DAVID'S FAITH

Then along came David. In contrast to the majority of his countrymen, David did not have a defective concept of God. When David saw Israel's armies retreating before Goliath, he asked, "Who is this uncircumcised Philistine that he should defy the armies of the living God?" (1 Sam. 17:26). He did not see God in the light of Goliath; instead, he saw Goliath in the light of God. David, the shepherd boy, told Saul, the giant of Israel:

> When a lion or a bear came and carried off a sheep from the flock, I went after it, struck it and rescued the sheep from its mouth. When it turned on me, I seized it by its hair, struck it and killed it. Your servant has killed both the lion and the bear; this uncircumcised Philistine will be like one of them, because he has defied the armies of the living God. The Lord who delivered me from the paw of the lion and the paw of the bear will deliver me from the hand of this Philistine.
>
> verses 34–37

David had the right concept of God, demonstrated by the fact that he ran *toward* Goliath as he called upon the Lord.

Who or what seems too much for you to handle today? Which seems larger in your eyes: God, or your problems? Like David, we should not see God in the light of our problems, but our problems in the light of God.

JUST ENOUGH

Even our small problems matter to God. In Mark's version of the feeding of the five thousand, we see just how Jesus tended to the needs of the crowd:

> Then Jesus directed [the disciples] to have all the people sit down in groups on the green grass. So they sat down in groups of hundreds and fifties. Taking the five loaves and the two fish and looking up to heaven, he gave thanks and broke the loaves. Then he gave them to his disciples to set before the people. He also divided the two fish among them all. They all ate and were satisfied, and the disciples picked up twelve basketfuls of broken pieces of bread and fish. The number of the men who had eaten was five thousand.
>
> Mark 6:39–44

Jesus blessed what he had, and as the disciples distributed the loaves and fish, the food just kept multiplying. One boy's lunch didn't explode into a mountain of bread and fish; it probably appeared to be the same amount even as the disciples handed it out. They simply could not exhaust the supply.

The same is true for us. God gives us what we need when we need it—not necessarily before, and never after, but when it is needed. So take what you have and start working with it, because gifts from God seldom come fully developed.

When I was boy, we once had a guest in our home who was an artist for Disney. I watched in amazement and admiration as he seemed to effortlessly sketch out Disney characters one after the other, right before my eyes. Our guest told me that he could draw this way because of his magic pencil. And much to my delight, he gave his magic pencil to me before he left. It didn't take long for me to discover there was nothing magical about that pencil, however. The so-called magic amounted to many hours of practice the artist had put in to develop his talent.

As we use the gifts God has given us, no matter how feeble or small we think they are, God will develop and even multiply them.

33

A Tale of Two Agendas

But the plans of the Lord stand firm forever,
the purposes of his heart through all generations.

Psalm 33:11

God often does his greatest work in quiet ways. We saw this when Jesus turned water into wine at the wedding in Cana (John 2:1–11). We see it in the Old Testament account of Elijah, after his dramatic showdown with the prophets of Baal on Mount Carmel:

> The Lord said, "Go out and stand on the mountain in the presence of the LORD, for the LORD is about to pass by." Then a great and powerful wind tore the mountains apart and shattered the rocks before the LORD, but the LORD was not in the wind. After the wind there was an earthquake, but the LORD was not in the earthquake. After the earthquake came a fire, but the LORD was not in the fire. And after the fire came a gentle whisper. When Elijah heard it, he pulled his cloak over his face and went out and stood at the mouth of the cave.
>
> 1 Kings 19:11–13

We find a lot of drama in the above passage: strong winds, an earthquake, a fire, yet God was not in any of these things. The Lord came with a still, small voice. And that's how God typically comes to us. Even so, we tend to ignore the quiet God and wait instead for the big show, the loud noise, the bright light.

Our Plans

We like to have an agenda. The problem is we would rather follow the one we make up ourselves than the one God has laid out for us. Take a look at what happened following the feeding of the five thousand. John writes, "After the people saw the miraculous sign that Jesus did, they began to say, 'Surely this is the Prophet who is to come into the world.' Jesus, knowing that they intended to come and make him king by force, withdrew again to a mountain by himself" (John 6:14–15). At the time this story took place, these people lived under Roman occupation. They wanted their freedom again, so they thought, "If we could get Jesus on our side, maybe we could drive out the Romans." They wanted to use God instead of be used by him.

Sometimes, we Christians do the same thing. We want God to serve our purposes. Some politicians invoke God's name in the hopes of being elected to office. Some businesspeople join large churches to "network." Some single people use Jesus to catch the attention of an attractive guy or girl. But Jesus will not be used by people. He didn't, and doesn't follow any agenda but his own.

GOD'S PLANS

Because of our desire for God to act in big, noisy ways, we often miss out on all the little ways God is working in our lives. These become particularly hard to see when we are in the midst of what feels like an enormous problem. But these are the times when we must trust God the most.

There will always be situations in life to which we have neither the resources nor the ability to respond. When that unexpected bill comes in the mail and you wonder, "How will we ever pay this?" When there is a crisis with your spouse and you think, "How will we ever get through this?" When your "perfect" child gets into trouble and you ask, "How will we survive this?" When there is that problem at work and you say to yourself, "I don't think I can make it another day."

We find such a situation in the Old Testament story of King Jehoshaphat. His enemies, who greatly outnumbered him, had joined forces and were coming to destroy him and his people. When he heard the news, his heart sank and he was filled with fear.

Jehoshaphat could have panicked or thrown a temper tantrum. But the Bible tells us that Jehoshaphat "resolved to inquire of the Lord, and he proclaimed a fast for all Judah" (2 Chron. 20:3). Then he prayed before all the people, "O our God, will you not judge them? For we have no power to face this vast army that is attacking us. We do not know what to do, but our eyes are upon you" (verse 12). And guess what happened? God delivered them.

Joining God's Agenda

God isn't only concerned about the big issues in our lives. In fact, the story of the feeding of the five thousand reminds us that God is involved in the most intimate, human aspects of our lives. Nothing is too small for God's care and concern.

The psalmist penned this prayer: "Hear my cry, O God; listen to my prayer. From the ends of the earth I call to you, I call as my heart grows faint; lead me to the rock that is higher than I" (Ps. 61:1–2). And 1 Peter 5:7 says to "cast all your anxiety on him because he cares for you." When we are overwhelmed, when we are worried and discouraged, we need to look at God's greatness—not the size of our problems.

Still, God is not just there to help us when times are difficult. God wants our involvement in the world. And so God has given all of us talents, abilities, gifts, and resources that we are to use for God's glory. No matter how insignificant these gifts may seem to you, God can use them. Think of the supposedly insignificant people God has used throughout history. Joseph was only a slave, but God used him to save both Egypt and Israel (see Gen. 45:3–7). He used a young slave girl to bring the powerful Syrian general Naaman to the prophet Elisha for healing (see 2 Kings 5). And he used an ostracized, immoral woman to bring a town to faith (see John 4:1–42).

God's agenda will always be more interesting, more fulfilling, more extraordinary than ours. Even when that agenda is played out in slow, quiet ways, it is the work of our amazing God. It is our privilege and our calling to join in.

34

HURRICANE GRACE

You intended to harm me, but God intended it for good
to accomplish what is now being done.

Genesis 50:20

You may remember the book and the film, *The Perfect Storm*, about a hurricane that hit off the coast of Gloucester, Massachusetts, in October 1991. Stronger than any other storm in recorded history, the "perfect" storm was actually two existing storms that converged with a hurricane, ironically labeled Hurricane Grace, to form a monstrous, two-thousand-mile-wide weather system that created waves up to one hundred feet high—the equivalent of a ten-story building.

John 6:16–18 tells the story of the disciples being hit by Hurricane Grace, so to speak. John writes, "When evening came, his disciples went down to the lake, where they got into a boat and set off across the lake for Capernaum. By now it was dark, and Jesus had not yet joined them. A strong wind was blowing and the waters grew rough." In effect, it was "the perfect storm." Matthew's Gospel tells us that Jesus made the disciples get into this boat and go to the other side of the Sea of Galilee (see Matt. 14:22). Why? He did it to change them. But that change couldn't come without the combination of the disciples' fear, the storm's fury, and God's faithfulness.

CAUGHT IN THE RAIN

As this story begins, Jesus had just performed the feeding of the five thousand. This miracle prompted the people to attempt to "make him king by force" (John 6:15). But Jesus wanted to diffuse this movement to make him king. He knew it would create a worst-case scenario for the disciples, who had the potential of going from suffering indifference and indignity to ruling over the people. It was a rags-to-riches story in the making. And that's exactly why Jesus had to get them out of town—as soon as possible. He knew such a change in status would have destroyed these disciples, who were already jockeying for position and arguing over who would get the best seat at the table.

Of course Jesus also knew he was not on Earth to set up a kingdom ruled by human power. He was here to establish the kingdom of God that would rule in the hearts of men and women. So Jesus acted quickly. According to Matthew, "*Immediately* Jesus made the disciples get into the boat" (14:22, emphasis mine), which suggests Jesus didn't give the disciples the option of sticking around. So off they went—into the storm.

THE STORMS WE FACE

You never know when a storm will come, and the same can be true for the storms of life. Sometimes out of nowhere, we find ourselves facing a difficult or broken relationship, a financial crisis, legal problems, or painful health issues. Maybe it is the death of someone we love. Maybe it is a rebellious child. Maybe it is the loss of a job. So common are such storms that it's been said there are only two kinds of people in the world: those who are *going* through a crisis, and those who are *going to* go through a crisis.

Life seems to bring about two kinds of storms. There are those that come as a result of our disobedience, like the one Jonah faced when he disobeyed God and tried to run. A great storm came, and the Lord took hold of this reluctant prophet and got him back on course. This storm was entirely the result of Jonah's own disobedience to God.

But there are also storms that come from our obedience. Moses, for example, wouldn't have had to put up with a large contingent of complainers had he not obeyed God at the burning bush. He could have simply stayed with his little flock of sheep in the desert, and we never would have known his name or been inspired by his story.

Daniel never would have faced a lions' den had he not been faithful to God.

Shadrach, Meshach, and Abednego never would have had to face a fiery furnace if they had simply bowed to the gold image King Nebuchadnezzar had set up. Then again, if they had bowed, they would have missed the privilege of experiencing God's presence in the fire with them.

THE SAFE SHORE

As believers, we know that God is also present and actively involved in everything that happens in *our* lives, using our storms to bring about victories for the kingdom. Romans 8:28 tells us, "And we know that in all things God works for the good of those who love him, who have been called according to his purpose." But we also need to remember the verse that follows it: "For those God foreknew he also predestined to be conformed to the image of his Son, that he might be the firstborn among many brothers and sisters" (verse 29 TNIV). What happens in our lives ultimately works to make us more like Jesus. In other words, although we are interested in what is *temporarily* good, God is interested in what is *eternally* good.

When I was a young boy, I lived with my grandparents, Charles and Stella McDaniel. All of our family called them Mama Stella and Daddy Charles. They were from Arkansas, so I ate good Southern cooking—fried chicken, black-eyed peas, collard greens, and mashed potatoes—for dinner almost every night. Mama Stella's crowning culinary achievement, however, was her biscuits. I have never had a better biscuit made by anyone, anywhere. She used vegetable oil, self-rising flour, and buttermilk. Of course, no ingredient she used for her mouthwatering biscuits was appealing on its own. But when she mixed all the ingredients together with expert hands and put them into a hot oven, the result was one good biscuit.

In the same way, God takes the events of our lives—the good things and the so-called bad things—and puts them into the oven of adversity. When it is all done, we say, "That's good." It may take time. It may even take a lifetime.

Like the disciples catching sight of Jesus through the waves, we can turn to the stories of our faithful brothers and sisters and see Jesus coming to us in the midst of our storms. We can trust that God is there watching us, caring for us, and ultimately guiding us through the turmoil and tumult to the safety of the shore.

35

RIGHT ON TIME

The Lord will open the heavens, the storehouse of his bounty,
to send rain on your land in season and
to bless all the work of your hands.

Deuteronomy 28:12

As a longtime resident of Southern California, I enjoy spending time at the beach when I can find the time. As a result, I have had the opportunity to see lifeguards at work. Any lifeguard knows there is a certain timing associated with saving the life of someone who is drowning. If a lifeguard approaches too soon, they can be pulled under by a panicked swimmer. A wise lifeguard will wait until someone is nearly exhausted before coming to his aid. Undoubtedly, the struggling swimmer—and even those standing on the beach watching—must wonder, "Where is that lifeguard? Why don't they do something?"

In the same way, God will sometimes allow us to come to the end of ourselves and our resources so we will learn to trust him, because when we get to the end of ourselves, we get to the beginning of God.

WAITING FOR GOD

We sometimes wonder, "Where is God?" We look at the state of our wicked world today and perhaps wonder, "When is he coming to execute judgment?" But as 2 Peter 3:9 reminds us, "The Lord is not slow in keeping his promise, as some understand slowness. He is patient with you, not wanting anyone to perish, but everyone to come to repentance." So let's not mistake God's timing for God's indifference. God sees us and he will intervene in his own time and according to his own plan.

The Gospel of John tells the story of Jesus and the disciples sailing through an intense storm. They were really scared. John 6:19–21 says, "When they had rowed about three or three and a half miles, they saw Jesus approaching the boat, walking on the water; and they were frightened. But he said to them, 'It is I; don't be afraid.' Then they were willing to take him into the boat, and immediately the boat reached the shore where they were heading" (TNIV).

The book of Matthew tells us that Jesus came to the disciples just before dawn (see Matt. 14:25). That suggests the disciples had been at sea for at least nine hours. Imagine what must have been going through their minds as they battled the wind, the waves, and their own exhaustion. *Why?* they might have wondered, *Why would Jesus leave us out here like this?*

Naturally, Jesus knew what he was doing all along. But why would Jesus wait? Why watch the disciples suffer so? I think it was probably because, like that well-trained lifeguard, Jesus knew it would take a while for the disciples to exhaust their resources and trust in him completely.

LOOKING FOR GOD

Not only was Jesus's timing important as he came to the disciples in the midst of the storm, but his method was important as well. I often wonder why Jesus chose to walk on the water. Why not just fly in, or suddenly appear in the boat? But I think he wanted to show his disciples that the very things they feared—the wind and the sea—were only a pathway for Jesus to use to come to them. Yet this scared them even more. Matthew tells us they thought Jesus was a ghost (see Matt. 14:26).

The disciples didn't recognize Jesus because they weren't looking for him. Had they been waiting in faith, they would have recognized Jesus immediately. Instead, they jumped to the false conclusion that this was a ghost. But there was Jesus, in the place they least expected him.

SEEING GOD

How often does the Lord speak to us, wanting to lead us, yet we don't see him? It isn't because he's not there, but because we aren't looking for him. So much is happening in our world today, from terrorism to war to political instability and the threat of nuclear conflict. Yet Jesus said, "When these things begin to take place, stand up and lift up your heads, because your redemption is drawing near" (Luke 21:28). We know that Jesus is here. But we look down at our troubles, not up toward our God. What a difference it makes to lift our heads and look for Jesus!

We had a German shepherd who used to like to sleep just outside our bedroom door at night. Or perhaps it would be more accurate to say that he leaned against our door. When I opened the door in the morning, he would come rolling in. Then he would anxiously jump up, tail wagging, ready for me to take him for a walk. He had been eagerly waiting for me to appear. All night long, he knew that his master would arrive at that door in the morning.

That is how our attitude should be toward Jesus. Are you looking for him right now? Do you know he is right here? You may know Jesus, but you never will know him deeply until you recognize him in the midst of the storms of life. That was Job's conclusion after the calamity that befell him: "My ears had heard of you but now my eyes have seen you" (Job 42:5). In other words, "I have heard how you deliver people and answer prayer. *Now* I know."

The disciples were about to know Jesus more deeply as he came to them in the midst of the storm. As they froze in fear at the sight of him, his reassuring voice pierced the darkness: "It is I; don't be afraid" (John 6:20). Note the order of the words. He didn't say, "Do not be afraid" before he said, "It is I." It reminds us that when we focus on Christ, we begin to find and receive his help. The disciples' fear gave way to faith. They knew it was Jesus, and they knew they would be all right.

36

Our Friend Failure

God is our refuge and strength, an ever-present help in trouble.

Psalm 46:1

I remember the first time I took my son Jonathan scuba diving in Hawaii. After we had gone through the training with the instructor, it was time for a real dive. But on that particular day, the waters were very rough. Jonathan looked at me, panicked. The instructor, sensing Jonathan's fear, turned to him and very calmly but firmly said, "Look at me, and remember what I told you." Jonathan relaxed, and as soon as we went below the surface, we discovered that all was calm.

That is how it was with Peter in the story of the disciples sailing in the storm (see John 6). As Jesus walked across the water to the boat, Peter experienced a great burst of faith. He was filled with love and devotion for the Lord, and he just wanted to be near him. Initially, Peter had gone from terror to boldness. Jesus had said, "Do not be afraid," and now Peter was ready to prove his courage. He was ready to do the impossible. And he did.

Matthew tells the story like this:

"Lord, if it's you," Peter replied, "tell me to come to you on the water." "Come," he said. Then Peter got down out of the boat, walked on the water and came toward Jesus. But when he saw the wind, he was afraid and, beginning to sink, cried out, "Lord, save me!" Immediately Jesus reached out his hand and caught him. "You of little faith," he said, "why did you doubt?" And when they climbed into the boat, the wind died down. Then those who were in the boat worshiped him, saying, "Truly you are the Son of God."

Matthew 14:28–33

There was Peter, suddenly walking on the water. He could do this because he was looking at Jesus. But when Peter took his eyes off Jesus, things fell apart.

FUMBLING AND FALLING

After Peter's great success came failure. But it was a spectacular failure. After all, if you are going to fail, then this is the way to do it. Have you ever tried to do something for God that turned out to be a complete failure? Maybe it was an attempt to share the gospel with someone. Perhaps it was a prayer for someone to get better, and the person actually got worse (this has happened to me!). Or maybe you started a home Bible study and no one showed up. If so, then let me say this: thank you for failures.

I would much rather try and fail than to never do anything at all. Besides, failure is not always such a bad thing; often the doorway to success has been entered through the hallway of failure. It has been said that if at first you don't succeed, relax. You're just like the rest of us.

There are many who failed initially, only to succeed later. Albert Einstein failed at math before he realized $E = mc^2$. An apple had to fall on Isaac Newton's head before he discovered the theory of gravity. And Michael Jordan failed to make his high school basketball team, only to later make the NBA and become a sports legend.

Peter's great fear turned to faith, and then back to fear again. Where faith reigns, fear has no place.

FIGHTING FEAR

Where fear reigns, however, faith is driven away. Fear is a powerful and very real emotion that can suddenly overtake us. When we take our eyes off God, we forget his promises to us. We forget that he is in control of our lives. Sometimes we forget him altogether. And then we start to sink.

Maybe you're sinking right now. Maybe you're filled with fear, worry, and defeat. You might be in the grip of some addiction. Maybe your marriage is in trouble. Maybe you feel like a complete failure because there was once a time when you were so strong spiritually, but then you took your eyes off Jesus and started looking toward the passing things of this world again.

Or maybe it was not anything outwardly sinful that drew your eyes away from the Lord. Perhaps it was your career or a relationship or some pursuit that became more important to you than your faith. And now you are sinking. So is this the end? Absolutely not! Follow Peter's example and cry out, "Lord, save me!" Jesus won't rebuke anyone who is trying to come to him by faith.

OUR RESCUER

Notice that Peter prayed as he was *beginning* to sink—better that than waiting until he had already sunk! There is no shame in asking for God's help. Crying out to God when you're in trouble does not mean that you are a big disappointment to God somehow. It simply means that you have learned a thing or two in life. And one of those things is that when you start sinking, you need to pray.

Do you think Peter's failure came as a surprise to Jesus? Do you think Jesus was shocked when Peter sank—or when he later denied him? Of course not. Jesus knew Peter. He knew him so well that he was ready to catch Peter the instant he started to sink. "Immediately Jesus reached out his hand and caught him. 'You of little faith,' he said, 'why did you doubt?'" (Matt. 14:31).

The phrase "little faith" is actually translated from one word in the original Greek, a word that has a quality of tenderness about it. It was as though Jesus were saying to Peter, "Oh, *Littlefaith*, you were doing so well! What happened?" And guess what? With his eyes back on Jesus, "Littlefaith" walked back to the boat. The storm was still raging, but Peter had his focus back, and with his eyes on Jesus he could once again do the impossible.

Jesus is saying, "Come." But you need to say, "Lord, save me!" And he will. Just as he reached out and took hold of Peter, Jesus will reach out and take hold of you. That doesn't mean the storm will instantly cease. But it's safer to be with Jesus in rough waters than it is to be without him in the boat.

37

Breakfast with Jesus

And my God will meet all your needs according
to his glorious riches in Christ Jesus.

Philippians 4:19

By 7:00 p.m. on October 20, 1968, only a few thousand spectators remained in the Olympic stadium in Mexico City. It was almost dark, and the last of the marathon runners were stumbling across the finish line. Finally, the spectators heard the wail of sirens from the police cars. As eyes turned to the gate, a lone runner, wearing the colors of Tanzania, staggered into the stadium. His name was John Stephen Akhwari, and he was the last of the seventy-four competitors. With a deep cut on his knee and a dislocated joint that was caused by a fall earlier in the race, he hobbled the final lap around the track. The spectators rose and applauded as though he were the winner of the race. Afterward, someone asked him why he had kept running. His now famous reply was "My country did not send me seven thousand miles away to start the race. They sent me seven thousand miles to finish it."

The Bible often compares the Christian life to running a race. The apostle Paul spoke of it on several occasions. Toward the end of his life, he concluded, "I have fought the good fight, I have finished the race, I have kept the faith" (2 Tim. 4:7). And to the believers at Corinth, he posed this challenge:

> Do you not know that in a race all the runners run, but only one gets the prize? Run in such a way as to get the prize. Everyone who competes in the games goes into strict training. They do it to get a crown that will not last; but we do it to get a crown that will last forever.
>
> 1 Corinthians 9:24–25

THE GOOD RACE

It's not always easy to finish a race. But any good runner will tell you that the only way to make it through a long run is to take it one mile at a time. To think of the whole race feels overwhelming. If you've ever read a passage from the Bible that just didn't seem to make any sense, or had a time in your life when it seemed as though God didn't come through for you, or were tempted to just give up trying to follow Jesus, you know that feeling. We might wonder how we'll ever hold on to our faith in the midst of all the complexities of life.

Jesus's disciples might have felt the same way. They just couldn't wrap their minds around what Jesus was saying and doing. Even though he performed miracles in their presence, they still wondered if they could trust him. So Jesus laid it on the line for them.

WHAT REALLY MATTERS

After the feeding of the five thousand, Jesus and the disciples headed to the opposite side of the lake so Jesus could get away from the crowd. That's where our story picks up.

> The next day the crowd that had stayed on the opposite shore of the lake realized that only one boat had been there, and that Jesus had not entered it with his disciples, but that they had gone away alone. Then some boats from Tiberias landed near the place where the people had eaten the bread after the Lord had given thanks. Once the crowd realized that neither Jesus nor his disciples were there, they got into the boats and went to Capernaum in search of Jesus. When they found him on the other side of the lake, they asked him, "Rabbi, when did you get here?"
>
> John 6:22–25

Jesus and his disciples had just endured a storm at sea. He had calmed the storm (and the disciples) and was perhaps hoping for some time alone for prayer. But on the other side of the lake, the stomachs of the well-fed multitudes began to growl. There were no restaurants to go to and no vendors selling bread from carts as they would have been in Jerusalem. There were no fishermen bringing in the catch of the day. So the people thought to themselves, "Where's Jesus this morning?" Realizing he was gone, they went searching for him.

But when they found Jesus, the crowd was confronted with their selfishness. He said, "Very truly I tell you, you are looking for me, not because you saw the signs I performed but because you ate the loaves and had your fill" (verse 26 TNIV).

The day before, Jesus had compassion on them and performed a miracle to feed them. They were so impressed they wanted to make him the king! But that awe faded fast as they grew hungry. They were standing in the presence of God Almighty, the very Bread of Life, and all they could think about was breakfast. Talk about missing the point!

There is a time to have breakfast and a time to wait on God—a lesson this multitude had not yet learned. So Jesus used this opportunity to remind them of what matters in life: "Do not work for food that spoils, but for food that endures to eternal life, which the Son of Man will give you. On him God the Father has placed his seal of approval" (John 6:27).

REAL HAPPINESS

Jesus didn't say, "Don't concern yourself with the necessities of life or plan ahead for your needs." What Jesus was saying was not to *worry* about these things or let them become the driving force of our lives. We are not to merely seek success, power, possessions, or happiness. Instead, as we seek God first and foremost, everything we need will be provided for us. Job had the right idea when he said, "I have treasured the words of his mouth more than my daily bread" (Job 23:12).

David Myers, professor of psychology at Hope College in Michigan, spent six years examining hundreds of studies on happiness and concluded that once a person gets beyond the poverty level, money doesn't help, no matter how much they buy: "The stockpiles of DVDs, the closets full of clothes, the big screen stereo TV systems . . . but clearly that doesn't do it. People having achieved that level of wealth have now adapted to it, and it takes new increments, a faster computer, a bigger TV screen, or whatever to 'rejuice the joy' that the initial purchase gained for them."[3]

This might be the most essential lesson we ever learn about following Jesus: He is all we need. The race might seem long, but Jesus is with us every step of the way.

38

THE MISUNDERSTOOD SAVIOR

> He was in the world, and though the world was made
> through him, the world did not recognize him.
>
> John 1:10

The more we read about Jesus, the more it becomes clear that people just didn't get him. Over and over, Jesus had to explain who he was and who he wasn't. He had to pull people away from their ideas about who God should be like so they could see who God was: Jesus, the Word made flesh.

The hungry crowd that followed Jesus to the other side of the lake was no exception. They had witnessed a miracle in the feeding of the five thousand, but they wanted more: It was morning and they were hungry.

I have to say I can understand this to a degree. I would like to say to you that the first thing that crosses my mind when I roll out of bed is the need to open the Bible and or to drop to my knees in prayer. But if I am honest, I would have to say that one of the first things on my mind in the morning is . . . breakfast!

It was the same with this multitude. "Then they asked him, 'What must we do to do the works God requires?' Jesus answered, 'The work of God is this: to believe in the one he has sent'" (John 6:28–29).

But the people weren't just looking for proof of Jesus's divinity, they were looking for food. John writes that the people asked Jesus, "What miraculous sign then will you give that we may see it and believe you? What will you do? Our forefathers ate the manna in the desert; as it is written: 'He gave them bread from heaven to eat'" (John 6:30–31).

Maybe they should have taken a more straightforward approach and asked, "Why don't you do that bread and fish miracle again? Better yet, why not show us how to do it, and we won't bother you anymore!" They had completely missed what Jesus said and went back to focusing on their stomachs.

THE TRUTH OF JESUS

At this point, Jesus pulled no punches with them. He explained:

> "I am the bread of life. He who comes to me will never go hungry, and he who believes in me will never be thirsty. But as I told you, you have seen me and still you do not believe. All that the Father gives me will come to me, and whoever comes to me I will never drive away. For I have come down from heaven not to do my will but to do the will of him who sent me. And this is the will of him who sent me, that I shall lose none of all that he has given me, but raise them up at the last day." . . . At this the Jews began to grumble about him because he said, "I am the bread that came down from heaven."
>
> John 6:35–41

This statement told the crowd—and us—what it means to follow God. First, we learn that knowing Jesus is not enough. We have to be willing to have our lives changed. This crowd wanted a king who would heal them when they were sick, who would conform to their plans and goals, and who would cater to their wants and whims.

The reaction of this hungry multitude indicates that a person can have a certain amount of spiritual insight, yet not necessarily see anything. We can, as the apostle Paul said in Acts 26:18, have our eyes opened. But we still must turn "from darkness to light, and from the power of Satan to God."

Second, we learn God chooses who will follow Jesus. This raises the question as to whether God chooses some and not others. In a sense, the answer is yes. God doesn't want anyone to fall away from him. Rather, he wants everyone to come to repentance (see 2 Peter 3:9).

So how do you know if you are chosen? Commit your life to Jesus Christ, and you will confirm you are. Reject him, and you will confirm you are not. If you think this is too hard to grasp, that you can't reconcile it in your mind, then welcome to the club. If God were small enough to understand, he wouldn't be big enough to worship.

EVERYONE IS WELCOME

Jesus also gives the crowd a beautiful promise: God will not reject anyone. No matter what sins you have committed, God will welcome and forgive you. There are no exceptions.

My friend Pastor Chuck Smith showed me a letter he received from someone who listened to his radio program, *The Word for Today*. It was signed by David Berkowitz, also known as the Son of Sam. Convicted of murdering six people, David Berkowitz was sentenced to 365 consecutive years in prison. He wrote:

> One night, I was reading Psalm 34. I came upon the sixth verse, which says, "This poor man cried, and the Lord heard him, and saved him from all his troubles." It was at that moment, in 1987, that I began to pour out my heart to God. Everything seemed to hit me at once. The guilt from what I did . . . the disgust at what I had become. . . . Late that night in my cold cell, I got down on my knees, and I began to cry out to Jesus Christ.

God graciously offered his forgiveness, even to the Son of Sam.

In John 10:28, we read, "I give them eternal life, and they shall never perish; no one can snatch them out of my hand." We don't need to live in fear of spiritually falling away. No one who has ever fallen away has done so against his or her will. Those who fall away make a series of choices that lead to spiritually destructive (and sometimes physically destructive) results.

UNDERSTANDING THE WORD

People often missed the point of Jesus's words because they had a literal interpretation of the symbolic language he used. So when Jesus said, "I am the bread that came down from heaven . . . ," it was a hard one for the crowd to grasp. John tells us that "many of his disciples said, 'This is a hard teaching. Who can accept it?'" (John 6:60). That doesn't mean Jesus's teachings are hard to understand, because really they're not. In reality, they are sometimes hard to keep. That's why we see a pattern in the Bible: when people didn't understand Jesus, they hung around and asked questions. It was when they *did* understand him that they either joined his ministry or went elsewhere. They left because what they heard was so contrary to their own ideas.

What about you? Are you willing to follow Jesus, to truly give your life to him? Or will you walk away?

39

CRAZY TALK

Jesus called the crowd to him and said, "Listen and understand."

Matthew 15:10

Jesus could be a difficult man to some. I don't mean he was unkind or hard to get along with. The fact is, he was Love incarnate. What I mean is, he did things that rubbed a lot of people the wrong way. He refused to play by the rules of the religious establishment. He challenged many popular ideas about who God was. And he said some things that were so difficult for people to accept that we still wrestle with them today.

THE LIVING BREAD

For example, Jesus said he was the bread of life, the living bread that came down from heaven (see John 6:33, 35, 51). This implies Jesus existed with God before his physical birth. At Christmas we celebrate the birth of Jesus, but we also celebrate the Incarnation—God coming in the flesh. God sent us Jesus so we would know God. This one truth—that we cannot know God without coming through his provision for us, Jesus—is perhaps the most difficult yet necessary concept of the Christian faith. But it's not possible to truly be a Christian and *not* believe it.

Maybe that sounds too narrow, too dogmatic, too intolerant. But in reality, it is simply believing what Jesus Christ plainly said: "I am the way and the truth and the life. No one comes to the Father except through me" (John 14:6). The Bible clearly teaches, "There is one God and one mediator between God and men, the man Christ Jesus" (1 Tim. 2:5), and "Salvation is found in no one else, for there is no other name under heaven given to men by which we must be saved" (Acts 4:12).

What sounds narrow to us is actually a wide embrace. This invitation to life with Jesus is open to all. No one who asks to join in is left out, no one who walks through the door is pushed away. All who come to meet the living God are welcome.

THE CRUCIFIXION

People in Jesus's day were also confused by his talk of giving up his life for others. He said, "I am the living bread that came down from heaven. If anyone eats of this bread, he will live forever. This bread is my flesh, which I will give for the life of the world" (John 6:51). We've heard this so often that we may have forgotten just how strange a statement it really is.

The cross is offensive, repulsive, and shocking—but necessary. It is an essential part of the Christian story. As 1 Corinthians 1:23–24 tells us, "We preach Christ crucified: a stumbling block to Jews and foolishness to Gentiles, but to those whom God has called, both Jews and Greeks, Christ the power of God and the wisdom of God." Yet those listening to Jesus had no idea what was coming. They could only listen and decide for themselves if this man was the Christ—or just crazy.

THE TRUE BELIEVERS

I believe Jesus made statements to intentionally thin out the ranks. I know that sounds strange, but I think Jesus wanted to rid himself of fair-weather followers who really weren't followers at all. John tells us that some of the people who walked with Jesus decided to drop out: "From this time many of his disciples turned back and no longer followed him" (John 6:66). And while I'm sure Jesus was sorry to see them go, I believe he preferred having a few true believers around him to a throng of fans who said they believed but did little to change their lives.

You see, God is more interested in quality than quantity. Are you a true disciple of Jesus or merely a fair-weather follower? Will you finish your race with joy or give up if it makes you unpopular or when things get a little tough?

When we first come to Jesus, it's all about our needs. We don't wake up one morning and say, "I need to glorify God and seek his will for my life!" Instead, we wonder, "Why is my life so empty and meaningless? What happens when I die?" So we come to Jesus. We discover prayer and start to talk with and hear from God. Initially, we pray for what we want and need in life. We come to church and want to learn all we can and be as blessed as possible. And there is nothing wrong with any of that.

But as we grow and mature spiritually, we start making some discoveries. One is that faith is about glorifying and seeking God. When we seek to be holy, we find we are happy—not from seeking happiness, but from seeking God. We discover that prayer is not about what we want, but about what God wants. We find that developing and using the gifts God has given us is a blessing at church. It is not that we don't need to keep learning and growing, but we also need to be serving and giving. That's when we become true disciples.

40

STANDING WITH JESUS

> When Jesus landed and saw a large crowd, he had compassion
> on them, because they were like sheep without a shepherd.
> So he began teaching them many things.
>
> Mark 6:34

People haven't changed much in the last two thousand years. Churches are still filled with people who are annoyed when the service runs long or there are too many children in the nursery. There are those who will witness literally thousands of people coming to Christ at a crusade, yet they complain that the line to get in the parking lot was too long or that the seats were uncomfortable. We are masters at missing the forest of faith because of all the little trees of our own selfish desires.

Yet for every one of the fair-weather faithful, there are those who walk with Jesus even when the road gets bumpy. The disciple Peter was one of them. Peter wanted Jesus to know he and his friends would not quit. When Jesus asked the disciples if they, too, were going to walk away from him, it was Peter who responded:

> "Lord, to whom shall we go? You have the words of eternal life. We believe and know that you are the Holy One of God." Then Jesus replied, "Have I not chosen you, the Twelve? Yet one of you is a devil!" (He meant Judas, the son of Simon Iscariot, who, though one of the Twelve, was later to betray him.)
>
> John 6:68–71

THE BEST LIFE

That is the mark of the true believer: he or she cannot quit. Peter first says, in effect, "Lord, we've been thinking about it. Sometimes we don't understand you. Others have laughed at us for following you. But we have looked at the alternatives and it comes down to this: we have never found anyone who can do what you do. Where else would we go? No one speaks like you do and no one understands life like you do. That holds us."

Peter speaks for many of us. We have tried life without Jesus and we know that life is empty and meaningless. But some of us have yet to fully commit ourselves to life with Jesus. We may say all the right things, show up at all the right church events, and spend time with all the right people, but still hold back pieces of our lives because we think we can manage them better than God can.

THE FAITHFUL FEW

In this conversation between Jesus and Peter, we see three kinds of disciples. These same levels of commitment exist in our churches today.

1. Those who won't quit, who can't quit, because their hearts have been captured by the love of God. Peter was one of these. Yes, he would make mistakes and even turn his back on Jesus. But Peter's heart never wavered. He sought Jesus constantly.

2. Those who start out well, who follow Jesus for a while, and then drop out and quit. The crowds who followed Jesus were filled with people like this. They enjoyed being part of something exciting, but when they realized they couldn't use Jesus for their own purposes, they got bored and left.

3. Those who are Judases. They appear to be Christians, but they are not. They are connivers, deceivers, and liars.

FINISHING THE RACE

Which group do you find yourself in today? Are you a true disciple who cannot quit? Then I want to encourage you to run this race with endurance, fixing your eyes on Jesus, "the author and perfecter of our faith" (Heb. 12:2).

Are you someone who started running well but dropped out of the race along the way? If you have been chasing after happiness, success, and fulfillment in life and keep coming up empty, remember that Jesus said, "I am the bread of life. He who comes to me will never go hungry, and he who believes in me will never be thirsty" (John 6:35). You can still return to the race and finish well.

And if you find yourself in the third category, then I want you to know that your eyes can be opened to the truth, but you must act upon that truth. Remember, Jesus said, "Whoever comes to me I will never drive away" (John 6:37). It isn't too late to enter the race. So why not do so today?

41

TURNING THE TABLES

Finally, all of you, live in harmony with one another;
be sympathetic, love as brothers, be compassionate and humble.

1 Peter 3:8

I once read a story about a hungry thief who grabbed some sausages in a meat market, only to discover they were part of a forty-five-foot-long string. As he tried to run away, he became tangled in the train of sausages and tripped. The police found him collapsed in a heap of fresh meat. He was literally caught in the act.

One of the central figures in the passage we're about to explore is a woman who was caught in the act of adultery. Under the law of Moses, she could have been put to death by stoning (see Lev. 20:10). But she didn't get what she deserved because she was brought before Jesus. What could have been the worst (and potentially last) day of her life turned out to be the best as she was transformed by her encounter with Christ.

THE TRAP

Before we find out what Jesus did for this woman, let's look at the events leading up to it. John 7 closes with, "Then each went to his own home" (verse 53), while John 8 opens with, "But Jesus went to the Mount of Olives" (verse 1). There is a stirring poignancy to those words. The Savior of the world, God in human form, was huddled under an olive tree, sleeping alone on a cold night on the Mount of Olives. He had no home to return to, but instead went to commune with his Father. He clearly left us an example to follow. There are many times in which we need to get away from the crowd and spend time in communion with our heavenly Father, because it is during those times that we find the resources to deal with the pressures that life can bring.

The Pharisees had probably been awake that night, hatching their scheme. Their decision to arrest Jesus was an easy one, but pulling it off was a problem. So some lawyer devised what they hoped would be a foolproof plan:

> At dawn [Jesus] appeared again in the temple courts, where all the people gathered around him, and he sat down to teach them. The teachers of the law and the Pharisees brought in a woman caught in adultery. They made her stand before the group and said to Jesus, "Teacher, this woman was caught in the act of adultery. In the Law Moses commanded us to stone such women. Now what do you say?" They were using this question as a trap, in order to have a basis for accusing him.
>
> John 8:2–6

As we will see, sometimes even foolproof plans can fail.

THE LAW OF JESUS

Much to the Pharisees' surprise, Jesus turned the tables on them:

> When they kept on questioning him, he straightened up and said to them, "If any one of you is without sin, let him be the first to throw a stone at her." Again he stooped down and wrote on the ground. At this, those who heard began to go away one at a time, the older ones first, until only Jesus was left, with the woman still standing there.
>
> John 8:7–9

The scribes and Pharisees may have looked holy spouting Scripture in front of Jesus. But let's not make the mistake of thinking that everyone who quotes the Bible is necessarily a true believer. Those who quote Scripture to heartlessly condemn others are frequently the guiltiest of all. Those who are quick to find fault with others usually have great fault in their own lives. This is precisely what Jesus was speaking of when he used the analogy of finding a speck in someone else's eye when you have a log in your own (see Matt. 7:3).

THE TRUE SIN

The sin that stands out here is not that of a woman who was unrighteous and knew it. The sin that stands out is that of the self-righteous men who did not know it. Yes, this woman who had been caught in the very act of adultery had clearly failed. But what was worse was that these men had no compassion for her.

Galatians 6:1 offers the appropriate response if we know someone who has fallen into sin: "Brothers, if someone is caught in a sin, you who are spiritual should restore him gently. But watch yourself, or you also may be tempted." If we know of someone who is falling in the area of sexual immorality, we should confront and restore them, not condemn them. The goal is to bring them back, not drive them away. We need to win the soul, not just the argument. That's how we love each other and that's how we bring each other closer to God.

42

SINS OF THE SPIRIT

> If you do what is right, will you not be accepted?
> But if you do not do what is right, sin is crouching
> at your door; it desires to have you, but you must master it.
>
> Genesis 4:7

We all have the potential to fall—and fall big. There is not a single one of the Ten Commandments that each of us could not break, given the right set of circumstances. That's why Hebrews 2:1 warns us, "We must pay more careful attention, therefore, to what we have heard, so that we do not drift away."

Sadly, most of us know at least one person—maybe more—who has fallen into adultery. Imagine the shock of the young pastor who heard a well-known evangelist say, "I have spent some of the happiest moments of my life in the arms of another man's wife. . . . " Then the evangelist added with a wink of the eye, "And that woman was my mother."

The young pastor thought, "That's so funny, I just have to use that!" So a few weeks later as he was speaking to his congregation, the phrase came to him. "I have spent some of the happiest moments of my life in the arms of another man's wife," he said. But then his mind went blank and he couldn't remember the punch line. So after a long pause, he muttered sheepishly, "But for the life of me, I can't remember who she was!"

THE SIN OF BETRAYAL

The real issue of adultery is no laughing matter. So many marriages and lives have been destroyed by it. Adultery goes beyond the mere sexual act. It almost always includes deception and betrayal.

I received a heartbreaking letter from a man who had fallen into this sin. He attended Harvest Christian Fellowship for a time, and once was active in ministry. In his letter, John (not his real name) told me:

> As you know, I'm sure, Mary and I are no longer husband and wife. Our marriage ended in divorce. . . . Bottom line, Greg, I took my eyes off of God and placed them on circumstances surrounding me. Pride, lust, and the Enemy had their way. Before long, Mary (God's gift to me) no longer satisfied me and I committed adultery. In fact, the very night that act took place, you and I crossed paths at the mall. I was there in a restaurant sitting with a coworker that I introduced as "Cindy." Remember? When I look back on that night, I'm reminded of when Judas came to Jesus in the garden with the band of soldiers to arrest Jesus. And before he [Judas] identified Christ with a kiss, Jesus said to him, "Friend, why have you come?" In that moment Jesus was giving to Judas one more opportunity to turn to him. Greg, you were that person God used to cross my path that evening to wake me up, to warn me, "Don't do this!" I didn't listen. Needless to say, that decision and those to follow would systematically destroy my life. . . . I had lost everything: my relationship with God, my marriage, my reputation. Everything was gone. To look back on my life and see the destruction that has been done through selfishness, because I failed to take God seriously at his word . . . I virtually destroyed what life I had at the time. Even worse, I destroyed Mary's life as well.

John went on to describe in his letter the extent of the destruction his wrong decision produced. God forgave John, but he paid a heavy price. My heart goes out to him, to Mary, and to any others who have gone down this sad road. Yes, God forgives, but there is still a "reaping of what you have sown" that follows.

SUBTLE SIN

You see, sin is not always obvious. Of course, some sins are, like murder, adultery, and stealing. But others are not as apparent, like pride, selfishness, and gossip. Sometimes we sin in ignorance or presumption. That is why David prayed, "Who can discern his errors? Forgive my hidden faults. Keep your servant also from willful sins; may they not rule over me. Then will I be blameless, innocent of great transgression" (Ps. 19:12–13).

According to Scripture, the sins of the heart can separate us from God just as easily as the sins of the body—and sometimes in a more destructive way because we are not aware of them. There are both sins of the flesh as well as sins of the spirit, as 2 Corinthians 7:1 tells us: "Since we have these promises, dear friends, let us purify ourselves from everything that contaminates body and spirit, perfecting holiness out of reverence for God."

KNOW SIN

A sin of the spirit is to go against what we know is true. Jesus made this distinction regarding the sin of the high priest, Caiaphas. To Pilate, Jesus said, "You could have no power at all against Me unless it had been given you from above. Therefore the one who delivered Me to you has the greater sin" (John 19:11 NKJV). Jesus was referring to Caiaphas or possibly Judas. Both of them knew the innocence of Jesus. Both deliberately did what they knew was wrong. When we have been schooled in the Scripture like Caiaphas or have been exposed to the truth and power of God like Judas, we are essentially without excuse. It is to knowingly sin against the light.

43

A NEW LEASE ON LIFE

And I will pour out on the house of David and
the inhabitants of Jerusalem a spirit of grace and supplication.

Zechariah 12:10

As I read the story of the woman caught in adultery, I often wonder what this woman must have been thinking. At first, Jesus bewildered her. Then she sensed that Jesus was more concerned with the sin and hypocrisy of her accusers than with the accusation they'd brought against her. Perhaps she looked up to see a flawlessness, a righteousness in his eyes, and at the same time, mercy, and genuine compassion. Maybe her heart began to soften and the rebellion, anger, and denial began to drain out of her.

She was left alone with Jesus, and he pierced the silence with a word she had not heard in a long time, if ever: "Woman." In the Greek language, this was a term of respect used toward a wife, a mother, a lady. It was the same word Jesus used when he spoke to his mother from the cross. Whenever Jesus used this term, it spoke of respect and great tenderness.

She had probably been called many things in her life, but never this.

Jesus continued, "'Has no one condemned you?' 'No one, sir,' she said. 'Then neither do I condemn you,' Jesus declared. 'Go now and leave your life of sin'" (John 8:10–11). How this must have shocked this undoubtedly hardened woman. Like the woman at the well, she probably had been used and abused by men all her life. And the very men who quite possibly had helped to condemn her soul had now demanded her execution. In reality, she was still immoral. She had been caught in the act.

But the reason Jesus could say, "Neither do I condemn you" was that, in a short time, he would personally take upon himself that very condemnation on the cross of Calvary.

FIRST, FORGIVENESS

Notice he didn't say, "Leave your life of sin, then I won't condemn you." Thankfully, that's not what Jesus said. We don't seek to live godly lives to win or find God's approval. But because we realize we have God's approval, we live godly lives. The goodness of God leads us to repentance. As followers of Jesus, we are not bound by rules and regulations. Rather, we are moved by his love. Paul said, "For Christ's love compels us" (2 Cor. 5:14).

"Go now and leave your life of sin," Jesus told her. He didn't just tell her she was forgiven and to be on her way. Implicit in his statement was a call to a better life. And he says the same to us: "Leave this lifestyle of sin!" This doesn't mean God expects perfection, because we will fail. There is a difference between being sinless and wanting to sin *less.*

FLASHES OF FAITH

When the convicting power of God's Holy Spirit drove her accusers away, the woman came closer. Just one look into Jesus's eyes answered all her questions, melted all her doubts, and drove away all her fears. Jesus saw in that moment, in a flash, that belief had poured into her once-hardened heart.

That is how belief can take place—in a flash, in a moment. We often assume that when we see someone walking forward during the invitation at a church service or an evangelistic event that, at that moment, he or she is becoming a believer. But the actual event of belief may have occurred much earlier. One statement may have brought it about, just a sudden realization of God's love washing over someone.

THE PROMISE OF GRACE

There are some implicit promises embedded in the forgiveness Jesus offered this woman. These same promises are there for all who come to Jesus seeking to turn away from a life of sin.

Promise #1: Her sins could be forgotten. Notice that Jesus never mentioned her past. A good definition for justification is "just as if it never happened." When we are justified through faith in Jesus Christ, it's as though our sins never occurred. God promises, "For I will forgive their wickedness and will remember their sins no more" (Jer. 31:34).

Promise #2: She did not need to fear God's judgment. The Lord did not condemn her; nor does he condemn us. As Romans 8:1–2 states: "Therefore, there is now no condemnation for those who are in Christ Jesus, because through Christ Jesus the law of the Spirit of life set me free from the law of sin and death."

Promise #3: She had new power to face her problems. "Go and sin no more," Jesus told her. If you've been caught in the midst of sin, or playing around with sin hoping you won't be caught, you need to come to Christ as fast as you can. Turn from your sin, and you will hear him say, "Neither do I condemn you; go now and leave your life of sin." Jesus didn't leave this woman in her sin. Yes, she had fallen down. But he helped her get up again. And he will do the same for you.

44

THE SOURCE OF SUFFERING

The Lord said, "I have indeed seen the misery of my people
in Egypt. I have heard them crying out because of their
slave drivers, and I am concerned about their suffering."

Exodus 3:7

When I came to faith in Jesus Christ, it was a pretty dramatic
conversion. I hung around with a group of guys who had no
interest in the things of God and were pretty surprised when
they heard I had become a Christian.

I had one friend that I had known since elementary school.
His name was also Gregg. He said, "Laurie, promise me you
won't become one of those Jesus freaks. Promise me you won't
carry a Bible and wear a cross around your neck and say, 'Praise
the Lord.'"

I said, "Gregg, I promise you I'll never do that."

Two weeks passed before I saw Gregg again. I was in Newport
Beach, standing on the corner telling people about Jesus, when
I saw Gregg walking toward me. There I stood with a cross
around my neck that someone had given me. I was carrying a
Bible. And before I could catch myself, the first statement out of
my mouth was "Praise the Lord." He laughed. And I laughed.
I said, "I know how this looks, Gregg. You think I've lost my
mind. But I'm telling you Christ has changed my life and it is
wonderful." He actually was listening to me, and I thought,
Well, maybe Gregg will come to the Lord.

As I was telling him about what had been taking place in my
life over the past two weeks, some guy was eavesdropping on
our conversation. He suddenly interrupted me and said, "I have
a few questions for you, Christian."

Who was this guy and where did he come from? I said, "Excuse me, but I'm just talking to my friend here."

"Yeah, but I have a few questions for you about God," he replied.

I had been a Christian for all of two weeks, but I felt I could handle whatever he asked me. So he started firing off question after question.

I had no idea what to say.

I don't remember exactly what that guy asked me, but I do remember being dumbfounded. I went home that day feeling pretty defeated. I prayed, "God, I'm sorry for not knowing." And I determined to study the Bible so that the next time someone came to me with tough questions about God, I would have some answers.

Easy to Ask, Hard to Answer

Most of us have found ourselves in the scenario like the one I just described. We have either been asked those questions or wondered about them ourselves—questions like, "Why is there suffering in the world?" or "Will God condemn someone who has never heard the gospel?" These questions are not necessarily new. In fact, many of them date all the way back to the time of Christ.

John tells the story of a blind man who was healed by Jesus and became a believer as a result. But before any of this took place, the first question was raised:

> As [Jesus] went along, he saw a man blind from birth. His disciples asked him, "Rabbi, who sinned, this man or his parents, that he was born blind?" "Neither this man nor his parents sinned," said Jesus, "but this happened so that the work of God might be displayed in his life."
>
> John 9:1–3

That seems like a rather tactless question on the part of the disciples. But there's a bigger issue behind their suggestion that the man's blindness is some kind of punishment for sin. The disciples' curiosity brings us to the often-asked question of why God allows suffering. Why does he allow babies to be born with disabilities? Why does he allow war, terrorism, illness, and tragedy?

BLAMING GOD

Many have turned against God because of a tragedy that occurred in their lives. They simply cannot reconcile the concept of a loving God coexisting with human suffering.

Our human intellects and notions of fairness reject the apparent contradiction between a loving God and a world of pain. The general tendency is to blame God for evil and suffering and to pass all responsibility for it on to him.

WHAT DID WE DO TO DESERVE THIS?

In a broad sense, sickness, disabilities, and even death are all the result of sin. But humans were not created to be sinful, but perfect, innocent, exempt from aging, immortal, and with the ability to choose right or wrong. Our first parents chose wrong. Had Adam and Eve never sinned, the curse of sin would not have come as a result: "Therefore, just as sin entered the world through one man, and death through sin, and in this way death came to all men, because all sinned" (Rom. 5:12). It is humanity, not God, who is responsible for sin.

Yet at the same time, we are not alone in our times of suffering. Jesus has promised, "I will never leave or forsake you."

45

The Power of Pain

For he has not despised or disdained the suffering
of the afflicted one; he has not hidden his face from him
but has listened to his cry for help.

Psalm 22:24

In the weeks and months following 9/11, the one question I was asked most often was "Why did God allow this?" Some even went as far as to say the attacks were God's judgment on the United States. But I disagree. In Luke 13, Jesus told a story about a tower that fell on a group of Gentiles, killing them. He asked the rhetorical question, "Do you think they were more guilty than all the others living in Jerusalem? I tell you, no! But unless you repent, you too will all perish" (Luke 13:4–5).

Jesus was addressing the fact that people die. Period. He was saying, in essence, "You had better be careful, because you are a sinner as well." The point was that those who died were not any worse than anyone else. It could happen to anyone. Everyone dies. There are no exceptions.

We have a hard time accepting that fact. We even shy away from the word by substituting phrases such as "passed away," "passed on," or "no longer with us." Even insurance salespeople avoid using the d-word in their sales pitches and instead say things like, "If something should happen to you. . . ." Our use of these very terms emphasizes the fact that we are basically afraid of death. It baffles, bothers, and frightens us.

THE GOOD IN THE BAD

But if you are a Christian, then you have hope. Yes, there are things in life that don't make sense. Good things happen to bad people. And bad things happen to good people. But we need to remember that when we suffer, God will always, in some way, bring good out of the situation (see Rom. 8:28).

Sometimes we can see God's hand in suffering, while at other times we can't. But suffering can have a corrective influence on us. In other words, sometimes the pain in our lives gets our attention. Many come to Christ because of an unexpected illness, tragedy, the death of a loved one, or a personal crisis such as a divorce or an addiction.

I had the opportunity to be a guest on *Larry King Live* in August 2005. Larry raised the question of why God allowed suffering, and I responded, "You know, Larry, I had a lady come into our office Sunday morning after the church service, and she has breast cancer. And it was that suffering that got her attention to get her to come back to church and to start seeking a spiritual life and getting right with God. And I think of the psalmist who writes, 'Before I was afflicted, I went astray. But now I have kept your word.' And C. S. Lewis said, 'God whispers to us in our pleasures . . . but he shouts to us in our pain.' Pain is God's megaphone—"

Larry interrupted, "How do you know it's not a crutch? I mean, 'I've got breast cancer. I've got to pray something.' You know—every believer in the foxhole."

I responded, "Thank God for that crutch, Larry. God's not a crutch to me, he's a whole hospital."

God can also use suffering to correct us. As David said, "Your rod and your staff, they comfort me" (Ps. 23:4). To me, it is a great comfort to know that God loves me enough to correct me. It proves that I am his child.

THE STRENGTH IN THE WEAKNESS

Sometimes suffering can be a direct road to a better life. As 2 Corinthians 4:17–18 reminds us, "For our light and momentary troubles are achieving for us an eternal glory that far outweighs them all. So we fix our eyes not on what is seen, but on what is unseen. For what is seen is temporary, but what is unseen is eternal."

Paul spoke of his physical suffering as his "thorn in the flesh":

> To keep me from becoming conceited because of these surpassingly great revelations, there was given me a thorn in my flesh, a messenger of Satan, to torment me. Three times I pleaded with the Lord to take it away from me. But he said to me, "My grace is sufficient for you, for my power is made perfect in weakness." Therefore I will boast all the more gladly about my weaknesses, so that Christ's power may rest on me.
>
> 2 Corinthians 12:7–9

Sometimes we ask the Lord to take something away, and he says, "No, I am working in the midst of this." That is what he did with Paul. And that thorn in his flesh made Paul all the more fervent in his ministry.

GOD'S PRESENCE IN THE PAIN

Sometimes when you go through hardship, you can bring a special measure of comfort to someone else who is going through a similar trial. We have seen this in the life of believers like Joni Eareckson Tada, Corrie ten Boom, and many others. There are also times when God will glorify himself by removing the suffering. And that is what he was doing in the life of the blind man in John 9, where John reports, " 'Neither this man nor his parents sinned,' said Jesus, 'but this happened so that the work of God might be displayed in his life. As long as it is day, we must do the work of him who sent me. Night is coming, when no one can work'" (verses 3–4). Instead of dealing with how this man ended up blind, Jesus was saying he would glorify himself through the situation. If we have eyes to see, we will find Jesus doing the same in our lives.

46

Is Healing Possible?

He prays to God and finds favor with him, he sees God's face
and shouts for joy; he is restored by God to his righteous state.

Job 33:26

The question of suffering is in many ways a question about
healing. If suffering is the result of human sin and free will, is it
reasonable for us to ask God for healing and help? The story of
Jesus healing the blind man gives us the answer. And the answer
is Jesus himself.

The prophet Isaiah spoke of the promise of Jesus's healing:
"But he was pierced for our transgressions, he was crushed for
our iniquities; the punishment that brought us peace was upon
him, and by his wounds we are healed" (Isa. 53:5). There are
multiple stories in the New Testament of people being healed
from various physical ailments—leprosy, blindness, paralysis,
even death itself. So it is clear that God *can* heal us. So why are
some of us still sick? The answer to that question is one of the
great mysteries of faith. We don't know why some people are
healed and others are not. But we do know healing isn't relegated
only to the physical part of our lives.

Healing the Outside

In the case of this blind man, Jesus healed the man's physical
sickness. John writes, "Having said this, he spit on the ground,
made some mud with the saliva, and put it on the man's eyes.
'Go,' he told him, 'wash in the Pool of Siloam' (this word means

Sent). So the man went and washed, and came home seeing" (John 9:6–7).

Think of all the ways Jesus healed people. Some would touch him, like the woman who touched the hem of his garment (Matt. 9:20–22). Some would hear his voice (Matt. 17:14–18). And some would receive his touch (Luke 4:40). And in the case of this blind man, it was Jesus's very saliva that brought about the healing. What a strange sight this man must have been as he hurried through the streets of Jerusalem, mud caked on his eyes. When he reached the pool of Siloam, he must have counted the steps as he descended, then washed the dirt from his eyes. And for the first time in his life, he could see.

A HEALING HERETIC?

Imagine what this no-longer-blind man must have felt at that moment. Who did this for him? Why? Would he ever see the one who healed him again? He didn't have much time to contemplate these questions or even to enjoy his newfound sight before he was called before the religious authorities and cross-examined:

> Now the day on which Jesus had made the mud and opened the man's eyes was a Sabbath. Therefore the Pharisees also asked him how he had received his sight. "He put mud on my eyes," the man replied, "and I washed, and now I see." Some of the Pharisees said, "This man is not from God, for he does not keep the Sabbath." But others asked, "How can a sinner do such miraculous signs?" So they were divided. Finally they turned again to the blind man, "What have you to say about him? It was your eyes he opened." The man replied, "He is a prophet."
>
> John 9:14–17

This man didn't know if he would ever see Jesus again and could have easily downplayed the truth. He knew these Pharisees were angry. I imagine he wouldn't want to provoke them and risk being barred from worship and ostracized by the community. The lives of the Jewish people revolved around the local synagogue, including their personal, business, and social lives. To be left out of religious life was to be left out, period. But this man simply could not deny what had happened to him. Jesus had opened his eyes. He could not deny it.

Meanwhile, these religious leaders could not let this go:

> A second time they summoned the man who had been blind. "Give glory to God," they said. "We know this man is a sinner." He replied, "Whether he is a sinner or not, I don't know. One thing I do know. I was blind but now I see!" Then they asked him, "What did he do to you? How did he open your eyes?" He answered, "I have told you already and you did not listen. Why do you want to hear it again? Do you want to become his disciples, too?" Then they hurled insults at him and said, "You are this fellow's disciple! We are disciples of Moses!"
>
> John 9:24–28

Let's put ourselves in this man's sandals for a moment. He was completely blind. He had never seen a blue sky, a cloud, or a sunset. He had never laid his eyes on the face of another person or knew what water, mountains, or trees looked like. Then one day, seemingly out of nowhere, this stranger named Jesus comes along and opens up the entire world of sight to him. Upon receiving this precious gift, he is of course overjoyed and elated. Yet all these Pharisees could do was argue about the things that didn't matter.

HEALING FROM THE INSIDE

The same thing happens to us when we come to Christ. Our world is changed overnight. The weight of sin is gone. The guilt in our hearts is replaced by peace. That's the kind of healing Jesus is all about. Yes, there are times when God will take away our physical suffering. But even when that suffering remains, we have God's promise—come to fruition in Jesus—that our hearts will be healed and restored.

47

SEEING AND BELIEVING

The secret things belong to the LORD our God,
but the things revealed belong to us and to our children
forever, that we may follow all the words of this law.

Deuteronomy 29:29

Anyone who has been a Christian for more than a few weeks is familiar with the story of Jesus healing the blind man. It's one of the Greatest Hits of the Bible, if you will. But we don't always know about the conversation Jesus had with the blind man — and the Pharisees — after he gave the man his sight. In fact, it's in what happened *after* Jesus healed the man that we find the point of this story:

Jesus heard that they had thrown him out, and when he found him, he said, "Do you believe in the Son of Man?" "Who is he, sir?" the man asked. "Tell me so that I may believe in him." Jesus said, "You have now seen him; in fact, he is the one speaking with you." Then the man said, "Lord, I believe," and he worshiped him. Jesus said, "For judgment I have come into this world, so that the blind will see and those who see will become blind." Some Pharisees who were with him heard him say this and asked, "What? Are we blind too?" Jesus said, "If you were blind, you would not be guilty of sin; but now that you claim you can see, your guilt remains."

John 9:35–41

The Pharisees mocked the blind man and were horrified when he suggested that they might want to follow Jesus themselves. But when "religion" turned this man away, Jesus took him in.

If you've been disillusioned with religion, or tried to keep all the rules and regulations but still come up empty, then Jesus is waiting for you with open arms, ready to open your eyes.

TRUE BLINDNESS

In telling the Pharisees, "If you were blind, you wouldn't be guilty," Jesus was saying, in essence, "If you were blind, then you would not be held accountable for truth you were unable to see. But you claim that you can see, and yet you willfully ignore the truth of my Word. That's why you are held accountable and found guilty. You saw the light but chose to live in darkness."

We often wonder what happens to people who have never heard about God. Will they be condemned because they have not accepted a truth they never had the chance to hear? The story of the blind man gives us an answer. God is perfectly holy and perfectly just. It goes against his nature to condemn someone who is ignorant of his truth. In fact, Scripture declares that God is loving, patient, and longing for fellowship (see 2 Peter 3:9). God will judge us according to the truth we have received. We will not be held accountable for what we do not know.

This, however, doesn't excuse us from all responsibility; otherwise we might claim that ignorance is bliss. No matter where we live, we humans are born with eternity in our hearts (see Eccles. 3:11). Each of us was born with a soul—a sense that life should have meaning and purpose. But if we turn away from what little we know to be true, this shows we don't really want to know God. It isn't ignorance; it's rebellion. Like the Pharisees, we want religion, not Jesus.

GOD REVEALED

I believe that if a person is a true seeker of God, then God will reveal himself to him or her. Jeremiah 29:13 promises, "You will seek me and find me when you seek me with all your heart." God doesn't hide from us. God wants us to know him and is waiting for us to open our eyes and hearts to the life he has for us.

The Bible tells us about a man named Cornelius who was very religious and prayed to God constantly. Cornelius had never heard of Jesus Christ, but he was asking God to reveal himself. God answered the prayers of Cornelius by sending Peter to him. Peter told Cornelius about Jesus and when Cornelius heard that wonderful message, he believed. That's because he was a true seeker.

THE SEEING SKEPTIC

There's nothing wrong with asking honest questions about God. It has been said that skepticism is the first step toward truth. But there's a big difference between skepticism and unbelief. Skepticism is open to believing, while unbelief is refusing to believe. Skepticism is honesty, while unbelief is stubbornness. Skepticism is looking for light, while unbelief is content with darkness.

An unbeliever has no intention of changing or believing. Unbelievers will offer up well-worn excuses and arguments, but even when confronted with evidence to refute their unbelief, they reject it out of hand. They don't want to believe.

Jesus put it this way: "This is the verdict: Light has come into the world, but men loved darkness instead of light because their deeds were evil. Everyone who does evil hates the light, and will not come into the light for fear that his deeds will be exposed" (John 3:19–20).

Perhaps something has happened in your life that has caught your attention. Maybe you have been going through a time of suffering. Maybe God has been making his presence clear to you. Whatever it may be, I would encourage you to pay attention. Like the blind man, be prepared to have your eyes opened. Look around you and ask yourself what God might be trying to show you.

48

An Abundant Life

He tends his flock like a shepherd: He gathers the lambs
in his arms and carries them close to his heart;
he gently leads those that have young.

Isaiah 40:11

Life. This is what I was searching for as a young man—not just existence, but life. My big question was not "Is there life after death?" It was "Is there life during life?" That is what we all want: a life that is worth living, a life that matters.

Many years ago, a young artist in Florence, Italy, had labored long and hard over a marble statue of an angel. When he finished, he asked the master artist, Michelangelo, to examine it. No master looked over the work more carefully than Michelangelo. It appeared perfect in every way. The artist waited for Michelangelo's response. His heart nearly broke when he heard, "It lacks only one thing." But Michelangelo didn't tell him what it lacked. For days the young artist could not eat or sleep, until a friend called on Michelangelo and asked him what he thought. Michelangelo said, "It lacks only life."

THE ENEMY OF LIFE

That could be said of so many people today. They have everything a person supposedly needs to be happy: a good job, a family, a house. But they lack life.

Most of us could say, at some point along the road of life, "If I had known what I know now, I would have lived differently. I would have done things differently so that I would have had a better life." Perhaps this statement from one ninety-year-old man says it best: "If I'd known I was going to live this long, I would have taken better care of myself."

We all want a better life. And in speaking of this, Jesus said, "The thief comes only to steal and kill and destroy; I have come that they may have life, and have it to the full" (John 10:10). The Bible often uses contrasts to make a point. We see this in the examples of Cain and Abel (Gen. 4:2–9) as well as Abraham and Lot (Genesis 11–19). Jesus spoke of a narrow road that leads to life and the broad road that leads to destruction (see Matt. 7:13). He also spoke of the wise man who built his house on the rock, and the foolish man who built his house on the sand (see Matt. 7:24–27).

And in John 10:10, we see both God's plan and Satan's plan. Satan's plan is to steal, to kill, and to destroy. He wants to ruin our lives. He accomplishes this through sin. And sin can be so alluring. But once the devil has his claws in us, he will pull us down so fast we won't even know what hit us. Satan's end game is destruction, misery, and death.

The Protector of Life

The thief this verse is referring to is the enemy of sheep—bears, lions, and wolves. Their goal is to kill and eat the sheep. But in contrast to that wicked agenda is the plan of our Shepherd, Jesus. He wants us to "have life, and have it to the full." In the next verse, Jesus offers a description of himself as the *Good* Shepherd: "I am the good shepherd. The good shepherd lays down his life for the sheep" (verse 11). The word "good" Jesus used here is full of meaning. Not only does it mean good as in morally good, but it also means "beautiful, winsome, lovely, attractive." So Jesus is the beautiful, winsome, lovely, attractive Shepherd. And this Good Shepherd's primary objective is to tend his flock as they flourish, are well-fed and cared for, are content and satisfied. He tells us as his followers, "Do not be afraid, little flock, for your Father has been pleased to give you the kingdom" (Luke 12:32).

And the kingdom of God, we are told in Romans 14:17, is one "of righteousness, peace and joy in the Holy Spirit."

THE ABUNDANT LIFE

So what exactly is the full, abundant life Jesus was speaking of? Let me first say what it isn't. The abundant life Jesus spoke of is not necessarily a long one. But it certainly is a full one. Breakthroughs in medical science can add years to our lives. But they cannot add life to our years. Nor is this abundant life one that is necessarily free from sorrow or sickness, although following God certainly does spare us many sorrows that we might otherwise have had. No, this abundant life Jesus promises is not a state of constant euphoria. I find it interesting how some people think Christians should have a permanent smile plastered across their faces. I've had people come up to me and say, "Greg, smile!!" Of course, the Christian life includes smiling, but not necessarily all the time.

Perhaps the best way to describe the abundant life is a *contented* life. This contentment comes from the knowledge that our Good Shepherd is capable of handling every emergency that will come our way. Our Good Shepherd is always looking out for our best interests, and it is his joy to lead us to green pastures, beside still waters, and through the valley of the shadow of death (Psalm 23).

Our English word *abundance* comes from two Latin words, which mean "to rise in waves" and "to overflow." The translation of the first word conveys the image of the constant, crashing of waves on a shore. It is endless. Surfers will check the surf report to see where the best swell is, but one thing is sure: those waves will keep coming, over and over and over again. The translation of the second word suggests the idea of a flood overflowing a river, caused by heavy rains. When we put it all together, here is what we have: The abundant life is one in which we are content in the knowledge that God's grace is more than sufficient for our needs, that nothing can suppress it, and that God's favor for us is unending. The abundant life means unending, consistent contentment.

49

LESSONS FROM A SHEPHERD

> I will search for the lost and bring back the strays.
> I will bind up the injured and strengthen the weak, but the sleek
> and the strong I will destroy. I will shepherd the flock with justice.
>
> Ezekiel 34:16

One of the most well-known and well-loved passages in the Bible is Psalm 23. Here, we find a picture of God as our loving Shepherd. The tenderness and care of the Shepherd gives life to the sheep. It's simply beautiful:

> The LORD is my shepherd, I shall not be in want.
>   He makes me lie down in green pastures,
> he leads me beside quiet waters,
>   he restores my soul.
> He guides me in paths of righteousness
>   for his name's sake.
> Even though I walk
>   through the valley of the shadow of death,
> I will fear no evil,
>   for you are with me;
> your rod and your staff,
>   they comfort me.
> You prepare a table before me
>   in the presence of my enemies.
> You anoint my head with oil;
>   my cup overflows.
> Surely goodness and love will follow me
>   all the days of my life,
> and I will dwell in the house of the LORD
>   forever.
>
> Psalm 23

David, a shepherd, penned these words that have brought comfort to millions. As one who observed and understood sheep, it dawned on him one day that he was just like those sheep he faithfully watched over. He probably was sitting against a rock, with rod and staff nearby, watching his flock. After a nice meal of grass, they were satisfying their thirst as they drank from a cool, refreshing stream. It was a picture of total contentment: *The Lord is my shepherd. I shall not be in want.*

This psalm about sheep has a great deal to teach us about living life to the fullest.

A SAFE PLACE TO REST

This psalm begins with contented sheep that are at rest. Sheep can be very skittish, but these sheep are content and willing to eat and rest because they feel safe. They have found their shepherd to be good, one who is able to meet their needs and ensure their freedom from anxiety. However, it is important to remember that these things are available only to those who belong to the Good Shepherd. Only the person who has said, "The Lord is my shepherd" can also say, "I shall not be in want."

There simply is no substitute for the knowledge that our Shepherd is near, because we live a most uncertain life. Any hour can bring disaster, danger, and distress. We never know what new trouble a day will bring, and it is often the unknown or unexpected that causes us the greatest anxiety. This is when we need to remember the Shepherd is near. And Psalm 121:4 promises, "Indeed, he who watches over Israel will neither slumber nor sleep." So take rest from the strains of life. You are saved and safe.

THE CLEAR PATH

The sheep are not put out to pasture, then left to their own devices. David writes, "He leads me beside quiet waters. . . . he guides me in the paths of righteousness for his name's sake." Sheep need to be led. On their own, they will wander off to dangerous places. They are creatures of habit and will never leave a place where they once found good grazing. Sheep have been known to completely destroy a pasture because they keep grazing until they've eaten every blade of grass and every root. In the same way, we so often will make the wrong decisions when left to ourselves. We hang out with the wrong people, go to the wrong places, and do the wrong things.

For some of us, it isn't that we want to go to the wrong place. It's that we don't want to go anywhere at all. We are fat, lazy, complacent sheep. So our Good Shepherd will periodically shake up our world and lead us on. It might be a move to start a new ministry. It might be a new business opportunity. But as followers of Jesus, it is important that we not live in the past, but in the present, and that we keep moving forward toward the future.

This psalm also assures us that God will keep us safe: "Even though I walk through the valley of the shadow of death, I will fear no evil, for you are with me . . . ." The Good Shepherd watches over us. When we belong to the Shepherd, we don't need to fear danger or death because God has conquered both on the cross. We are just as vulnerable to sickness and accidents as those who don't know God, but we have the assurance that whatever happens to us in this life is temporary. We have a greater life ahead of us in heaven with our Lord.

Notice that David said, "Though I *walk* through the valley . . ." (emphasis mine). Walking requires movement, which means that we need to keep moving in this Christian life. And remember, those valleys won't last forever.

THE BEST PROMISE OF ALL

David tells us of the Good Shepherd's provision for us: "You prepare a table before me in the presence of my enemies. You anoint my head with oil; my cup overflows." God will always provide for our needs, no matter what.

My dog always wants "people food," but that can hurt, even kill, him. For example, chocolate can kill a dog. So I wouldn't be a very good pet owner if I gave my dog what he wants instead of what he needs. God gives us what we need—not necessarily what we want.

As the psalm ends, we have the most blessed assurance of all that we are loved and cared for by our Shepherd: "Surely goodness and love will follow me all the days of my life, and I will dwell in the house of the LORD forever." We not only have life during life, but we also have life after death. Are you experiencing life during life? Are you prepared for life after death? Are you content? This can only happen when the Lord is your Shepherd. Remember, Jesus said, "I am the good shepherd. The good shepherd lays down his life for the sheep" (John 10:11).

50

ALL IN GOD'S TIME

"Therefore wait for me," declares the LORD, "for the day
I will stand up to testify. I have decided to assemble the nations,
to gather the kingdoms and to pour out my wrath on them—
all my fierce anger. The whole world will be consumed
by the fire of my jealous anger."

Zephaniah 3:8

Has it ever seemed like God has let you down? Have you ever felt as though he didn't come through for you in your hour of need, that he forgot about you somehow, or that he was simply too late? If you've ever felt this way, then you're in good company, because some of God's servants have felt the same way.

Let's look at a story that beautifully illustrates how what can appear to be a mistake on God's part is actually part of his perfect plan for us. It's a story that shows us God is always right on time—God's time.

> Now a man named Lazarus was sick. He was from Bethany, the village of Mary and her sister Martha. This Mary, whose brother Lazarus now lay sick, was the same one who poured perfume on the Lord and wiped his feet with her hair. So the sisters sent word to Jesus, "Lord, the one you love is sick." When he heard this, Jesus said, "This sickness will not end in death. No, it is for God's glory so that God's Son may be glorified through it." Jesus loved Martha and her sister and Lazarus. Yet when he heard that Lazarus was sick, he stayed where he was two more days. Then he said to his disciples, "Let us go back to Judea."

John 11:1–7

The village of Bethany was not far from Jerusalem, and Jesus spent a lot of time with Lazarus and his sisters—eating meals and enjoying their friendship. Martha, Mary, and Lazarus really could say Jesus was their personal friend. So when Lazarus grew seriously ill, the sisters knew that Jesus would heal him. They sent word to Jesus that the one he loved was sick. They probably expected Jesus to drop whatever he was doing and rush to Bethany to help out his friend.

TIME FOR ACTION?

Notice, however, that this was not an invitation or even a request. They didn't say, "Lord, please come immediately." They just assumed that because Lazarus was a personal friend of Jesus, that Jesus would hurry there. However, they didn't tell Jesus what to do. They simply told him about the situation. They believed Jesus would know what to do.

Also notice the basis of their appeal. They said, "Lord, the one you love is sick." They did not say, "Lord, the one who *loves you* is sick." Of course Lazarus loved Jesus as did his sisters. But they didn't base their prayer on their worthiness or even their friendship. They didn't say, "Hey, Lord, the one that loves you and is your *good friend* is sick." And that's something we should keep in mind. We shouldn't appeal to God on the basis of our worthiness. Rather we come to God on the basis of his love for us.

TIME'S UP

So, Jesus heard their request . . . and stayed put. Immediately, this sounds like a contradiction. After all, if Jesus really loved Lazarus, why didn't he go immediately and heal him? When hardship, tragedy, or even death comes into our lives, we might ask the same. It is hard to see through eyes filled with tears. Even though we can't see how a situation will end or why it has happened to us, we can know that our lives are in the hands of the God who loves us. We should interpret what seems like delays through the lens of God's love, not the other way around.

Jesus wanted to do above and beyond what Martha, Mary, and Lazarus could imagine. They wanted a healing. But he wanted a resurrection. They thought only of friendship, but he thought of ultimate, sacrificial love. They thought only of temporal comfort, but he thought of eternal comfort.

Meanwhile, Lazarus was getting worse and worse and worse. Then suddenly he died. He was gone. It was over with, and Jesus was nowhere to be found. Then four days later, there was Jesus, strolling into town after Lazarus was dead, buried, and in the process of decomposition.

ANOTHER'S TIME

Martha rushed out to meet him, unable to contain her disappointment and hurt and pain. The Bible tells us Martha said, "Lord, . . . if you had been here, my brother would not have died. But I know that even now God will give you whatever you ask" (John 11:21–22). Allow me to loosely paraphrase: "Lord, you blew it. We pinned our hopes on the fact that you would heal our brother, and you didn't even show up for the funeral. You missed everything."

Now in her defense, she still addressed Jesus as "Lord." She was still speaking to him. She still acknowledged that he was in control. She also expressed a measure of hope.

There is nothing wrong with going to God and saying, "Lord, I love you, but I don't quite know why you're letting this happen to me. I don't know why you haven't taken this away from me. Where are you?" When we experience a tragedy, difficulty, or the death of a loved one, we are hard-pressed to make sense of God's plans. But Paul offers us this word of hope: "For our light and momentary troubles are achieving for us an eternal glory that far outweighs them all" (2 Cor. 4:17).

Jesus wanted to help Martha get an eternal perspective on her problems. Jesus simply wanted to do more than Mary and Martha asked him to.

51

Our Friend in Sorrow

Then maidens will dance and be glad, young men and old
as well. I will turn their mourning into gladness;
I will give them comfort and joy instead of sorrow.

Jeremiah 31:13

Lazarus's sister Martha wasn't the only sister who was surprised and confused when Jesus failed to heal their brother's illness. When Lazarus died, each sister comes to Jesus with her anger, her sorrow, and her questions. But rather than answering them with mere words, Jesus does something amazing—he cries.

Here we are given a glimpse into the utter humanity of Jesus. We typically celebrate his deity—and rightly so. But Jesus was also a man, one with feelings and compassion and friends. And as he faced the sisters of his dead friend, Jesus was overcome with the sadness of the moment.

When Mary reached the place where Jesus was and saw him, she fell at his feet and said, "Lord, if you had been here, my brother would not have died." When Jesus saw her weeping, and the Jews who had come along with her also weeping, he was deeply moved in spirit and troubled. "Where have you laid him?" he asked. "Come and see, Lord," they replied. Jesus wept. Then the Jews said, "See how he loved him!"

John 11:32–36

Jesus, Moved

I've often wondered why Jesus reacted this way. I mean, he knows the end of the story. But there's something about this situation that moves him and I think I know what it might be. I think Jesus was angry with death. I think he was angry with the fact that humanity has to go through something like this, that we have to attend funerals for people we love, that we have to say good-bye to them. I think he wept because he hurt for these people, hurt for the pain of living in a world broken by sin.

Jesus was touched by the tears of his friends. He was affected by their sorrow. And he joined in their suffering. In the same way, when Jesus sees our tears, he is moved. He weeps with us. He aches with us. He hurts with us. The Bible says God makes a record of our tears (see Ps. 56:8).

A Strange Suggestion

Now what Jesus suggests next almost seems a bit morbid. John writes, "Jesus, once more deeply moved, came to the tomb. It was a cave with a stone laid across the entrance. 'Take away the stone,' he said. 'But, Lord,' said Martha, the sister of the dead man, 'by this time there is a bad odor, for he has been there four days'"(John 11:38–39).

Today when a person dies, he or she is usually embalmed. But in the first century, once a body was placed in a tomb, the process of decomposition was immediate. Four days had passed. So to say "by this time there is a bad odor" was kind of an understatement.

The whole thing did seem a little insensitive. Here Jesus had seemingly ignored the fact that Lazarus was sick. Once his friend died, Jesus didn't even come for the funeral. Then, four days later, he comes walking into town and tells the family to open up the grave. I wouldn't have been surprised if the sisters had been a little put out by this suggestion.

Life Returns

There must have been something in Jesus's words that instilled confidence in them instead, because they moved that massive stone from Lazarus's tomb:

Then Jesus looked up and said, "Father, I thank you that you have heard me. I knew that you always hear me, but I said this for the benefit of the people standing here, that they may believe that you sent me." When he had said this, Jesus called in a loud voice, "Lazarus, come out!" The dead man came out, his hands and feet wrapped with strips of linen, and a cloth around his face. Jesus said to them, "Take off the grave clothes and let him go."

verses 41–44

What a moment! It is a good thing Jesus called Lazarus by name, because if Jesus had just said, "Come forth," *everybody* in every grave would have come out at once! Here was Lazarus, bound in his grave clothes, inching his way out of the tomb. No doubt, it was a little difficult for Lazarus to get around. So Jesus gave the command to undo his grave clothes. "Set the poor guy free!" He was saying. Jesus hadn't forgotten Lazarus after all. He had a plan all along—a plan that Martha, Mary, and the others just couldn't see at the time.

From tremendous pain came a glorious moment. Can you imagine the celebration Lazarus and his sisters had that day? Can you imagine how much greater the celebration in heaven on the day when we see God's perfect plan revealed in all its fullness? Then, like Mary and Martha, we will see that God's timing is perfect after all.

52

WHEN GOD SEEMS LATE

O God, you are my God, earnestly I seek you;
my soul thirsts for you, my body longs for you,
in a dry and weary land where there is no water.

Psalm 63:1

The story of Jesus raising Lazarus from the dead reminds us that God is never late. His so-called delays are delays of love. Even God's silence can be a silence of love. That's why it's never dangerous to pray, "Not my will, but yours be done." We might not be able to see the Lord's wisdom and plan unfolding until we are in heaven. Until then, we must trust God and know that he wants to enter into our sorrows and into our pain and into our hurt.

The three Hebrew teenagers, Shadrach, Meshach, and Abednego, could have been tempted to believe that God was late, that he had forgotten about them. Their king had given a decree that all should bow before a golden image of himself—or die in a blazing furnace of fire. So when the theme music played, all the people obediently fell prostrate before the image—all the people except the three Hebrew boys, that is.

The king was so enraged that he commanded the fire to be heated seven times hotter than it already was. The boys were given another chance to change their minds, but they would not. The heat from the fire was so intense that it killed the guards who had been assigned the unpleasant task of throwing Shadrach, Meshach, and Abednego into it.

GOD'S PROTECTION

Why didn't the Lord come and scorch this idolatrous king and his followers? Where was he?

We discover that God was waiting for Shadrach, Meshach, and Abednego *in* the furnace. And when they were thrown in, much to the king's surprise, he saw four figures—not three—walking around in the furnace: "He said, 'Look! I see four men walking around in the fire, unbound and unharmed, and the fourth looks like a son of the gods'" (Dan. 3:25).

Sometimes God delivers us *from* the trial, and sometimes he delivers us *through* it. In the case of Shadrach, Meshach, and Abednego, God received greater glory by allowing them to go through this fiery trial instead of delivering them from it.

GOD'S ESCAPE ROUTE

We also find this to be true when the Israelites crossed the Red Sea. Moses had demanded the release of the Israelites time and time again, but Pharaoh resisted, making their existence in Egypt more miserable than ever. Finally, after God's judgment came, Pharaoh relented and let the people go. Joy filled their hearts as they began their massive exodus out of Egypt and toward the Promised Land.

But soon they realized a major obstacle was before them. It was called the Red Sea. The Israelites must have wondered how God could possibly rescue them from this dead end. But God did: "Then Moses stretched out his hand over the sea, and all that night the LORD drove the sea back with a strong east wind and turned it into dry land. The waters were divided" (Exod. 14:21).

God caused this mighty sea to part and hover on each side of the Israelites, forming massive, liquid walls. Things were looking good when, much to their horror, they turned to see the heavily armed Egyptian army coming after them in their chariots. As the army got closer and closer, the Israelites thought all was lost. Then God came through again. The waters closed back in, drowning the Egyptian army.

GOD'S REASONS

So you see, God is never late; he is always on time. As we look at the world around us, we see horrible violence, perversion, and people not only breaking God's laws but also flaunting their wicked lifestyles. And we wonder when God will return to put an end to all of the suffering and sorrow. That's when we need to trust in God's perfect timing.

The apostle Peter wrote:

First of all, you must understand that in the last days scoffers will come, scoffing and following their own evil desires. They will say, "Where is this 'coming' he promised? Ever since our fathers died, everything goes on as it has since the beginning of creation. . . ." But do not forget this one thing, dear friends: With the Lord a day is like a thousand years, and a thousand years are like a day. The Lord is not slow in keeping his promise, as some understand slowness. He is patient with you, not wanting anyone to perish, but everyone to come to repentance.

2 Peter 3:3–4, 8–9

The day will come when God will make all things right. And until that day, we can find hope in the promise that God is with us, weeping for justice, aching for righteousness, and holding us firmly in his loving grasp.

53

No Regrets

This is what the Lord says—Israel's King and Redeemer,
the Lord Almighty: I am the first and I am the last;
apart from me there is no God.

Isaiah 44:6

In the 1960s, at the zenith of The Beatles' popularity, John Lennon said, "Christianity will go. It will vanish and shrink. I needn't argue about that; I'm right and I will be proved right. We're more popular than Jesus now; I don't know which will go first—rock 'n' roll or Christianity."[4]

Dear John: Who's more popular now?

Jesus was popular in the first century too, especially after he raised Lazarus from the dead. His name was on everyone's lips. Wherever he went, people thronged him. The problem was the same people who made him popular soon turned on him, because they never understood his real mission.

Even his handpicked disciples never fully understood Jesus. That is, until his crucifixion and resurrection from the dead. But there was one exception among his followers. It wasn't John, who was known for his spiritual perception. It wasn't Peter, James, Matthew, or Andrew. This person wasn't even one of the twelve disciples. In fact, it wasn't a man at all. This woman had greater spiritual insight than those who had spent every waking hour in Jesus's presence for nearly three years. *Her* name was Mary—the same Mary of Mary-and-Martha fame, the friend of Jesus, and the sister of Lazarus.

THE RIGHT CHOICE

It is worth noting that every time we read about Mary in Scripture, she is at the feet of Jesus. Perhaps that's why she had such insight. When the Lord came to visit at her house, she wisely sat at his feet, even as Martha was slaving away in the kitchen. Jesus said to Martha, "You are worried and upset about many things, but only one thing is needed. Mary has chosen what is better, and it will not be taken away from her" (Luke 10:41–42).

Mary, no doubt led by the Holy Spirit, seemed to grasp a truth that was largely missed by the others: the fact that Jesus had to die. Not only did she have a unique understanding of who he was, but she also gave him a wonderful gift. She gave him the most precious thing she owned. For this, she not only was commended, but her gift was a memorial that would never be forgotten.

GOD'S POINT OF VIEW

It's interesting to see which miracles, teachings, and events were recorded by Matthew, Mark, Luke, and John. In his Gospel, John wrote, "Jesus did many other things as well. If every one of them were written down, I suppose that even the whole world would not have room for the books that would be written" (John 21:25).

Some writers would have gravitated toward the more dramatic miracles, or the great empires and leaders that coexisted with Jesus and the apostles in their day: the Caesars, the wonders of Rome, the great battles that were fought. But the Bible says very little about these things. Rome is presented merely as a backdrop for the most important story ever told. The great King Herod is a bit player. Caesar is briefly referenced. God chose to record Mary's gift to show us that he sees things differently than we do.

So what great thing did Mary do? What was it that so impressed Jesus? It wasn't necessarily a practical thing, but it was a heartfelt one. Mary decided to seize the moment and once again sit at his feet. Then she offered her gift to Jesus:

Six days before the Passover, Jesus arrived at Bethany, where Lazarus lived, whom Jesus had raised from the dead. Here a dinner was given in Jesus's honor. Martha served, while Lazarus was among those reclining at the table with him. Then Mary took about a pint of pure nard, an expensive perfume; she poured it on Jesus's feet and wiped his feet with her hair. And the house was filled with the fragrance of the perfume.

John 12:1–3

Things had been coming to a head in Jesus's ministry. There had been a number of increasingly confrontational exchanges between Jesus and the religious leaders. They wanted him dead, plain and simple. But Jerusalem was swarming with visitors for Passover. If they arrested Jesus, who was very popular among the people at this point, it could cause a riot.

Jesus was aware of all this, and he was looking forward to an evening with friends in Bethany. He and the disciples would be having dinner with Mary, Martha, and the newly resurrected Lazarus at the home of Simon the leper. I'm sure there must have been a lively conversation going on. Perhaps different people shared their story of how Jesus had touched them. And I'm sure that more than one wanted to know the details from Lazarus about his resurrection.

Mary was moved by the Holy Spirit to do something unusual, outstanding, and extravagant, to demonstrate her total devotion to Christ. So, Mary came bearing this imported perfume, most likely a family heirloom. However, she didn't just sprinkle a few drops of it on Jesus. With complete abandon, she poured the entire bottle on his feet, and then wiped them with her hair.

THE FIRST PRIORITY

I think what motivated such devotion on Mary's part was nothing less than Jesus himself. She felt, and rightly so, there was nothing too good to give him. What amazes me about Mary is that she did not have the privilege of spending as much time in Jesus's physical presence as the apostles did. She didn't personally hear all his teachings. But whenever he was around, she would stop what she was doing and listen and absorb every single detail—the expression on his face, the nuance in his voice, and of course, his every word. She didn't want to miss a thing. Sure, she could have helped her sister Martha in the kitchen. But how often do you have the privilege of sitting at the feet of the Creator? How often can you hear the Word of God spoken by the Word of God himself (see John 1:1, 14)?

We can't pour perfume on the feet of Jesus, but we can show our love and adoration just the same. We can make God a priority, just like Mary did, putting work, hobbies, even family in their proper place. Doing so doesn't mean those activities and people aren't important. But nothing can come close to the importance of our precious Lord. Mary knew that. Do you?

54

MARY'S INSIGHT

What is more, I consider everything a loss compared
to the surpassing greatness of knowing Christ Jesus my Lord,
for whose sake I have lost all things.
I consider them rubbish, that I may gain Christ.

Philippians 3:8

Mary had a perception no one else seemed to have. She listened in rapt attention as the Lord spoke to the group that had gathered in Simon's home. But with an intuition often inherent in women, she saw and heard something else. She saw the lines etching Jesus's face and read correctly the troubles reflected in his eyes. An inner sense told her the disciples were wrong in expecting a kingdom. The Master meant exactly what he had said. He was not speaking metaphorically; he was literally going to Jerusalem to be crucified.

She couldn't understand something so terrible, but she accepted it because he said it. She would not wait to pay a floral tribute at his funeral. She would bring her flowers now. She would give the very best she possibly could. So she lavished the beautiful and costly perfume on Jesus.

AT THE FEET OF JESUS

How is it that Mary had this incredible spiritual perception? Perhaps it was because of her willingness to set aside all practicality to be close to Jesus, to stop what she was doing, choose what was better, and simply sit at his feet.

Danish sculptor Thors Walden captured this idea well in a life-sized granite carving of Jesus. Walden sculpted the body of Christ in such a way that the face cannot be seen from a standing position. A sign next to the sculpture reads, "If you want to see the face of Jesus, you must sit at his feet." And sure enough, those who sit at the foot of the statue can look up and see the face of Jesus perfectly.

Mary had a clear view of Jesus. After all, he had raised her brother from the dead. There was no way to ever repay a debt like that. So she no doubt decided to give the most precious thing she had. But it wasn't the gift that was so significant as much as the attitude that was behind it. It wasn't the cost that was so important, but what it cost her.

THE CYNICAL CRITIC

However, not everyone appreciated her generosity and sacrifice:

> But one of his disciples, Judas Iscariot, who was later to betray him, objected, "Why wasn't this perfume sold and the money given to the poor? It was worth a year's wages." He did not say this because he cared about the poor but because he was a thief; as keeper of the money bag, he used to help himself to what was put into it. "Leave her alone," Jesus replied. "It was intended that she should save this perfume for the day of my burial. You will always have the poor among you, but you will not always have me."
>
> John 12:4–8

Judas, a man who knew the price of everything and the value of nothing, instantly calculated the waste, which in terms of today's economy, would have been around $30,000. On the surface, it seemed like Judas had a legitimate complaint. Was this practical? Was it good stewardship?

But John tells us what was really going on. Judas wasn't concerned about the poor, but about himself. As Mary poured out her perfume, Judas saw his own take of the profit slipping away. Soon after this moment, Judas approached the chief priests with his plan of betrayal. Was there a connection? Probably.

Judas's attitude is not so different from many people today. Like the Pharisees, many will give only what is required by God. We will try to get by with the bare minimum, asking ourselves, "What's the least I can do and still technically be a Christian?" We will go to church, but out of a sense of duty, not a desire to worship. We will read the Bible for a few minutes a day, if we can find the time. We will pray briefly before meals and before bed. We will put something in the offering—if we have any spare change.

Over the years, I've noticed that the people at church who complain the most are often the ones who do the least, while those who complain the least are the ones who do the most. And frequently the criticism will tell you more about the people themselves than about those whom they are criticizing.

This was true in Judas's case. He didn't care for the poor. His motives were greed and selfishness. "It was a waste!" Judas complained. Yet in a few hours, Jesus would call Judas "the son of perdition," or literally, "the son of waste."

THE TRUE BELIEVER

Although he could be found in the company of the other disciples, Judas was never a true believer. He appeared to be a spiritual man, especially when he made statements like this one. But things are not always as they seem. At this moment, Mary may have seemed wasteful and frivolous because of her gift, while Judas appeared to be thrifty, compassionate, and spiritual.

Yet Mary was the one who was spiritual and sacrificial, while Judas was wicked and greedy. Mary would spare no expense, because she had a glimpse of what Jesus had really come to do: "to give his life as a ransom for many" (Matt. 20:28).

In Mark's account of the same event, Jesus answered Judas by saying, "She did what she could. She poured perfume on my body beforehand to prepare for my burial. I tell you the truth, wherever the gospel is preached throughout the world, what she has done will also be told, in memory of her" (Mark 14:8–9). Mary did what she could because she understood that Jesus would do what he did.

55

GIVING OUR BEST

You also, like living stones, are being built into a
spiritual house to be a holy priesthood, offering
spiritual sacrifices acceptable to God through Jesus Christ.

1 Peter 2:5

Nothing is ever wasted when it is borne out of a heart that wants
to glorify God. In the eyes of unbelievers, what we Christians
do may seem wasteful and silly. Going to church seems like a
waste of a perfectly good weekend morning. Reading the Bible
sounds more boring than watching grass grow. And missions?
Who wants to leave all the luxuries of home to live with the
poorest people in the world?

We do all of this because we all have a part to play in the
advancement of God's kingdom. Mary did what she could, and
we must do what we can. She couldn't do everything, but she
could do something. In the same way, we can't do everything,
but we can do something. We must all do what we can, while
we can.

THE BIGGEST REGRET

When you come to the end of your life and look back, what
will you see? Will you regret not using the gifts and talents God
gave you in service to him? God will not hold you accountable
for what he called others to do. He will hold you accountable
for what he called you to do, which is to love others and serve
God with all your heart, soul, and mind (Matt. 22:37–39).

The Bible tells us there is coming a day of judgment for Christians in this very area:

> For no one can lay any foundation other than the one already laid, which is Jesus Christ. If any man builds on this foundation using gold, silver, costly stones, wood, hay or straw, his work will be shown for what it is, because the Day will bring it to light. It will be revealed with fire, and the fire will test the quality of each man's work. If what he has built survives, he will receive his reward. If it is burned up, he will suffer loss; he himself will be saved, but only as one escaping through the flames.
>
> 1 Corinthians 3:11–15

This passage is telling us that two classes of believers will stand at the judgment seat of Christ. First, there will be those who built on the right foundation using, gold, silver, and gems. These are the believers who invested their lives and used their time and money wisely. And they will be rewarded.

Then there will be those who built with the wrong materials, who didn't do anything of great value for God with the time and resources he gave them, but still they will be saved. These believers will have a saved soul, but a lost life.

This will not be a judgment concerning our salvation, because that has been given to us when we responded to the gospel and put our faith in Christ. Rather, this judgment has to do with how our believing the gospel has affected our lives—what it has resulted in. Speaking to believers, the apostle Paul wrote, "For we must all appear before the judgment seat of Christ, that each one may receive what is due him for the things done while in the body, whether good or bad" (2 Cor. 5:10).

TWO MILLIONAIRES

I'd like to tell you about two men whose lives illustrate what it means to use our resources for God. As a graduation gift from his parents, William Borden, heir to the Borden dairy estate, received a trip around the world. As he traveled through Asia, the Middle East, and Europe, he felt a growing burden for people who did not know the Lord. Finally, he wrote home to say, "I'm going to give my life to prepare for the mission field." Upon making his decision, he wrote two words in the back of his Bible: "NO RESERVES."

Upon graduation from Yale, Borden turned down some high-paying job offers. But he was determined to fulfill the call God had placed on his life. He wrote two more words in the back of his Bible: "NO RETREAT." Borden went on to do graduate work at Princeton Seminary, and upon completing his studies, he sailed for China to work with Muslims. But first, he stopped in Egypt to study Arabic. While he was there, he came down with spinal meningitis. Within a month, twenty-five-year-old William Borden was dead. In the back of his Bible, two more words had been written: "NO REGRETS."

No reserves. No retreat. No regrets. These six words encompassed the principles of William Borden's life.

A LIFE WASTED

Contrast Borden's life with that of millionaire Howard Hughes. The film about his life, *The Aviator*, chronicles his amazing achievements in aviation and other exploits. Yet a few important details were left out, including the fact that Hughes was a very immoral man who had been involved with many, many women. In *The Aviator*, Hughes's eccentricities were attributed to a vague form of mental illness, triggered by his mother's behavior.

The real Howard Hughes contracted syphilis, no doubt from his philandering, which attacked his brain in the form of neuro-syphilis, causing him to go insane. He spent the last two decades of his life bedridden and alone in a hotel room, covered in his own excrement. Having survived on a diet of candy and cake, he had lost all his teeth, and his fingernails were so long they curved under his fingers.

Hughes took his last breath on a plane heading back to the U.S. from Mexico. Afterward, the few people who had been loyal to him went to war for his estate, creating several fake wills to bolster their greed.

In contrast to William Borden, Howard Hughes had many regrets, I'm sure. But you won't see a movie about William Borden. His life didn't have the sizzle or the sex appeal of Howard Hughes's life. Nor did it have the same ending. William Borden is in heaven. And where is Howard Hughes? Only God knows.

We need to follow the example of people like William Borden and Mary. We need to do what we can. God has given each of us influence, opportunities, resources, and time. Let's choose what is best so that we can say of our lives: No reserves. No retreat. No regrets.

56

FINDERS, WEEPERS; LOSERS, KEEPERS

> But godliness with contentment is great gain.
>
> 1 Timothy 6:6

What makes us happy? *Time* magazine ran a cover story called, "The New Science of Happiness." The article offered some surprising answers to the question of where people find happiness. The piece reported, "Research has shown that once your basic needs are met, additional income does little to raise your sense of satisfaction."[5] Neither youth, nor education, nor wealth changed people's sense of happiness.

An article from the same issue, entitled "The Real Truth about Money," states, "If you made a graph of American life since the end of World War II, every line concerning money and the things money can buy would soar upward. But if you made a chart of American happiness since the end of World War II, the lines would be as flat as a marble tabletop."[6]

THE WRONG PLACE

So if we don't find happiness in wealth, youth, or education, where *do* we find it? Let me first tell you where we *won't* find it. It will not come from this world. The fleeting happiness this world has to offer comes and goes, depending on our circumstances. If things are going reasonably well, we are happy. If they are not, then we are unhappy. But we need to remember, "There are two sources of unhappiness in life. One is not getting what you want. The other is getting it."

Money can buy us some things, but not the most important things. Money can buy you a bed, but not sleep; books, but not brains; a house, but not a home; medicine, but not health; finery, but not beauty; and amusement, but not happiness. And to quote Saint Paul, John, George, and Ringo, "Money can't buy [you] love."

THE RIGHT PLACE

So where do we find the meaning and purpose in life that we all crave? How can we be truly happy people? In the *Time* article and elsewhere, an interesting fact was mentioned regarding the search for happiness: Scandinavians are the happiest people on Earth, followed by the Americans at a close second. Faith, family, and friends all contributed to happiness. According to *Time*, "Love, friendship, family . . . the belief that your life has purpose—these are the essentials of human fulfillment, and they can't be purchased with cash."[7]

Those of us who weren't born into Scandinavian families can't do much about that factor. But the belief that our lives have purpose—that's something we can work with.

A SENSE OF PURPOSE

Does your life have purpose? According to the Bible, if we seek to know God and discover his plan for our lives, then we'll find the happiness that has eluded us for so long. Happiness comes not as a result of seeking *it*, but seeking *God*. Psalm 144:15 says, "Blessed are the people whose God is the LORD." And as C. S. Lewis observed:

God designed the human machine to run on himself. He himself is the fuel our spirits were designed to burn, or the food our spirits were designed to feed on. There is no other. That is why it is just no good asking God to make us happy in our own way without bothering about religion. God cannot give us a happiness and peace apart from himself, because it is not there. There is no such thing.[8]

According to Scripture, happiness is never something to be sought directly. It is always something that results from seeking something else. If we seek holiness, we'll find happiness. Jesus said, "Blessed are those who hunger and thirst for righteousness, for they will be filled" (Matt. 5:6). The word "blessed" in this verse also could be translated, "happy." As our will becomes aligned with God's, and as we walk in harmony with him, the other areas of our lives will find their proper balance. We find what we are looking for in life not by seeking it in and of itself, but by seeking God.

57

UPSIDE-DOWN KINGDOM

> He said to them, "Let the little children come to me, and do not
> hinder them, for the kingdom of God belongs to such as these.
>
> Mark 10:14

Toward the end of his life, Jesus's popularity and notoriety were literally exploding. All kinds of people began seeking him out, including a group of Greek men. Perhaps it was their disillusionment with their pagan ways that sent them searching. Perhaps they had heard that Jesus raised people from the dead. It might have been mere curiosity. Whatever the case, Jesus revealed to them—and to us—the meaning and purpose of life, the secret to living a happy and meaningful life.

John records their story for us: "Now there were some Greeks among those who went up to worship at the Feast. They came to Philip, who was from Bethsaida in Galilee, with a request. 'Sir,' they said, 'we would like to see Jesus.' Philip went to tell Andrew; Andrew and Philip in turn told Jesus" (John 12:20–22).

LOOKING FOR JESUS

This inquiry from these Greeks triggered an important event in Jesus's life. Something about these men and their request drew this response from Jesus: "The hour has come for the Son of Man to be glorified" (verse 23).

This "hour" Jesus spoke of was the day of his crucifixion. On many occasions prior to this, Jesus would resist the pressure of others to completely reveal himself. He would say, "My hour has not yet come." But now, it had. These Greek men were but the beginning of millions who would follow, who would find life because of Christ's death on the cross for the whole world.

But why would these men come to Jesus in the first place? At the time this story took place, Greece was the center of human wisdom, the fountainhead of philosophy, the matrix of mythology, and the cradle of civilized society. It was an open and free society, devoid of absolutes, where people were encouraged to live as they please. Immorality was pervasive, marriage was crumbling, and justice was lacking. These men most likely had chased after the promises of hedonism and come back empty-handed. So, they came to Jerusalem looking for answers.

THE STRANGE SECRET

To them, and to all of us, Jesus revealed the meaning of life, the secret of happiness. But it wasn't what we might expect. He said, "I tell you the truth, unless a kernel of wheat falls to the ground and dies, it remains only a single seed. But if it dies, it produces many seeds. The man who loves his life will lose it, while the man who hates his life in this world will keep it for eternal life" (verses 24–25). Now this flies in the face of conventional wisdom. *The one who loves his life will lose it.* This seems so hard to understand, so unnatural, and so impossible. But when you stop and think about it, it makes complete sense.

Think of all the people who are trying to live life to its fullest but are going about it in the wrong way. They think it's ridiculous to wait until marriage to engage in sexual activity. And if you are married and the thrill is gone, spice it up and have an affair, they say. If your spouse finds out, just terminate the marriage and move on. If you want to get ahead in school, just cheat here and there, but don't get caught. If you want to get a good job, exaggerate about your experience on that résumé. File that false claim to get an insurance payout. If someone bothers you, sue them. When those taxes are due, lie to save some money. The list goes on and on—and so do the repercussions.

But God's wisdom says that if you love your life, you will lose it. If you live for yourself, you never will really find yourself. God's plan for finding meaning, purpose, and yes, happiness, is this: lose your life to find it. This isn't always easy to do, because it means you have to let go. You have to submit to the will of God for your life.

LIVING THE KINGDOM PARADOX

Are you willing to take your future and place it in God's hands? If you are, then you'll discover that the Christian life is paradoxical in so many ways. What we really want will not come by the ways this world teaches us.

Everyone wants more power in their lives, from the most powerful computer to the most powerful car to the most powerful position or the most powerful body. After all, we reason, with power, we can rule, influence, and control. But God said to the apostle Paul, "My grace is sufficient for you, for my power is made perfect in weakness" (2 Cor. 12:9). *If you lose your life, you will find it.*

Leaders want others to listen to what they have to say and to follow their leadership. But Jesus says, "You want to lead? Learn first to follow and serve." Speaking in Mark 9:35, Jesus said, "If anyone wants to be first, he must be the very last, and the servant of all." *If you lose your life, you will find it.*

We want our marriages to be successful, but it won't come through the conventional wisdom of a 50–50 commitment. No, it's a 100–100 commitment. Without any thought of our own gain, we must put our spouse's needs above our own. Husbands, do you want a good marriage? Then God says, "Love your wives, just as Christ loved the church and gave himself up for her" (Eph. 5:25). Wives, do you want a good marriage? Then "submit to your husbands as to the Lord" (Eph. 5:22). *If you lose your life, you will find it.*

In the Christian life, the way to greatness is through humility, the way to power is through weakness, the way to life is through death, and the way to up is down. And the way to happiness is to stop looking for it and look instead to God. This is life in the upside-down kingdom.

58

THE DO'S AND DON'TS
OF A HAPPY LIFE

To the man who pleases him,
God gives wisdom, knowledge and happiness.

Ecclesiastes 2:26

Life in the kingdom of God isn't about all the trappings of a so-called happy life. But that doesn't mean it's a miserable, restricted life either. Psalm 1:1 speaks of how to live a happy life: "Blessed is the man who does not walk in the counsel of the wicked or stand in the way of sinners or sit in the seat of mockers." The world "blessed" can also be translated "O how happy." So if you want to be a happy person, you need to do what this psalm encourages. Psalm 1 begins not with the power of positive thinking but with the power of negative thinking. It's telling us that if we want to be happy, we can begin by avoiding certain things that make it impossible for happiness to flourish. These things are poisonous and counterproductive. "Blessed is the man who does not walk in the counsel of the wicked. . . ." Happiness is found in what we *don't* do.

PRACTICING HAPPINESS

But it is also found it what we *do.* Psalm 1 continues, "But his delight is in the law of the LORD, and on his law he meditates day and night. He is like a tree planted by streams of water, which yields its fruit in season and whose leaf does not wither. Whatever he does prospers" (verses 2–3). The happy person of Psalm 1 stays in God's Word.

Amazingly, at the time this psalm was written, "the law of the Lord" consisted only of the first five books of Moses. So how much more should we Christians today practice meditating on God's Word? After all, we have sixty-six books to read! Keep in mind too that this verse doesn't say "his drudgery is in the law of the Lord," or "his dread is in the law of the Lord," not even "his duty is in the law of the Lord," although one could make a case for the dutiful study of Scripture. Instead, it is our delight and privilege to read the words of our God each day.

FOUR SIMPLE QUESTIONS

A number of Christians I know have a hard time reading the Bible. They don't quite know how to apply its truths to their lives today.

I encourage people to learn how to read the Bible in a methodical, meaningful, meditative way, asking certain questions as we meditate on God's Word:

- Is there any *sin* here for me to avoid?
- Is there any *promise* for me to claim?
- Is there any *victory* to gain?
- Is there any *blessing* to enjoy?

This psalm tells us that happiness is found in being both reactive and proactive, resisting what's wrong *and* embracing what's right. If we do this, the Bible says, we will find happiness.

THE TRUE GOSPEL

This is the great Christian paradox. In fact, if this element is not present, then it is not the authentic gospel, because the gospel begins with a cross. If you hear a so-called gospel proclaimed from a pulpit, on TV, or on the radio, and that gospel does not begin with a cross and the fact that some part of you has to die, then it is not the true gospel. If it tells you to believe but not to repent, then it is not the true gospel. If it promises heaven but does not warn of hell, then it is not the true gospel.

There is the so-called prosperity gospel of today that says you can have it all. You don't have to be sick or in debt. But Jesus says that if you are living to please yourself, you will lose yourself. This means we must see ourselves for what we really are. We need to realize that living for ourselves never will supply what we want out of life.

Remember, Jesus said, "The man who loves his life will lose it, while the man who hates his life in this world will keep it for eternal life" (John 12:25). Only when Jesus Christ is in total control of your life, only when God becomes your everything and your self becomes nothing, only when your love for God is so great that your self-love seems like hate in comparison, only then will you truly find yourself.

59

LOVING TO THE END

You have heard that it was said,
"Love your neighbor and hate your enemy." But I tell you:
Love your enemies and pray for those who persecute you,
that you may be sons of your Father in heaven.

Matthew 5:43–45

The final hours of Jesus's earthly life were filled with intense activity—meals with the disciples, time in fervent prayer, the betrayal of a friend. John records the last Passover service Jesus would celebrate with his disciples, along with the first-ever communion service. John gives us a closing glimpse of Judas before he slinks into the night with betrayal on his mind. He takes a somewhat comical look at Simon Peter as Jesus tries to wash this disciple's feet. Through John's report, we get a better look at ourselves as we discover more about what Jesus desires for us.

The story of these final moments begins with a powerful opening verse in John 13: "It was just before the Passover Feast. Jesus knew that the time had come for him to leave this world and go to the Father. Having loved his own who were in the world, he now showed them the full extent of his love" (John 13:1).

THE SERVANT KING

The disciples were alone with Jesus. The crowds were gone, along with all the pushing and pulling that accompanied them. The world was locked out, and the disciples relaxed around a low-slung table. But something was up. They could clearly see that Jesus was troubled. Very troubled. Something wasn't right, but no one knew quite what. Then Jesus did something completely unexpected:

The evening meal was being served, and the devil had already prompted Judas Iscariot, son of Simon, to betray Jesus. Jesus knew that the Father had put all things under his power, and that he had come from God and was returning to God; so he got up from the meal, took off his outer clothing, and wrapped a towel around his waist. After that, he poured water into a basin and began to wash his disciples' feet, drying them with the towel that was wrapped around him.

John 13:2–5

With all the pressure of Calvary closing in, this is a touching and disarming portrait of Christ as he washed the disciples' feet, loving them to the end. Perhaps as he dried the feet of Andrew and Mark, he thought, "These precious feet will spread the gospel to the world!" Perhaps the words of the prophet Isaiah came to mind: "How beautiful on the mountains are the feet of those who bring good news" (Isa. 52:7).

THE HUMBLEST ACT

Then Jesus came to the feet of the outspoken fisherman, Simon Peter. Peter protested, "Lord, are you going to wash my feet?" (John 13:6).

I don't think Peter was being disrespectful. He just didn't understand. You see, foot washing was the role of a servant. If you were a relatively affluent person living in that time, you would have a household servant whose job it was, among other things, to wash the feet of someone who came to your home. So Peter was confused. *You are the Master, not just of the house, but of the universe. Why are you washing my feet?*

But Jesus told him, "Unless I wash you, you have no part with me" (John 13:8).

Once Peter grasped this, he wanted Jesus to give him a bath: "Lord, . . . not just my feet but my hands and my head as well!" (verse 9).

SERVE ONE ANOTHER

Peter's enthusiasm is rather funny. But Jesus was being a serious example to them. He was demonstrating that if they wanted to be greatest in the kingdom of God, they must be the servant of all (see Mark 9:35). And later, he would instruct them to do this for one another—to serve one another, help one another, and encourage one another. Ironically, Luke's Gospel tells us that an argument broke out in Jesus's presence as to who would be the greatest in the kingdom (see Luke 9:46–48). They were willing to fight for the throne, but no one wanted the towel.

I often wonder, as I read this story, what Jesus must have felt as he washed the feet of Judas. It's one thing to serve those we love—that seems to come easy for most of us. But here was Jesus, humbling himself not only before the disciples who had been his faithful friends but before the one who was about to betray him. When we speak of serving one another, are we willing to include serving our enemies? Are we willing to embrace them with the love of God, just as Jesus himself showed his love to Judas? Can we make room in the servant heart we want to cultivate to include those who wrong us? If we want to be like Jesus, we must.

60

THE TRAITOR IN THEIR MIDST

Those who cling to worthless idols
forfeit the grace that could be theirs.

Jonah 2:8

Jesus showed himself to be the ultimate servant king when he washed the feet of those who thought they were serving him. Yet in the middle of the act of extraordinary love, there was sorrow in Jesus's heart. John wrote, "Jesus was troubled in spirit and testified, 'I tell you the truth, one of you is going to betray me.' His disciples stared at one another, at a loss to know which of them he meant" (John 13:21–22).

Jesus was fully God, but he also was fully man. He knew anger and sorrow, but he wasn't necessarily angry or sorrowful over the same things we would be. In this case Jesus wasn't troubled for himself, but for another. Specifically, he was troubled for the very one who was going to deliver him up to a cruel death. He was troubled over the soul of the one who would betray him.

THE GREAT PRETENDER

While the disciples didn't know Judas was the betrayer, they understood the force of Jesus's words: there was a traitor in their midst. To their credit, they looked at one another and asked, "Is it me?" (see Mark 14:19). But none of them suspected their friend and brother Judas.

Judas was an imitator extraordinaire, one of the most mysterious and paradoxical individuals ever found in the pages of Scripture: His very name is synonymous with evil and treachery. He was the traitor's traitor. His life ended miserably in suicide, because he sold out Jesus for thirty pieces of silver. But there is more to Judas than that.

If we could have known Judas, we might have been surprised that he didn't come across as a sinister, evil man. In fact, Judas probably appeared rather upright, seemingly considerate, and very religious. Remember his loud protest over Mary's so-called waste as she anointed the feet of Jesus with the costly oil (see John 12:1–6)? That appeared so considerate and compassionate on his part, but in reality, as John points out, he said this not because he cared about the poor, but because he wanted to pocket the profit that would have come from selling the perfume.

Judas was an actor, and in fact, like one of many tremendous actors in the church today. They talk the talk, quote their Bibles, and sing the songs. But underneath, they are phony. And they are fooling only themselves.

A TRAITOR REVEALED

The disciples didn't know which of them would betray Jesus, but they wanted to bring the truth to light. John, who always stayed close to Jesus, was given the assignment to find out who it was:

> One of them, the disciple whom Jesus loved, was reclining next to him. Simon Peter motioned to this disciple and said, "Ask him which one he means." Leaning back against Jesus, he asked him, "Lord, who is it?" Jesus answered, "It is the one to whom I will give this piece of bread when I have dipped it in the dish." Then, dipping the piece of bread, he gave it to Judas Iscariot, son of Simon.
>
> John 13:23–26

Judas was sitting at the left hand of Jesus, the place of honor. No doubt Jesus had invited him to come and sit next to him on this particular night. In that culture, it was a gesture of friendship, trust, and closeness to dip a piece of bread into a common dish and offer it to another. And that's what Jesus did for Judas. To offer this food to Judas was an act of friendship. It was an act of fellowship. It was an act of mercy. It was an offer of forgiveness. Jesus was reaching out to Judas, as if to say, "Old friend, we have walked a lot of roads together. You don't have to go through with this. You don't have to betray me. Here is my friendship. I still offer it to you. All you have to do is take it." Jesus was showing that he knew exactly what Judas was up to. He was demonstrating his love to the very end. But Judas slammed the door in Jesus's face. John wrote, "As soon as Judas took the bread, Satan entered into him. 'What you are about to do, do quickly,' Jesus told him" (John 13:27).

An Offer of Grace

In spite of Judas's willful and deliberate wickedness, Jesus continued to offer him the opportunity to repent and not go through with his plan. In fact, Jesus offered Judas opportunity after opportunity to repent. When Jesus was in the Garden of Gethsemane and Judas arrived on the scene with the temple guard to arrest him, Jesus asked, "Friend, do what you came for" (Matt. 26:50). Notice how Jesus called this betrayer "friend." Yet Judas went on to betray Jesus with a kiss. The original language could be translated to say that he kissed Jesus again and again. It wasn't just a peck on the cheek. Rather, it was a demonstration of affection. This made what Judas did all the more wicked.

Some have tried to paint Judas as a victim, even a pawn in the hand of God. But nothing could be further from the truth. Every step of the way, Judas was complicit in his betrayal of Jesus, falling increasingly under the power of the devil, culminating in actual possession by Satan himself (John 13:27). If ever Satan had a son, it was Judas. Yet Judas had fooled everyone . . . except Jesus.

What about you? Are you the person others believe you to be—or are you living a life of lies? If you are, this is the time to give up the deception and be who God made you to be—his child, his beloved, his friend.

The grace Jesus extended to Judas is there for you too. Will you take it?

61

No Excuses

I have strayed like a lost sheep. Seek your servant,
for I have not forgotten your commands.

Psalm 119:176

Have you ever known someone who had everything, then lost it all because of a foolish or selfish mistake? When that happens, we find it incomprehensible that a person would squander a life many of us long for. That's how I feel when I read about Judas.

Judas spent hours walking and talking with God incarnate. What an incredible privilege that was! Unbelievers often will say it's the hypocrisy of Christians that keeps them away from Christianity. But that's just an excuse. Judas saw faith lived out in the person of Jesus and turned away just the same.

THE ULTIMATE EXAMPLE

Jesus was the ultimate example, to say the least. He never did a single, inconsistent thing. He never lost his temper, never said an unkind thing, and never told a lie. He never had a single thought out of harmony with God. He was the perfect, flawless example. Yet Judas not only refused to believe, he turned against Jesus, selling him out for thirty pieces of silver—a price commonly paid in those days to purchase a slave.

It is amazing to consider that Judas was even one of the original disciples. Keep in mind that he had been chosen by Jesus himself. Still, the foreknowledge of God does not change the responsibility of man. Even though Jesus already knew what would take place, Judas, of his own choosing, deliberately betrayed the Lord. This was in spite of the fact that Judas had personally heard the great teachings of Jesus. He had listened as Jesus delivered the Sermon on the Mount, heard firsthand the story of the prodigal son. He had heard Jesus's words and teachings on hypocrisy and his warning about the wheat and the tares. He had personally witnessed some big-time miracles, such as the feeding of the five thousand, the blind receiving their sight, and the resurrection of Lazarus from the dead. With his own ears, he heard Jesus say, "Not everyone who says to me, 'Lord, Lord,' will enter the kingdom of heaven, but only he who does the will of my Father in heaven" (Matt. 7:21). He had countless opportunities to believe. And like Pharaoh in Moses's day, the more he saw, the harder his heart became.

ALL THE WRONG REASONS

In the same way, some unbelievers will come to church for some "relief." The worship music and teaching of God's Word bring them a measure of comfort, but then they continue to live in sin, with no desire to change. They think worship, Bible study, and even communion will do them some good. And they will—if these people follow the Lord. The apostle Paul warned against receiving the elements of communion without knowing and following the God those elements represent:

> For anyone who eats and drinks without recognizing the body of the Lord eats and drinks judgment on himself. That is why many among you are weak and sick, and a number of you have fallen asleep. But if we judged ourselves, we would not come under judgment.
>
> 1 Corinthians 11:29–31

The same sun that softens the wax hardens the clay. The same sun that makes a living tree grow makes a dead tree dry up. And the same gospel message that transforms one life drives another deeper into sin, if he or she doesn't respond in the appropriate way. It is really frightening that someone could be exposed to so much truth and yet remain in, even be strengthened in, unbelief. If a person can habitually commit sin without any sense of conviction or remorse, he or she simply does not know God.

GOOD GUILT

We are missing the point if we go to church for a little relief. Faith is more than that. It is walking with God. The true child of God, though still a sinner, will not live in a pattern of sin. As 1 John 3:9–10 tells us,

> No one who is born of God will continue to sin, because God's seed remains in him; he cannot go on sinning, because he has been born of God. This is how we know who the children of God are and who the children of the devil are: Anyone who does not do what is right is not a child of God; nor is anyone who does not love his brother.

If you find yourself under immediate conviction when you start to cross a line you know you shouldn't, if you find that deep guilt sets in when you have sinned, then rejoice. Why? Because it proves you are indeed a child of God. If one of my sons does something wrong, it is my right, even my responsibility, as his father to correct and even discipline him if necessary. That is not my right with someone else's child (though I wish it were at times). The same is true of God. He convicts and disciplines those who are his.

The writer of Hebrews reminds us,

> And you have forgotten that word of encouragement that addresses you as sons: "My son, do not make light of the Lord's discipline, and do not lose heart when he rebukes you, because the Lord disciplines those he loves, and he punishes everyone he accepts as a son." Endure hardship as discipline; God is treating you as sons. For what son is not disciplined by his father? If you

are not disciplined (and everyone undergoes discipline), then you are illegitimate children and not true sons.

Hebrews 12:5–8

Judas was able to do the wicked things he did because he really never knew Jesus. Sure, he knew more *about* him than most people, but he never *knew* him. His life could be summed up in the phrase from Luke's account of these tragic circumstances: "And Judas went to the chief priests . . ." (Luke 22:4). As Proverbs tells us, "There is a way that seems right to a man, but in the end it leads to death" (14:12).

Which way are you going?

62

THE AGE OF STRESS

Peace I leave with you; my peace I give you.
I do not give to you as the world gives.
Do not let your hearts be troubled and do not be afraid.

John 14:27

One of the downsides of living in this age of technology—cell phones, PDAs, BlackBerries, iPhones, and even watches that can give us sports scores, the weather, and the latest news—is that we are inundated with information. As a result, we have even more to be worried about. It's more accurate to say we live in the age of stress.

When we're young, we're stressed out about getting older. We wonder what we'll do for a living, where we'll go to college, who we're going to marry. When we actually are older, we wish we were younger again. We may have reached some of our goals, but we look back on our youth as the "good old days" of no worries, no stress.

THE SOURCE OF THE TROUBLE

Obviously we'll have stress in our lives no matter how old we are. I read about a survey of adults and their teenage children in which they were asked the stressors in their lives. The results were telling:

The top stressor for parents was fighting with their kids. And the top stressor for teenagers was fighting with their parents.

The second biggest stressor for parents was getting their teen-agers to study. The second biggest for teenagers? Doing their homework.

Next on the list for parents was teenagers themselves. For the teenagers? Their parents.

The parents said they were stressed out by their efforts to get skinny. The teenagers, in turn, were stressed out by their efforts to stay skinny.

Further, parents were stressed about promotions and raises, while their teenagers were stressed about grades.

The parents were stressed out by chaos and noise, but the teenagers were stressed out by peace and quiet.

Finally, parents were stressed out by work, and teenagers were stressed out by chores.

Stress can be serious stuff. Studies suggest that high levels of stress lead to a number of health problems, including obesity, heart attacks, ulcers, depression, nervous breakdowns, even can-cer. And the Centers for Disease Control and Prevention says that in the USA, up to 90 percent of visits to physicians may be triggered by stress-related illnesses.[9]

Some of the worry and anxiety we experience is avoidable, but much of it is just part of life. The book of Job tells us, "Man is born to trouble as surely as sparks fly upward" (Job 5:7). Holding on to our jobs, keeping our families together, paying our bills—these are the experiences stress is made of. Even when we generally enjoy our lives, stress can come along. One study suggests that some 70 percent of American moms find moth-erhood "incredibly stressful," while 30 percent of mothers of young children suffer from depression.[10]

Then there are the situations where life takes an unexpected turn—a job loss, an illness, a move. Or maybe the stress comes because we are disappointed with ourselves since we are not always what we want to be. We want to be strong, but we are weak. We want to be successful, but we experience many failures. We want to be loved, but we struggle to connect with others.

THE PROBLEM WITH WORRY

Without a doubt, we're living in stressful times. But worrying doesn't empty tomorrow of its sorrow; it empties today of its strength. God will give us the strength to face each day with enough grace to manage. Whatever you may face, God will not abandon you. But if you worry about your circumstances, you only will compound your troubles.

Does this mean that Christians never should feel anxious, pressured, or afraid? Does this mean such feelings are sinful? Are we supposed to feel cheerful and confident all the time? That's not what the Bible teaches. Our Lord himself experienced stress and concern. Stress is a normal human response to changes and problems in our lives. When Jesus said, "Don't let your heart be troubled," he wasn't saying the disciples would never be troubled by life. He was saying there is a way to overcome it.

THE CURE

The Bible is a practical book that speaks to our lives and tells us how to deal with issues like stress, agitation, fear of the unknown, and much more. And that brings us to Jesus's words to those of us who struggle with stress. These words offer help to hearts that are unsettled. He said:

> Do not let your hearts be troubled. Trust in God; trust also in me. In my Father's house are many rooms; if it were not so, I would have told you. I am going there to prepare a place for you. And if I go and prepare a place for you, I will come back and take you to be with me that you also may be where I am.
>
> John 14:1–3

The word that Jesus used for "troubled" could be translated "agitated, disturbed, or thrown into confusion." It is a picturesque word. The idea behind it is "Don't let your heart shudder." Interestingly, it was the same word used in John 13:21 to describe Jesus's emotions as Judas went astray.

It is a strong word, and Jesus was specifically saying to the disciples, in light of the imminent cross, "It may look like your world is falling apart and that darkness will overtake you, but don't let your hearts be troubled!"

In other words, he was showing them that although there was cause to be troubled, there was even greater cause *not* to be. The same is true for us today. In spite of all the reasons to worry, we have the very best reason not to, for our lives are in the hands of a loving God who conquered death and sin.

63

Looking Homeward

We have heard of your faith in Christ Jesus and of the love you
have for all the saints—the faith and love that spring from the hope
that is stored up for you in heaven and that you have already
heard about in the word of truth, the gospel that has come to you.

Colossians 1:4–6

This life is filled with problems to worry about. If we choose
to we could easily spend every waking hour worrying—and
some of us do just that. But when we are followers of Jesus,
we know there is far more to life than the struggles we see in
front of us every day. We know there is a life to come that will
be worry-free.

When Jesus told his disciples to trust him, he was reminding
them to look at the big picture of life with God. Jesus said, "In
my Father's house are many rooms" (John 14:2). One of the
assurances Jesus gives his friends is the hope of heaven. He was
telling them that no matter what happened to them on earth,
it would pale in comparison with the life to come. The words
of the apostle Paul remind us of this truth: "For our light and
momentary troubles are achieving for us an eternal glory that
far outweighs them all. So we fix our eyes not on what is seen,
but on what is unseen. For what is seen is temporary, but what
is unseen is eternal" (2 Cor. 4:17–18).

Longing for Home

Deep inside, we all long for this place we have never been. In
his book *The Problem of Pain*, C. S. Lewis calls this the incon-

solable longing, "the secret signature of each soul, the incommunicable and unappeasable want."[11] We all have a longing for heaven, whether we know it or not. And heaven is waiting for the child of God. We have God's Word on it.

Jesus has gone to prepare a place for us (John 14:3). That's a key element in our comfort here on earth. When you're expecting guests in your home, you prepare the room ahead of time. You might know they like certain books or treats, so you customize the room. That way, when your guests arrive, they feel at home. If we put that kind of effort into preparing a place for our friends, imagine the care God has put into preparing our eternal home.

OUR DWELLING PLACE

When Jesus spoke of the place he had prepared, I don't think he was talking about bunk beds or cozy cabins. I believe Jesus was referring to the new bodies we will have when we go to heaven. Paul alludes to our new bodies in 2 Corinthians 5:1–3:

> Now we know that if the earthly tent we live in is destroyed, we have a building from God, an eternal house in heaven, not built by human hands. Meanwhile we groan, longing to be clothed with our heavenly dwelling, because when we are clothed, we will not be found naked.

The Bible doesn't tell us a lot about heaven, probably because it is so far beyond our comprehension. It would be like taking a three-month-old baby, propping him up with pillows, and saying to him, "Now I am going to tell you about Hawaii. Are you ready?" You get out a big book with gorgeous photos of the Hawaiian islands. "Look. This is the island of Maui. See how nice it is?" The baby is just going to sit there, because he doesn't have the capacity to comprehend the information you're conveying.

In the same way, as God speaks of the glories of heaven, there is no way—in this life at least—we can fully grasp what awaits us. Even the apostle Paul, who personally caught a glimpse of heaven, said, "And I know that this man—whether in the body or apart from the body I do not know, but God knows—was caught up to paradise. He heard inexpressible things, things that man is not permitted to tell" (2 Cor. 12:3–4).

HEAVENLY HEARTS

Jesus is preparing wonderful homes for each of us, and I find that to be a great comfort. Some may call that pie-in-the-sky escapism, but I believe the reality of our future heavenly home helps us through the trials of this life. And the fact of the matter is that when we truly are heavenly minded, we are the *greatest* earthly good.

Those who have done the most for this world have usually had their hearts set on the next one. Any honest look at history will reveal that those who have done the most for others are Christians who know the hope of eternal life. They are the ones who have started universities, built shelters and hospitals, and have gone into the war-torn and famine-ridden areas of the world with food, medicine, and clothing. I've heard of a lot of church-affiliated hospitals, but personally, I've never heard of an atheist hospital.

When we have the comfort of heaven, we can put our worries aside and live our lives for others. We are no longer bound by fear and anxiety, but freed by the promise of new life with God. When our hearts are lightened by this promise, there is no end to the good we can do.

64

The Return of the King

> But our citizenship is in heaven.
> And we eagerly await a Savior from there, the Lord Jesus Christ.
>
> Philippians 3:20

In our fallen world, we find relief for our troubled hearts in the fact that Jesus is coming back to receive us to himself. He told the disciples, "And if I go and prepare a place for you, I will come back and take you to be with me that you also may be where I am" (John 14:3).

Our Lord has said to us, "I will come again." Some day, in the not-too-distant future, he will set his foot back on earthly soil and say, "I have returned!" And it might be sooner than we think. The Lord will not merely send for us but will come in person to escort us to our Father's house:

> For the Lord himself will come down from heaven, with a loud command, with the voice of the archangel and with the trumpet call of God, and the dead in Christ will rise first. After that, we who are still alive and are left will be caught up together with them in the clouds to meet the Lord in the air. And so we will be with the Lord forever. Therefore encourage each other with these words.
>
> 1 Thessalonians 4:16–18

As Paul points out, these are words of encouragement for Christians. We can manage the trials of this life because we know there is more than what we see in front of us. We know that our Rescuer is coming to bring peace and justice to a broken world.

WORDS FROM A SKEPTIC

Jesus then offered a somewhat mysterious statement, perhaps to elicit a response from the disciples: "You know the way to the place where I am going" (John 14:4). Yet Thomas was the only one bold enough to ask Jesus what he meant. Thomas has been given the title, "Doubting Thomas," but he was really more of a skeptic. The doubter doubts, even when the facts are clear. But the skeptic looks carefully, wanting to see for himself. Thomas wasn't the kind of guy to let others do his thinking for him. He was behaving more like "Honest Thomas" than "Doubting Thomas." He didn't understand and said so: "Lord, we don't know where you are going, so how can we know the way?" (John 14:5).

I often wonder if the disciples had a tendency to act as though they understood something Jesus was telling them, when, in fact, they did not. Thomas was honest enough to speak out and say, "Lord, we don't know where you're going." Jesus didn't rebuke him, but instead used Thomas's question as an opportunity to expand this revelation of himself. His reply to Thomas is one of the most famous and profound statements in all of Scripture: Jesus said to the disciples, "I am the way and the truth and the life. No one comes to the Father except through me" (John 14:6).

JUST ONE WAY?

This statement also is one of the most controversial aspects of our faith. By believing this we are saying that Jesus Christ is the only way to know God. This is hard for some people to accept. They choke on this, arguing that Christians are narrow-minded. "How dare you suggest that your faith is the only true faith?" they say. "How dare you say that not all religions are true and that not all roads lead to God?"

Personally, I say it because Jesus said it. If I offer anything less or anything more than this, then I am not offering the true gospel message. The Bible says, "Salvation is found in no one else, for there is no other name under heaven given to men by which we must be saved" (Acts 4:12). It also says, "He saved us, not because of righteous things we had done, but because of his mercy. He saved us through the washing of rebirth and renewal by the Holy Spirit" (Titus 3:5). Jesus said he was the way, the truth, and the life. No one comes to the Father except through him. It's as simple as that.

What Belief Looks Like

I know so many people who come to church, read their Bibles, and go through the motions of Christianity. But they are missing the heart of what it means to follow God. This is what it means to be a Christian: The moment you acknowledge Jesus as your Savior, you are saying you believe he died on the cross for you and paid the price for your sins. It means you have turned from that sin and are putting your faith in him. It means you have become a child of God and have a guaranteed residence waiting for you on the other side in heaven. And it means when Christ comes back again, even if it happens in your lifetime, he will take you with him. It is belief in Jesus—and Jesus alone—that will save you. Period.

Although good works won't save you, they are good evidence that you are saved. If you have really embraced Christ as Savior and Lord, it will affect the way you want to live. You will want to go to church. You will want to study the Bible and do what it says. You will want to pray. This is a result of your salvation.

If you're not sure about your salvation, Jesus can give you the hope of heaven right now, along with the forgiveness of your sins and the assurance that if he comes in our lifetime, you will be ready to meet him. Jesus died on the cross. He shed his blood for our sins. He rose from the dead. And he is standing at the door of your life, knocking. If you hear his voice and open the door, he will come in.

65

Why We Exist

Live such good lives among the pagans that,
though they accuse you of doing wrong, they may see
your good deeds and glorify God on the day he visits us.

1 Peter 2:12

If there is one universal desire among people around the world and throughout history it is this: We all want to know the meaning of life. Having a sense of purpose is one of the fundamental human needs. We desperately want to believe our lives matter.

This is not just a religious person's quest. Well-known atheist Bertrand Russell said, "Unless you assume a God, the question of life's purpose is meaningless." Interestingly, the Bible tells us this as well. Romans 8:19–21 tells us, "The creation waits in eager expectation for the sons of God to be revealed. For the creation was subjected to frustration, not by its own choice, but by the will of the one who subjected it, in hope that the creation itself will be liberated from its bondage to decay and brought into the glorious freedom of the children of God." In other words, all of creation, including human beings, longs for fulfillment and purpose.

God-Shaped Hole

If you are seeking it from this world, however, you won't find it. The world itself has been broken by sin. After Adam's sin, God said, "Cursed is the ground because of you; through painful toil you will eat of it all the days of your life" (Gen. 3:17).

Solomon said, "Yet when I surveyed all that my hands had done and what I had toiled to achieve, everything was meaningless, a chasing after the wind; nothing was gained under the sun" (Eccles. 2:11). We won't find fulfillment in this world. Only God can fill the empty place inside us.

A while back I attended two funeral services, both for faithful followers of Jesus Christ who died in their early 70s. One was for a woman named Carmen who had dedicated her life to helping orphans in Mexico. The other was for a man named Perry, who was an usher at the church where I pastor. He worked tirelessly behind the scenes as a volunteer at our radio broadcast, at our Harvest Crusades, and on mission trips. And he did it all *after* he retired. Both Carmen and Perry lived their lives to glorify and honor God. And I have no doubt that God said to both of them, "Well done, good and faithful servant." Neither of them had the trappings of a "fulfilled" life as we would define it in worldly terms. But they were both deeply fulfilled because they lived their lives for Jesus.

Even the most powerful among us can have meaningless lives if we live without God. Thousands of years ago, the prophet Daniel interpreted the writing on the wall for the rebellious Babylonian king, Belshazzar: "You have been weighed on the scales and found wanting" (Dan. 5:27). Daniel provided the reason for Belshazzar's wasted life:

> You have set yourself up against the Lord of heaven. You had the goblets from his temple brought to you, and you and your nobles, your wives and your concubines drank wine from them. You praised the gods of silver and gold, of bronze, iron, wood and stone, which cannot see or hear or understand. But you did not honor the God who holds in his hand your life and all your ways.
>
> Daniel 5:23

The root of his problem was that he failed to glorify God. And a life that doesn't glorify God is a life wasted.

FRUITFUL LIVES

When I talk about glorifying God, I don't just mean giving God praise. I don't just mean honoring God with our words. I mean living in a way that shows others the love of God. The Bible calls this "bearing fruit." John 15:16 says, "You did not choose me, but I chose you and appointed you to go and bear fruit—fruit that will last. Then the Father will give you whatever you ask in my name" (John 15:16).

John 15 opens with a metaphor in which Jesus said, "I am the true vine, and my Father is the gardener. He cuts off every branch in me that bears no fruit, while every branch that does bear fruit he prunes so that it will be even more fruitful" (John 15:1–2). A vine is intended to bear fruit. God intended his people to bear fruit to glorify his name before all the nations of the world.

WHAT'S YOUR FRUIT?

Yet far too many people, even professing Christians, fail to live this way. They are far more interested in what God can do for them than in what they can do for God. The Bible gives us this contrast between a life lived following the sinful nature and a life that bears spiritual fruit:

> The acts of the sinful nature are obvious: sexual immorality, impurity and debauchery; idolatry and witchcraft; hatred, discord, jealousy, fits of rage, selfish ambition, dissensions, factions and envy; drunkenness, orgies, and the like. I warn you, as I did before, that those who live like this will not inherit the kingdom of God.
>
> Galatians 5:19–21

In contrast, the fruitful believer lives a life of peace and joy. "But the fruit of the Spirit is love, joy, peace, patience, kindness, goodness, faithfulness, gentleness and self-control. Against such things there is no law" (Gal. 5:22–23).

Is this what others see in your life? Or is the opposite true? If instead of love, there is hatred and bitterness; if instead of joy there is gloom; if instead of peace there is turmoil and guilt; if instead of faith, there is worry; if instead of gentleness, there is harshness and a short temper; if instead of self-control, there is lust and greed, then either you don't know God at all, or you are living outside of fellowship with him. If that's the case, this is the day to make a change, to connect your life to the Vine who gives us our purpose.

66

BEARING FRUIT

The fruit of the righteous is a tree of life,
and he who wins souls is wise.

Proverbs 11:30

Glorifying God and living a fruitful life . . . this is why we're here. But we aren't always sure what this fruit might look like. Thankfully, the Bible tells us what we need to know.

For example, the first fruit is a life that points to Jesus. As Paul wrote in Romans, "What benefit did you reap at that time from the things you are now ashamed of? Those things result in death! But now that you have been set free from sin and have become slaves to God, the benefit you reap leads to holiness, and the result is eternal life" (Rom. 6:21–22). Whether you have been a Christian since you were a child or have become a Christian as an adult, the biggest, most obvious fruit in your life will be your life itself.

REAPING THE HARVEST

When our lives glorify God, others will notice. Sharing our faith and helping our brothers and sisters in Christ grow in theirs is another way we bear fruit. The apostle Paul wrote to his friends at Rome, "I planned many times to come to you (but have been prevented from doing so until now) in order that I might have a harvest among you, just as I have had among the other Gentiles" (Rom. 1:13). And Proverbs tells us, "The fruit of the righteous is a tree of life, and he who wins souls is wise" (Prov. 11:30). Sometimes God gives us the privilege of personally leading someone to Christ. Other times, it simply means sowing a seed. We have a part to play, but it is—and always will be—God who gives the increase.

Sharing God's love with others isn't limited to our words. We also share God's love when we share God's blessings. When Paul collected an offering from the Gentiles for the poor saints in Jerusalem, he called that offering "fruit": "So after I have completed this task and have made sure that they have received this fruit, I will go to Spain and visit you on the way" (Rom. 15:28). Once we recognize that all we have comes from God, even our very breath, we can happily share it with others. Whether we share our food, our homes, our money, we are investing in the kingdom of God.

TENDING THE SOIL

I realize all of this is a tall order: being holy, leading people to Christ, giving, serving . . . so how do we produce this fruit Jesus desires? Jesus said, "Remain in me, and I will remain in you. No branch can bear fruit by itself; it must remain in the vine. Neither can you bear fruit unless you remain in me" (John 15:4). To "remain" involves a permanence of position, not some flash-in-the-pan, "try God" approach. It requires a continuing commitment. Jesus said, "If anyone would come after me, he must deny himself and take up his cross *daily* and follow me" (Luke 9:23, emphasis mine).

It takes a lot of time to become more like Jesus and bear fruit. The Bible speaks of slowing down, taking root, studying, denying, and obeying. That might sound like an unexciting life, but really, what better way is there to spend your life than growing closer to the one who loves us best?

DOING OUR SHARE

Here in John 15, Jesus described a two-sided process: his side and our side. We have a responsibility to remain in Jesus, and he has promised to remain with, and indeed live in, us. For a believer to be fruitful, both sides of this process must be operational. There's no doubt Jesus will hold up his end. But we have to commit ourselves to holding up ours. This relationship works like a marriage. Imagine being married, then breaking your wedding vows again and again. One day, your marriage falls apart and you wonder why. A marriage cannot survive, or indeed flourish, with only one partner doing his or her part. So it is with our responsibility to remain in Jesus.

This means following Jesus each and every day. We need to stay as close as we can to him, talking with him, reading his Word, doing his will, obeying his commands, and worshiping him. We need to avoid sin and stay away from relationships and situations that might dull our hunger for spiritual things.

Living that kind of life isn't hard; it's impossible—*without God's help, that is.* Of course, this doesn't mean nothing can happen without Christ. A person could still run a business without Christ, get married and raise a family without Christ, go to church on Sunday without Christ, and even preach sermons without Christ. We can be very busy without Christ. But if we have done it all apart from Jesus, it will be ultimately fruitless. We may have impressed hundreds, even thousands, of people. But without God, it will have counted for nothing.

67

REAPING THE REWARDS

> But I said, "I have labored to no purpose; I have spent my strength in vain and for nothing. Yet what is due me is in the LORD's hand, and my reward is with my God."
>
> Isaiah 49:4

A life centered on Christ looks different from one centered on selfish desires. A person who is focused on glorifying God, testifying about his faith with others, and spreading the blessings he's been given will find that life itself changes.

POWERING UP OUR PRAYER

The Bible tells us that those whose lives bear fruit have a special closeness with Jesus. Christ said, "Remain in me, and I will remain in you. No branch can bear fruit by itself; it must remain in the vine" (John 15:4). One of the best ways to remain in Christ is through prayer. Daily conversations with Jesus help us develop the heart of Jesus. Our prayers become tuned in to the will of God. And when that happens, we see our prayers answered in ways we never did before.

I'm not suggesting prayer is a way of getting God to do what we want. Prayer is a process of joining in partnership with God so he can achieve his promises through us. Nothing lies outside the reach of prayer except that which lies outside the will of God. Prayer is surrender—surrender to the will of God and cooperation with that will. It's like being on a boat, throwing the boat hook to the shore, and pulling. Do I pull the shore to me? Or do I pull myself to the shore? Prayer is not pulling God to my will, but aligning my will with the will of God.

LIVING IN OBEDIENCE

The same thing happens when it comes to following God's commandments. The closer we get to Jesus, the more in tune we are with God's will. Jesus said, "If you obey my commands, you will remain in my love, just as I have obeyed my Father's commands and remain in his love" (John 15:10). The fruit of the Spirit grows only in the garden of obedience. Knowing and loving God is not merely believing in Christ, attending church, or even reading the Bible and praying. It is doing what he tells us to do—not perfectly, of course. We will sin, and we will fail. But if we are true children of God, then we will repent and return to him.

The person who truly seeks God comes to understand that when God tells us to do or not to do something, it is for our own good. It would be like a child complaining to his parents, "Why won't you let me play on the freeway? Dylan's mom lets *him* play on the freeway!" When our lives are about glorifying God, obedience becomes second nature.

FINDING JOY

In that obedience, we find something surprising: joy. Jesus said, "I have told you this so that my joy may be in you and that your joy may be complete" (John 15:11). The joy of a Christian runs deeper than mere happiness. It does not depend on circumstances; it only depends on God.

Notice the progression of Jesus's words in verse 11, from "*My* joy" to "*your* joy." Do you have joy in your life right now? You often can tell someone is a Christian by his or her countenance. I recently ran into someone who had gone to our church for years, but hadn't been around in some time. You could just tell something was different. The joy was gone. As he had fallen away from God, he had lost the joy he once had.

Of course I don't mean we as Christians should walk around with phony smiles plastered across our faces. Rather, we have the joy that comes from knowing that true life is bigger than the troubles of this world.

Sin strips us of that joy. After committing adultery and causing the death of his mistress's husband, King David wrote, "Restore to me the joy of your salvation and grant me a willing spirit, to sustain me" (Ps. 51:12). It is not that David's salvation was lost, but his joy had evaporated. God wants our joy to be continual, but he also wants it to overflow, that your joy might be full.

Answered prayer, a life glorifying the God who made us, a life of obedience, a life of joy, a life of purpose . . . these are all evidence of a fruitful Christian life.

May God help us to bear fruit for him and to fulfill our purpose in life.

68

The Holy Spirit

Guard the good deposit that was entrusted to you—
guard it with the help of the Holy Spirit who lives in us.

2 Timothy 1:14

A Sunday school teacher was speaking on the subject of sin and asked the class if they knew the difference between the sins of commission and omission. A little girl in the front of the class raised her hand, so the teacher called on her and asked, "Do you know the definition of the sin of commission?"

"Yes, I do," the girl said. "The sin of commission is when we do what we are not supposed to do."

"That is exactly right," the teacher said. "Now, does anyone know what the sin of omission is?"

A little boy in the back of the room was frantically waving his hand. So the teacher called on him.

He stood up and said, "The sin of omission? Well, those are the sins you want to do, but you just haven't gotten around to them yet."

Not quite. But it does bring up an interesting subject about sin in general. Are some sins worse than others? And if so, what is the worst sin a person can commit? You might be surprised by the answer.

The Helper

In John 16, Jesus tells the disciples he is leaving them. Naturally, they're worried about how they'll function without their Lord and their leader. But he offers them this assurance:

But I tell you the truth: It is for your good that I am going away. Unless I go away, the Counselor will not come to you; but if I go, I will send him to you. When he comes, he will convict the world of guilt in regard to sin and righteousness and judgment: in regard to sin, because men do not believe in me; in regard to righteousness, because I am going to the Father, where you can see me no longer; and in regard to judgment, because the prince of this world now stands condemned.

John 16:7–11

Jesus was talking about the Holy Spirit. While the disciples didn't really understand what Jesus meant, we have the benefit of the Bible to tell us more about this "Counselor." Through Scripture, we clearly see that the Holy Spirit has a will, emotion, and intelligence. The Holy Spirit is one of the ways God is present in the lives of Christians. The Spirit acts as a guide and helper to those who are already followers of Jesus.

The Holy Spirit seals us, teaches us, and leads us to truth. Jesus said, "But the Counselor, the Holy Spirit, whom the Father will send in my name, will teach you all things and will remind you of everything I have said to you" (John 14:26). The Holy Spirit can, in an incredible way, open up passages of Scripture for us. Paul said:

However, as it is written: "No eye has seen, no ear has heard, no mind has conceived what God has prepared for those who love him"—but God has revealed it to us by his Spirit. The Spirit searches all things, even the deep things of God. For who among men knows the thoughts of a man except the man's spirit within him? In the same way no one knows the thoughts of God except the Spirit of God.

1 Corinthians 2:9–11

The Holy Spirit brings God's truth alive in our hearts in a personal way.

CONVERSION AND CONVICTION

The Holy Spirit is incredibly active: The Spirit is with us. The Spirit empowers us. The Spirit seals us. And the Spirit teaches us. But the Holy Spirit also has work to do in the world and in the life of the unbeliever. John 16:8 says, "When he comes, he will convict the world of guilt in regard to sin and righteousness and judgment." Ignorance of sin, righteousness, and judgment can ultimately bring about a person's destruction, so God has sent the Holy Spirit to make unbelievers aware of their need for God. People need to be convicted by the Holy Spirit, because there is no conversion without conviction.

Sadly, Christianity is often presented as a self-help program. The gospel of Jesus is reduced to a message of feeling better about ourselves: "If you want a little more spring in your step, or a better marriage, or if you want to be a happy person, all you need to do is believe in Jesus!"

Don't get me wrong: Jesus can make a marriage better. Jesus can make us happy. But the work God has come to do for us is so much more than these things—they're just the fringe benefits. The ultimate work of God is to save us from our sin and its ramifications.

THE "WORST" SIN

This brings us back to our earlier question: What's the worst sin a person can commit? Is it murder, adultery, or stealing? Is it taking the Lord's name in vain? Rape? Incest? While these are all terrible sins, the "worst" sin—and the one with the most far-reaching consequences—is not believing in Jesus Christ.

Other sins are the result of not knowing God or living in rebellion against him. But those sins can be dealt with and forgiven if we believe in the saving blood of Jesus. The worst possible sin we can commit is not believing, because that's what we'll be judged for.

The Holy Spirit has come to bring us to Jesus: "When he comes, he will convict the world of guilt in regard to sin and righteousness and judgment: in regard to sin, because men do not believe in me" (John 16:8–9). Once we've heard the gospel, we are accountable for our sin. Jesus said, "If I had not come and spoken to them, they would not be guilty of sin. Now, however, they have no excuse for their sin" (John 15:22).

A refusal to believe in Jesus Christ as the Son of God, who bore the sins of the world, is a rejection of the very work of the Holy Spirit (see John 16:13–14).

69

Our Need for Conviction

> But you, dear friends, build yourselves up
> in your most holy faith and pray in the Holy Spirit.
> Keep yourselves in God's love as you wait for the mercy
> of our Lord Jesus Christ to bring you to eternal life.
>
> Jude 20–21

Those who don't yet believe in Christ aren't the only ones in need of the conviction of the Holy Spirit. When we believe in Jesus and are saved, his righteousness is deposited into our spiritual account. In order to truly appreciate the incredible love of God, we must first see our utter depravity and desperate need for a Savior.

Naturally, this is very hard for most of us. We like to think we're pretty close to saving ourselves through our good works or committed Bible study. We like to think we just need a little extra push from Jesus to get us all the way to salvation. We're like the man who was out hiking in the mountains, lost his footing, and slipped over the side—a hundred-foot drop. He grabbed hold of a branch on the way down and hung on to it for dear life. Knowing he was in real trouble, he cried out for help. But there was no answer. Again he cried out. Again it was quiet. The third time he yelled, "Is there anybody out there?"

A voice responded, "Yes, I am here."

"Who are you?" the man called back.

"I am the Lord," the voice said.

"Well, Lord, help me!"

"I will. But I need you to do something first."

"What?" he yelled back.

"Let go of the branch."

"That's crazy!" the man shouted. "If I let go of the branch, I'll fall to my death."

"No," the Lord said, "I will catch you."

There was a moment of silence, then the man yelled out, "Is anybody *else* up there?"

A USELESS BRANCH

Like that hiker, we are clinging firmly to our branch of self-righteousness. We don't want to let go. We think, "I'm a moral person. I'm a good person. I'm a religious person."

But God says, "That's not what matters. You have to realize your need for forgiveness. You need to admit you are a sinner." As difficult as it is, we must let go of the flimsy branch of self-righteousness, the very thing that keeps us from the true righteousness of God. True righteousness is not available to us until we have an awareness of sin, and the Holy Spirit has come to help us discover this.

On the day of Pentecost, Peter preached the gospel, and the Holy Spirit was at work. The Bible tells us that the people who were listening were "cut to the heart" (Acts 2:37). The word "cut" used in this verse means "to pierce," or "to stab," indicating something sudden and unexpected occurred, something only the Holy Spirit could bring about. The people then asked Peter, "What shall we do?" So Peter led them to Christ.

These people were so moved by the power of the Holy Spirit, they couldn't help but step into new life with Christ. Is the same true for you?

PRESERVING AND SHINING

Once we are walking with Jesus, we are to act as salt and light in this world (see Matt. 5:13–16). In ancient times, salt functioned as a preservative. In the same way, God uses us to stand up for what's right and good and to try to prevent the wholesale spread of evil in our culture. This means living as true, Bible-believing Christians, allowing our faith to influence everything we do and say—the friends we choose, the media we expose ourselves to, and the decisions we make. Jesus warned, "But if the salt loses its saltiness, how can it be made salty again? It is no longer good for anything, except to be thrown out and trampled by men" (Matt. 5:13).

To be light means we are to let others know of our faith in Christ. Jesus said, "Let your light shine before men, that they may see your good deeds and praise your Father in heaven" (Matt. 5:16). In our attempt to avoid being perceived as fanatical Christians, we often try to bury our faith. But they can plainly see there's something different about us—something major. And that's exactly what the Holy Spirit will use to turn a person's heart toward God.

LIGHTING THE WAY

The apostle Paul recognized the difference between believers and unbelievers when he wrote to the Corinthians, "Do not be yoked together with unbelievers. For what do righteousness and wickedness have in common? Or what fellowship can light have with darkness? What harmony is there between Christ and Belial? What does a believer have in common with an unbeliever?" (2 Cor. 6:14–15). Try as you may to relate as hard as you can, unbelievers simply won't understand your faith and commitment to Christ until their spiritual eyes are opened. The Bible tells us, "The man without the Spirit does not accept the things that come from the Spirit of God, for they are foolishness to him, and he cannot understand them, because they are spiritually discerned" (1 Cor. 2:14).

Before unbelievers can see their desperate need for the light, they must first see they are living in a miserable darkness. Before there can be conversion, there must be conviction—and that partly will come through believers as the Holy Spirit works through us, as we live godly lives, and as we share the gospel. We make a mistake if we try and undo the very thing God is using in the lives of unbelievers to show them their need for him. So let your light shine! Let it light the way for the Holy Spirit to convict the hearts of those God wants to join him in eternity.

70

Sin and the Spirit

How could you turn away from the Lord and
build yourselves an altar in rebellion against him now?

Joshua 22:16

The Holy Spirit is surely the most misunderstood member of the Trinity. We can at least partially grasp the idea of God as a Father. And certainly, with the help of Gospels like John, we can grasp the idea of God as the Son. But the Holy Spirit is much harder to wrap our minds around. That may be because in Scripture he is compared to both wind and fire, among other things, so we may begin to think of him as an "it" more than a "him."

Know this: not only does the Holy Spirit God have a distinct personality, he also can be specifically sinned against!

Six Sins

The New Testament mentions six offenses that can be committed against the Holy Spirit. Some specifically apply to unbelievers, while others apply to believers. Still others apply to both.

1. We lie to the Holy Spirit. Acts 5:1–5 tells the story of Ananias and Sapphira, two so-called Christians who tried to cheat the church out of some money. Peter caught them in the act and rebuked them, telling them in lying to the Holy Spirit, they had lied to God. Immediately, Ananias dropped dead.

2. We grieve the Holy Spirit. This offense applies to believers. Ephesians 4:30–31 tells us, "And do not grieve the Holy Spirit of God, with whom you were sealed for the day of redemption. Get rid of all bitterness, rage and anger, brawling and slander, along with every form of malice." The phrase "to grieve" means "to make sad or sorrowful." When we allow bitterness, rage, anger, harsh words, slander, and any type of malicious behavior to take place in our lives, we grieve the Holy Spirit. Are you harboring a grudge against someone? Have you been slandering (speaking lies about) anyone lately? Have you been flying into fits of rage? All of this grieves the Holy Spirit.

3. *We quench the Holy Spirit.* This, too, applies to believers. The apostle Paul exhorted the Thessalonians, "Do not put out the Spirit's fire" (1 Thess. 5:19). Unbelief certainly can hinder the working and moving of God's Holy Spirit. This happened in Jesus's hometown as the people questioned his authority. We read that "He did not do many mighty miracles there because of their lack of faith" (Matt. 13:58). Quenching the Spirit can occur when the Holy Spirit is leading you to do a certain thing, such as sharing your faith with someone, praying more, or taking a step of faith in a certain area, and you flatly refuse to do it. Has God called you to serve him with your life? Has he led you to do something? Are you doing it? If not, then you're quenching the Holy Spirit.

TURNING OUR BACKS ON GOD

The list continues with sins that involve pushing the Spirit away.

4. *We resist the Holy Spirit.* Stephen, as he spoke to the unbelieving Sanhedrin, said, "You stiff-necked people, with uncircumcised hearts and ears! You are just like your fathers: You always resist the Holy Spirit!" (Acts 7:51). The Holy Spirit seeks to speak to the heart of the unbeliever and lead him or her to God. The Holy Spirit is incredibly patient and persistent, but it is possible to resist all the Spirit's pleadings, as we discover from Genesis 6:3, where God said, "My Spirit will not contend with man forever." Apparently the spiritual leaders of Israel whom Stephen was addressing had resisted the Holy Spirit. It seems they were convinced of the truth of what Stephen was telling them, yet they would not yield their hearts.

5. *We insult the Holy Spirit.* When someone refuses to accept Jesus Christ, he is denying the very mission of the Holy Spirit. He's saying he doesn't need salvation or doesn't believe Jesus Christ can save him or that Jesus's work on the cross was unnecessary. Hebrews warns, "How much more severely do you think a man deserves to be punished who has trampled the Son of God under foot, who has treated as an unholy thing the blood of the covenant that sanctified him, and who has insulted the Spirit of grace?" (Heb.10:29). Therefore, to resist the Holy Spirit's appeal is to insult God and cut off all hope of salvation. The Bible poses this alarming question: "How shall we escape if we ignore such a great salvation?" (Heb. 2:3).

The Most Serious Offense

6. *We blaspheme the Holy Spirit.* This is the unpardonable sin, which can be committed only by unbelievers. In speaking of this sin, Jesus said,

> And so I tell you, every sin and blasphemy will be forgiven men, but the blasphemy against the Spirit will not be forgiven. Anyone who speaks a word against the Son of Man will be forgiven, but anyone who speaks against the Holy Spirit will not be forgiven, either in this age or in the age to come.
>
> Matthew 12:31–32

This is the most serious offense against the Holy Spirit, because there is no forgiveness for the one who commits it. So what *is* blasphemy against the Holy Spirit? Again, the work of the Holy Spirit is to convict us of sin and bring us to Jesus Christ. To blaspheme the Spirit is similar to insulting the Spirit by resisting the Spirit's work altogether. This sin should not be the concern of any Christian because it is not a sin a believer can or will commit.

But for the person who is playing some silly religious game, there is great cause for concern, because this is a point of no return. Where and when this would occur in an individual's life, only God could say.

So instead of lying to, grieving, quenching, or insulting and resisting the Holy Spirit, we should be open to the Spirit's work in our lives. The Spirit wants to show us our need for Jesus Christ and then fill and empower us to be the people God wants us to be.

71

Jesus in Prayer

> But Jesus often withdrew to lonely places and prayed.
>
> Luke 5:16

We want others to pray for us, and so we should, because clearly there is power in united prayer. Jesus said, "Again, I tell you that if two of you on earth agree about anything you ask for, it will be done for you by my Father in heaven" (Matt. 18:19).

We all should remember to pray for one another, but even if we forget, there is good news: Jesus Christ himself is praying for us. Hebrews tells us, "Therefore he is able to save completely those who come to God through him, because he always lives to intercede for them" (Heb. 7:25). And we read in Romans 8:34, "Who is he that condemns? Christ Jesus, who died—more than that, who was raised to life—is at the right hand of God and is also interceding for us."

The Greatest Prayer

It's good to know that Jesus is praying for us. It's even better to know *what* Jesus is praying for us, because this is where we find God's plan and purpose for our lives. After all, that's the objective of prayer—to align our will with the will of God.

In John 17, we find Jesus praying for his disciples—past, present, and future. It is Jesus's prayer for you. And it is the greatest prayer ever prayed.

We call the prayer Jesus gave to his disciples in Matthew 6:9–14 "The Lord's Prayer," but in reality, it is "The Disciples' Prayer." That prayer contains petitions Jesus would never need to make, such as "Forgive us our debts, as we also have forgiven our debtors."

In John 17 we find the true "Lord's Prayer," with petitions only Jesus could ask. It shows God's heart, his desire, and his purpose for us.

WHY JESUS PRAYED

If you think about it, it's quite extraordinary that Jesus prayed at all. Why would Jesus, a member of the Trinity, need to pray? Yet throughout the gospels, we see that he prayed regularly. After a dizzying, busy day of ministry, he would spend the entire evening coming before his Father in prayer. He would often spend all night in prayer. And before he selected the twelve disciples, we're told he prayed all night (see Luke 6:12–13). He was praying when he was transfigured with Moses and Elijah. Later, we see him praying in anguish in the Garden of Gethsemane. The first words that fell from his lips when he hung from the cross formed a prayer. And later on the cross, he also prayed, "My God, my God, why have you forsaken me?" (Mark 15:34). Without a doubt, Jesus was a man of prayer.

But why? Because although he was God, Jesus submitted to the Father. Not only that, but he was leaving us an example to follow. If Jesus, who was perfect and sinless, took time to pray, then how much more should we, as imperfect and sinful people, do the same?

A PRAYER FOR HIMSELF

Jesus started by praying for himself, which by the way, isn't a bad thing to do. Jesus began, "Father, the time has come" (John 17:1). Jesus had used this phrase again and again throughout his earthly ministry. When his mother wanted him to show his power at the wedding in Cana, he responded, "Dear woman, why do you involve me? . . . My time has not yet come" (John 2:4). In John 7, we read that the religious leaders were angry with Jesus and wanted to arrest him: "At this they tried to seize him, but no one laid a hand on him, because his time had not yet come" (John 7:30).

But now, the hour had come, the hour of his betrayal, arrest, crucifixion, and resurrection from the dead. It was the hour of both darkness and light, the hour of Satan's attack, and the hour of our purchased salvation. Jesus had finished the work the Father had given him to do. Earlier in this Gospel, Jesus said, "The one who sent me is with me; he has not left me alone, for I always do what pleases him" (John 8:29). And that was 100 percent true. Jesus had glorified the Father in all he said and did, from the beginning to the end of his earthly ministry. And certainly he left us an example to follow. The Bible tells us, "Your attitude should be the same as that of Christ Jesus" (Phil. 2:5).

We can never fully have the mind of Christ. But as we look at his life, the way he followed his Father, and the way he asked us to do the same, we see what it means to walk in the will of God.

72

PRAYER WHEN YOU NEED IT MOST

> May your unfailing love be my comfort,
> according to your promise to your servant.
>
> Psalm 119:76

Jesus turned to prayer in all kinds of situations. He prayed when he wanted God's guidance, and he prayed when he wanted God's comfort. Yet many of us forget to pray, even when it's the one thing that might make a difference in our lives.

DESPERATE PRAYERS

Think of someone like Dave Dravecky, a great athlete and former major league baseball pitcher. Dave was diagnosed with cancer, which claimed his right arm and shoulder. Obviously, it was a devastating setback, yet Dave has now committed his life to ministering to people. I had the opportunity to talk at length with him about how he was feeling and asked him if he had any pain. He said he had phantom pain where his arm used to be and is in pain throughout the day. But God gives him the strength to endure it. He visits cancer wards in hospitals, speaks in churches, and glorifies God, in spite of his infirmity.

Then there is Lt. Col. Brian Birdwell, who was working at the Pentagon on September 11, 2001, when American Flight 77 was commandeered by terrorists and crashed into the Pentagon building. Birdwell was severely burned, and a number of his co-workers were killed. He went through very painful skin grafts, enduring more than thirty operations. Now he travels the country ministering and glorifying God, despite his infirmity.

The apostle Paul, in writing about his own "thorn in the flesh," said, "Therefore I will boast all the more gladly about my weaknesses, so that Christ's power may rest on me. That is why, for Christ's sake, I delight in weaknesses, in insults, in hardships, in persecutions, in difficulties. For when I am weak, then I am strong" (2 Cor. 12:9–10).

Why We Pray

There are times when God is glorified in the midst of our infirmities, and there are times when he is glorified by their removal. That was the case with the blind man from John 9. But our objective should be to glorify God, regardless of the temporary outcome. Again, we can look to the apostle Paul as an example. He wrote, "I know what it is to be in need, and I know what it is to have plenty. I have learned the secret of being content in any and every situation, whether well fed or hungry, whether living in plenty or in want. I can do everything through him who gives me strength" (Phil. 4:12–13).

Let me be clear: I don't want to come across as cavalier about personal tragedies, because if you're the one who is suffering, it's not easy to believe there might be relief. But God truly will give you the power you need to face that challenge or obstacle. Many of us wonder why God allows certain things in our lives, but what we fail to see is what God is doing *internally* to change us. These verses help put things into perspective:

> For our light and momentary troubles are achieving for us an eternal glory that far outweighs them all. So we fix our eyes not on what is seen, but on what is unseen. For what is seen is temporary, but what is unseen is eternal.
>
> 2 Corinthians 4:17–18

This brings us back to the "why" of prayer. I believe God allows certain circumstances in our lives to keep us dependent on him. If life were all blue skies and green lights, would we turn to

God in prayer? If there was never an illness in your life or the life of someone you knew, would you still pray? If there was never a need for provision or never a prodigal child, would you still pray? You might, but probably not as often or as fervently.

THE PRAYER CONNECTION

In his book *When God Prays*, my friend Skip Heitzig tells the story of a father whose son was leaving for college. This father came up with an effective way to maintain contact with his son. He agreed to pay his son's tuition and also give him a monthly allowance so he could fully concentrate on his studies. But before the boy left home, his father sat him down for a talk.

"Your mom and I are really glad that you're going to school," he told him. "And just as I promised, I'll be taking care of your financial needs for the next four years. But I won't be sending you a monthly check."

The boy was puzzled. "What? But you said—"

"What I said was that I would provide for your needs on a monthly basis," his father answered. "If you want the money, you'll have to come home at least once a month to get it. I want you to come in person."

This wise father knew his son might get caught up in his new environment and not come home very often. So to preserve a relationship with his son and enjoy his occasional fellowship, he made sure the boy would come around often enough to touch base.[12]

God allows challenges in our lives so we will not forget him and will come to him in prayer. If there is a sin we are all probably guilty of, it is the sin of prayerlessness.

73

A Prayer for Our Preservation

You who are trying to be justified by law have been
alienated from Christ; you have fallen away from grace.

Galatians 5:4

We all know people who seem to have made a commitment
to follow Jesus, only to become spiritual casualties. Some of
them might even have been people you looked to as role mod-
els. Maybe their downward spiral has caused you to question
your faith as well, "Am I next? Will I, too, become a spiritual
failure?"

Jesus knew how hard it can be for us to hold on to our faith.
So he prayed for our preservation: "I will remain in the world
no longer, but they are still in the world, and I am coming to
you. Holy Father, protect them by the power of your name—
the name you gave me—so that they may be one as we are one"
(John 17:11). In Luke's Gospel, Jesus turned to Simon Peter and
said, "Simon, Simon, Satan has asked to sift you as wheat. But
I have prayed for you, Simon, that your faith may not fail. And
when you have turned back, strengthen your brothers" (Luke
22:31–32). Here in John 17, we find Jesus doing the same. He
was praying our faith would not fail.

When Faith Fails

When people fall away spiritually it is, for all practical purposes, because they chose to. It is not that they said, "Hey, I
think I'll stop being a Christian today." Rather, the problem is
they have stopped moving forward spiritually. In essence, they

have put their lives on spiritual cruise control. And if you're not moving forward spiritually, it's only a matter of time until you fall backward.

Scripture clearly tells us God will keep us:

I lift up my eyes to the hills—where does my help come from? My help comes from the LORD, the Maker of heaven and earth. He will not let your foot slip—he who watches over you will not slumber; indeed, he who watches over Israel will neither slumber nor sleep. The LORD watches over you—the LORD is your shade at your right hand.

Psalm 121:1–5

Scripture also tells us how, time and again, the Lord instructed the Jewish priests to pronounce a blessing over the people. He wanted them to hear it so many times that it would be etched in the banks of their memories: "The LORD bless you and *keep you*; the LORD make his face shine upon you, and be gracious to you; the LORD turn his face toward you and give you peace" (Num. 6:24–26, emphasis mine).

We find the same truth in the New Testament as well. In 1 Peter, we see that believers "are shielded by God's power until the coming of the salvation that is ready to be revealed in the last time" (1 Peter 1:5). And Jude begins, "Jude, a servant of Jesus Christ and a brother of James, To those who have been called, who are loved by God the Father and kept by Jesus Christ" (Jude 1). In the original language, this verse uses the perfect tense, of which the nearest equivalent is "continually kept." It is a continuing result of past action. So whatever your difficulties may be, know that you are preserved in Jesus Christ.

KEEPING US CLOSE

When you possess something valuable, you're usually aware of where it is. And certainly you don't lose someone you love. You wouldn't go to Disneyland with your kids and then completely forget about them and leave them there. In the same way, God never forgets what he loves. He will protect those he has called to himself. A few chapters earlier in John's Gospel, we read that "Jesus knew that the time had come for him to leave this world and go to the Father. Having loved his own who were in the world, he now showed them the full extent of his love" (John 13:1). If it were not for the preserving grace of God, not a single one of us would make it. But thankfully, Jesus loves us, preserves us, and intercedes for us.

STAYING WITH GOD

Although God will keep us, we must *want* to be kept. Which brings up an interesting aspect of Jesus's prayer. He mentioned Judas Iscariot, who had already left to betray him: "While I was with them, I protected them and kept them safe by that name you gave me. None has been lost except the one doomed to destruction so that Scripture would be fulfilled" (John 17:12). It wasn't that Judas was a believer who fell away. Judas was never a believer to begin with. Jesus *keeps* all whom the Father has given to him.

Even so, the Bible tells us, "Keep yourselves in God's love as you wait for the mercy of our Lord Jesus Christ to bring you to eternal life" (Jude 21), showing us that faith isn't a free pass to do whatever we want with our lives. If we want the joy and abundance Jesus offers, we need to live the life Jesus calls us to. We don't keep ourselves saved, but we do keep ourselves *safe*. Though God's love is unsought, undeserved, and unconditional, it is possible for us to be out of harmony with his love.

So what does Jude mean by telling us to "keep ourselves in the love of God"? Simply put, it means that we are to keep ourselves from all that is unlike God. We are to keep ourselves from any influence that would violate his love and bring sorrow to his heart. It means keeping ourselves in a place where God can actively show and pour out his love in our lives. Some people, places, and activities make it easier for the devil to tempt us. So now that we've been delivered from the kingdom of Satan, we should have no desire to deliberately put ourselves back into his clutches.

When we pray "Lead us not into temptation," we're asking our heavenly Father to help us so we won't tempt ourselves by deliberately placing ourselves in volatile situations. We are in the Lord's safekeeping, but if we run away from him, we are rejecting the protection he provides.

74

A Prayer for Our Hearts

Do not conform any longer to the pattern of this world,
but be transformed by the renewing of your mind.
Then you will be able to test and approve what God's will is—
his good, pleasing and perfect will.

Romans 12:2

When I became a certified scuba diver a number of years ago, I had to learn about all kinds of equipment. There is your B.C., which is your inflatable vest. Then you have your regulator, your aqualung that you breathe through, which is hooked up to your tanks. You have gauges that you have to watch. Then you have fins, a mask, a snorkel for when you are not using your regulator, a weight belt, and so forth.

As part of my training, I had to go underwater, take off my weight belt, and put it back on again. Then I had to take my tanks off and put them back on. Then there was buddy breathing, so in case I lost air, I could share with another diver. The funny thing is, I was able to cruise through all those drills. Then it came time to take my mask off, put it in a little pile, reach down and find it, put it back on, and clear the water out—all while under water. There was something about having that mask ripped off my face that suddenly woke me up to the reality of being underwater. Of course I already knew that, but there was a false sense of security behind the glass and air. But when my mask was removed, it was a wake-up call that said, "You're in the ocean, buddy. And you don't belong down here."

In the same way, sometimes we get a little bit too comfortable in this world. We start blending in and becoming too much like people around us. So we need our masks removed, so to speak. We need to be reminded that we're not of this world. We sometimes forget the world doesn't love those of us who are followers of Christ. That's why Jesus prayed for our consecration:

> I am coming to you now, but I say these things while I am still in the world, so that they may have the full measure of my joy within them. I have given them your word and the world has hated them, for they are not of the world any more than I am of the world. My prayer is not that you take them out of the world but that you protect them from the evil one. They are not of the world, even as *I am not of it*. Sanctify them by the truth; your word is truth.
>
> John 17:13–17, emphasis mine

ALIENS IN THE WORLD

Jesus said of his disciples, "The world has hated them" (verse 14). Why? Because if we are true followers of Jesus Christ, then our light will shine in a dark world. And those who live in darkness don't welcome bright, searing light. People are not always going to appreciate your stand.

This doesn't mean that we should try and isolate ourselves. Living in seclusion won't remove you from the temptations of this life. In fact, no matter where you go, temptation will be there waiting for you. Therefore, we must learn to take hold of God's divine resources to resist temptation. We should seek to influence others as we live our lives for the glory of God.

A UNITED FRONT

As we listen in on Jesus's prayer, we might feel overwhelmed by all that the Christian life demands. But God not only gave us the Holy Spirit, he gave us one another to support and encourage one another.

I love being involved in our Harvest Crusades. In addition to carrying out the obvious task of proclaiming the gospel, these events bring churches together. There is something wonderful about worshiping and praying with five thousand people. You realize you—and those in your local church—aren't the only believers out there.

Jesus prayed we would be unified:

> My prayer is not for them alone. I pray also for those who will believe in me through their message, that all of them may be one, Father, just as you are in me and I am in you. May they also be in us so that the world may believe that you have sent me. I have given them the glory that you gave me, that they may be one as we are one: I in them and you in me. May they be brought to complete unity to let the world know that you sent me and have loved them even as you have loved me.
>
> John 17:20–23

Jesus also said, "By this all will know that you are My disciples, if you have love for one another" (John 13:35 NKJV). And the psalmist wrote, "How good and pleasant it is when brothers live together in unity!" (Ps. 133:1).

THE DEVIL'S DIVISION

Yet the devil loves to bring about division. His strategy always has been to divide and conquer. We even see it in the early church: "In those days when the number of disciples was increasing, the Grecian Jews among them complained against the Hebraic Jews because their widows were being overlooked in the daily distribution of food" (Acts 6:1). Satan immediately came in to challenge what the Lord had done. As the Lord is blessing a local church or a certain group of believers who are doing his work, divisions sometimes will come from those who want to stir things up. Yet the Bible says that among the seven things God hates are "a false witness who pours out lies and a man who stirs up dissension among brothers" (Prov. 6:19). Don't be one of those people the enemy uses to create division. Christian unity stands as a powerful witness to a divided world when we overcome our generational, racial, socioeconomic, and cultural differences and are unified around Christ.

Finally, Jesus prayed for us and for the ones who we will reach: "My prayer is not for them alone. I pray also for those who will believe in me through their message" (John 17:20). As we live lives that glorify and honor God, as we seek to be holy and set apart for his service, as we love one another, the world will take notice.

75

The Agony of Jesus

For we do not have a high priest who is unable to sympathize
with our weaknesses, but we have one who has been
tempted in every way, just as we are—yet was without sin.

Hebrews 4:15

Have you ever felt lonely? Cut off? Abandoned? Misunderstood? Then you have a faint idea of what Jesus went through as he agonized in the Garden of Gethsemane.

We all will face our Gethsemanes in life, times when it seems as though the whole world is closing in on us. We all will face times of ultimate stress, when the circumstances in which we find ourselves seem too much to bear, when it feels like we can't go on another day.

Jesus has provided a model for us of what to do in times of uncertainty. We don't always know the will of God in every situation. And there are times when we do know it, but we don't like it. At other times, God's will doesn't make sense. Yet we must never be afraid to place an unknown future into the hands of a known God.

The Bible says Jesus was "a man of sorrows, and familiar with suffering" (Isa. 53:3). But the sorrow Jesus experienced in Gethsemane on the night before his crucifixion seemed to be the culmination of all the sorrow he had ever known. Other than his death itself, his prayer in the Garden was the loneliest moment of Jesus's life.

THE TERRIBLE DECISION

Much is said about the cross, and rightly so. But here in the Garden of Gethsemane, we see the agony Jesus went through as he made the decision to go to the cross. The ultimate triumph that would take place at Calvary was first accomplished beneath the gnarled, old olive trees of Gethsemane.

I find it interesting that sin began in a garden, and the commitment to bear that sin took place in one as well. In Eden, Adam and Eve sinned; in Gethsemane, Jesus conquered. In Eden, Adam and Eve hid themselves; in Gethsemane, our Lord boldly presented himself. In Eden, the sword was drawn; in Gethsemane, it was sheathed.

At this point in his life, Jesus had preached his last public sermon and had eaten his last meal with the disciples. And now, the final events in his journey toward the cross began to unfold.

THE LONELY LORD

John wrote, "When he had finished praying, Jesus left with his disciples and crossed the Kidron Valley. On the other side there was an olive grove, and he and his disciples went into it. Now Judas, who betrayed him, knew the place, because Jesus had often met there with his disciples" (John 18:1–2).

We find a bit more insight into Jesus's state of mind in Mark 14:32–34: "Jesus said to his disciples, 'Sit here while I pray.' He took Peter, James and John along with him, and he began to be deeply distressed and troubled. 'My soul is overwhelmed with sorrow to the point of death,' he said to them. 'Stay here and keep watch.'"

Jesus desired the companionship of Peter, James, and John because he was in agony. We often think that being a strong Christian means not bothering others with our fears or troubles. But here was Jesus, the Savior, asking his friends to stay with him and help him get through this horrible night. We should never be ashamed to ask our brothers and sisters in Christ to support us when we're facing difficulties.

THE BITTER CUP

In one of the most dramatic descriptions of Jesus's suffering in Gethsemane, Luke wrote,

> He withdrew about a stone's throw beyond them, knelt down and prayed, "Father, if you are willing, take this cup from me; yet not my will, but yours be done." An angel from heaven appeared to him and strengthened him.
>
> Luke 22:41–43

Jesus knew he would be denied by the one whom he had invested the most in: Simon Peter. He knew he would become the object of Peter's shame and the cause of his cursing. He knew he would be rejected by the people he had come to save. He knew his disciple Judas Iscariot was about to betray him with a kiss. He knew he would be vilified in a kangaroo court of injustice and subjected to unfair treatment, ironically all in the name of God. But worst of all, he who had been in constant communion with the Father and the Holy Spirit would find himself forsaken by the Father as he became sin for the whole world. This is why he prayed, "My Father, if it is possible, may this cup be taken from me" (Matt. 26:39).

Jesus, who was holy, righteous, and pure, was about to bear every vile, perverse sin of humanity. Everything in his thirty-three years on earth had been building to this event. From the moment of his birth, Jesus lived in the shadow of the cross. From the moment the prophet Simeon told Mary, "A sword will pierce your own soul too" (Luke 2:35), it was clear that Jesus was destined to die—and not only die, but die under the wrath of God.

Jesus knew exactly what lay ahead as he prayed. In Mark's Gospel the first recorded words of Jesus's prayer were "Abba, Father" (Mark 14:36), the affectionate cry of a child. He was confident in his Father's will and direction. Yet there was this struggle, which Jesus referred to as "this cup." What was "this cup" he recoiled from? Isaiah called it "the cup of his wrath" (Isa. 51:17). Have you ever tasted something that turned your stomach? Imagine having to drink it all down. That is what Jesus had to do. He had to drink "this cup."

On one occasion, the mother of James and John came to Jesus with an ambitious request: "Grant that one of these two sons of mine may sit at your right and the other at your left in your kingdom" (Matt. 20:21).

So he asked James and John, "Can you drink the cup I am going to drink?" (Matt. 20:22).

Jesus indeed drank that cup. He made that final sacrifice, saying to the Father, "Not what I will, but what you will" (Mark 14:36).

76

THE PURPOSE IN GETHSEMANE

> For if, by the trespass of the one man, death reigned
> through that one man, how much more will those who
> receive God's abundant provision of grace and of the gift of
> righteousness reign in life through the one man, Jesus Christ.
>
> Romans 5:17

Luke offers additional insight into what Jesus was going through in Gethsemane: "And being in anguish, he prayed more earnestly, and his sweat was like drops of blood falling to the ground" (Luke 22:44). Luke is the only one who mentions this detail. It may be that Luke was describing the fact that Jesus's sweat had become so thick and concentrated, it was like blood dropping to the ground.

There is a rare phenomenon known as *hematridrosis*, in which a body is under such emotional stress that the tiny blood vessels in the sweat glands rupture and produce a mixture of blood and sweat. Clearly Jesus was under incredible spiritual and physical strain at this moment. And I have no doubt the devil was there in full force as well. We know that he had already entered the heart of Judas (see John 13:2), who was in the garden and approaching.

THE TEMPTING TO TURN

But from the biblical accounts of Jesus coming back to talk to the disciples three times, we might conclude that he was facing waves of temptation to turn from the cross, similar to what he faced during his temptation in the wilderness (Matt. 4:1–11). But

Jesus would have nothing to do with it, not then, and not now. He knew there was only one way to settle this sin issue; he had to taste death for everyone.

This is why it's insulting to God to suggest that all religions are true, and that Jesus is just one of many ways to God. If that were true, do you think God would have allowed his Son to go through this?

THE JOY SET BEFORE HIM

Still, something kept Jesus moving forward, toward excruciating pain and torture and abandonment. Hebrews 12:1–2 tells us:

> Therefore, since we are surrounded by such a great cloud of witnesses, let us throw off everything that hinders and the sin that so easily entangles, and let us run with perseverance the race marked out for us. Let us fix our eyes on Jesus, the author and perfecter of our faith, who for the joy set before him endured the cross, scorning its shame, and sat down at the right hand of the throne of God.

The writer of Hebrews spoke of joy. Is it possible Jesus found hope and help in the promise of joy? Jesus once told the story of a shepherd who had a lamb that went astray. The shepherd went and found the lamb and brought it back, wrapped around his shoulders. Jesus then said, "There will be more rejoicing in heaven over one sinner who repents than over ninety-nine righteous persons who do not need to repent" (Luke 15:7). We are that joy. We are the reason he went through this pain and agony.

FACING OUR GETHSEMANES

Jesus prayed, "Not as I will, but as you will" (Matt. 26:39), and every one of us must come to this point. We all will face times of ultimate stress in which the cup we must drink appears to be too much for us. That's when we must say the one thing God wants to hear each of his children say: "Not as I will, but as you will."

Are you willing to take your future, place it into God's hands, and let him choose for you? I came across a poem that expresses well what our mind-set should be when we face our Gethsemanes:

> All those who journey, soon or late,
> Must pass within the garden's gate;
> Must kneel alone in darkness there,
> And battle with some fierce despair.
> God pity those who cannot say,
> "Not mine, but thine," who only pray,
> "Let this cup pass," and cannot see
> The purpose in Gethsemane.[13]

There was a purpose in Gethsemane for Jesus . . . and for us as well. It is a place where we realize obedience overrules personal desire, where Spirit becomes more important than flesh, and where the glory of God is more important than our own glory and desires.

Jesus said, "Whoever loses his life for my sake will find it" (Matt. 10:39), and "Take my yoke upon you and learn from me, for I am gentle and humble in heart, and you will find rest for your souls" (Matt. 11:29). So don't be afraid to pray, "Abba, Father" and surrender yourself to God's perfect will for your life.

77

NOT VICTIM, BUT VICTOR

> But thanks be to God! He gives us the victory
> through our Lord Jesus Christ.
>
> 1 Corinthians 15:57

Imagine watching the story of Jesus in the Garden of Gethsemane on a split screen showing simultaneous action. On one screen you see Jesus in anguished prayer, facing the most painful decision a man could make. On the other screen, you see the Roman soldiers pressing in, led by the wicked Judas. In just a moment, these two scenes will merge as the crowd surrounds Jesus and Judas betrays his Lord. If this was a movie, you'd be tempted to yell at the screen, "Run, Jesus! They're coming for you!"

But this wasn't a movie. This was the moment our Savior was arrested like a criminal.

THE CROWD ARRIVES

Matthew tells us this was a large crowd (see Matt. 26:47), which would have included the temple police, as well as a cohort of Roman soldiers, which at full strength numbered six hundred. There may have been as many as a thousand armed people coming to arrest one individual and his eleven peaceful disciples. From the midst of this crowd came Judas:

> So Judas came to the grove, guiding a detachment of soldiers and some officials from the chief priests and Pharisees. They were carrying torches, lanterns and weapons. Jesus, knowing all that was going to happen to him, went out and asked them,

"Who is it you want?" "Jesus of Nazareth," they replied. "I am he," Jesus said.

John 18: 3–5

Rather than falling back or hiding, Jesus stepped toward them, asking, "Who is it you want?" Then John tells us, "And Judas the traitor was standing there with them. When Jesus said, 'I am he,' they drew back and fell to the ground" (John 18:5–6).

Jesus was using his divine title as God. When Moses was called by God, the Lord identified himself as "I AM." Jesus's response here in Gethsemane was the last exercise of the same power he used to calm the seas, still the winds, and heal the sick. He was not a hapless victim, but a powerful victor who could have easily gotten out of this situation. He was warning them that they were in way over their heads. He could have called on thousands of angels or could have simply spoken these people out of existence. But remember, Jesus said,

The reason my Father loves me is that I lay down my life—only to take it up again. No one takes it from me, but I lay it down of my own accord. I have authority to lay it down and authority to take it up again. This command I received from my Father.

John 10:17–18

THE BETRAYAL

Judas then betrayed Jesus with a kiss. Why a kiss? Why not simply point at Jesus? Because Judas was the hypocrite extraordinaire. Even in this, the hour of ultimate betrayal, he wanted to appear spiritual.

Peter was fuming as he watched this and decided to save the day:

Then Simon Peter, who had a sword, drew it and struck the high priest's servant, cutting off his right ear. (The servant's name was

Malchus.) Jesus commanded Peter, "Put your sword away! Shall I not drink the cup the Father has given me?"

John 18:10–11

Poor Peter. He just couldn't get it right. He was boasting when he should have been listening, and sleeping when he should have been praying. Now he was fighting when he should have been surrendering. He wasn't thinking; he was reacting—as if Jesus could not have gotten out of this with one word to heaven!

Jesus told Peter, "All who draw the sword will die by the sword. Do you think I cannot call on my Father, and he will at once put at my disposal more than twelve legions of angels?" (Matt. 26:52–53). I can imagine that even those angels were waiting with swords drawn, ready for the word from Jesus.

ONE FINAL MIRACLE

So Peter, in an impulsive moment, cut off the guard's ear. Jesus stopped him, and then stooped down to heal the man's injury. Amid this flurry of activity in the garden, very few noticed the last miracle of Jesus's earthly ministry. It wasn't a big, flashy, go-out-with-a-bang miracle, but a quiet one. This final miracle showed his true heart. He healed the ear of one of the first people who came to arrest him. He received no thanks from this man that we know of. Yet as he faced this lynch mob, Jesus hadn't forgotten about the needs of an individual. And hours later on the cross, he would pray for the forgiveness of the men who were crucifying him.

78

INDECISION

> So, because you are lukewarm—neither hot nor cold—
> I am about to spit you out of my mouth.
>
> Revelation 3:16

We've all experienced it at one time or another, some more so than others. It's called indecision. Most of the time, I'm pretty decisive. But then there are those times when I simply can't make a choice, like when I go into certain restaurants and their menus are pages long. That's why I like a drive-through place we have here in Southern California called In-N-Out Burger. The choices are burgers, fries, and beverages, period.

We are about to look at the story of an indecisive man, someone who let others do the thinking for him, who tried to appease a bloodthirsty, fickle crowd and his own troubled conscience. He tried to find middle ground and make everyone happy. His name was Pontius Pilate.

The indecisive person tries to maintain moral neutrality by insisting there are two sides to every issue. And that is true. But it's also true that there are two sides to a sheet of flypaper. It makes a big difference to the fly as to which side he chooses.

Pilate definitely landed on the wrong side of the flypaper, so to speak. In spite of his position of great power, Pilate had to answer a question we all must eventually come to grips with: "What am I going to do with Jesus?" When you get down to it, this is not the story of Jesus before Pilate as much as it is the story of Pilate before Jesus.

THE UNJUST TRIAL

At this point, Jesus already had been cruelly beaten and rushed through a hasty appearance before the religious elite, the Jewish Sanhedrin. One wonders how these religious leaders could become so corrupt that they would actually try, convict, and execute God in human form. Even if they didn't accept Jesus as their Messiah, why their venomous hatred toward him and the desire for such a quick execution?

In the minds of the religious leaders, Jesus was bad for business. He had blown their cover, and they wanted to get rid of him. The fact of the matter is that all of it was playing right into the will and plan of God.

Before Jesus was taken to the house of Caiaphas, the high priest, he was taken to the house of Caiaphas's father-in-law, Annas (see John 18:12–13). Annas was a godfather figure of sorts, wielding great influence in temple affairs. Annas was the first to question Jesus:

> Meanwhile, the high priest questioned Jesus about his disciples and his teaching. "I have spoken openly to the world," Jesus replied. "I always taught in synagogues or at the temple, where all the Jews come together. I said nothing in secret. Why question me? Ask those who heard me. Surely they know what I said." When Jesus said this, one of the officials nearby struck him in the face. "Is this the way you answer the high priest?" he demanded.
>
> John 18:19–22

Jesus was then taken, bound, to Caiaphas, who accused the Lord of blasphemy. Mark's Gospel tells us, "Then some began to spit at him; they blindfolded him, struck him with their fists, and said, 'Prophesy!' And the guards took him and beat him" (Mark 14:65).

Undeniably, there was a lot of pent-up hostility toward Christ. His life and ministry exposed their religious hypocrisy. His most scathing words were reserved for them and their ilk. Pilate later observed they wanted Jesus dead because of envy. But they didn't want to kill Jesus themselves; rather, they wanted Pilate to do it for them.

PILATE'S DILEMMA

So Jesus was brought to Pontius Pilate. Pilate was the Roman governor, or procurator, of Judea. Governors in this time weren't elected by the people, but were appointed by Rome. Pilate was one of the many regional representatives who reported to Rome. Normally, Pilate would have been kicking back at his beautiful palace on the Mediterranean, but he had to be in Jerusalem during Passover week because the crowds were so large.

Pilate was already in hot water with Rome. He had already had a number of run-ins with the Jews, whom he hated. He was being investigated by Rome. This is why the otherwise unbending, brutal, prejudicial Pilate appeared so vacillating and indecisive in his dealings with Jesus. And this explains why he didn't throw the Jewish religious leaders out of the palace when they came asking for Jesus's death. Pilate was scared, plain and simple. I think Pilate would have liked to free Jesus, just to spite them. I also think Pilate knew Jesus was innocent.

GOD AT WORK

The scene was set for high drama. But there was more taking place that day than met the eye. The forces of good and evil were at work. Both God and Satan were mysteriously moving in the same direction but with very different objectives. Satan wanted Jesus dead, so he gathered his forces and played his wicked hand. God wanted the sin of the world dealt with. That would only happen through the death of his Son.

As Pilate stood in front of the Son of God, he had a choice to make. Like us, Pilate had to decide what to do with Jesus. What he couldn't know is that no matter what he chose, God was about to win. Big.

79

THE FINAL DECISION

If you fully obey the LORD your God and carefully follow
all his commands I give you today, the LORD your God
will set you high above all the nations on earth.

Deuteronomy 28:1

Sometimes, the path our lives should take is clear. Should I be
faithful to my wife or cheat on her? Pretty simple answer. Should
I skim a little off the top of the offering each week or use the
money for God's glory? Also a no-brainer. But other times,
there is no easy decision. That's the position Pilate was in as he
tried to figure out what to do about Jesus.

John's report says:

> Then the Jews led Jesus from Caiaphas to the palace of the Roman
> governor. By now it was early morning, and to avoid ceremonial
> uncleanness the Jews did not enter the palace; they wanted to be
> able to eat the Passover. So Pilate came out to them and asked,
> "What charges are you bringing against this man?"

John 18:28–29

Revealing the complete sham of their so-called "faith," the
Jewish leaders didn't want to go into Pilate's headquarters for
fear they would be defiled, yet they were in a rush to crucify an
innocent man, which was against everything the Torah stood
for. These religious leaders really wanted Pilate to do their dirty
work for them, without even examining Jesus.

So Pilate asked, "What are the charges against this man?"

As though their dignity were being impugned, they retorted, "If he were not a criminal we would not have handed him over to you" (John 18:30).

"Take him yourselves and judge him by your own law," Pilate told them (verse 31).

THE FULFILLMENT

Pilate was, in essence, giving them permission to execute Jesus, because he knew that according to their laws, the most serious religious offenders were punished by death. Their design, however, was not simply to have Jesus put to death, but to avoid responsibility for it, as well as possible reprisals from their own people. Not only were they wicked, but they were cowards as well.

Satan, working through the Jewish leaders (regardless of their motives), was playing into God's hands. By demanding a Roman crucifixion instead of stoning, which was the Jews' usual practice, these religious leaders unwittingly made certain the prophecy of Psalm 22, and other passages that specifically address the kind of death Jesus would die, would be fulfilled: "They have pierced my hands and my feet" (Ps. 22:16).

Then there were Jesus's own repeated references as how he would die. Jesus told his disciples earlier, "We are going up to Jerusalem, and the Son of Man will be betrayed to the chief priests and the teachers of the law. They will condemn him to death and will turn him over to the Gentiles to be mocked and flogged and *crucified*. On the third day he will be raised to life!" (Matt. 20:18–19, emphasis mine). How much more specific can you be than that?

PILATE BEFORE JESUS

By the time Jesus was brought to Pilate, he had already been beaten. With a touch of sarcasm, Pilate asked him, "Are you the king of the Jews?" (John 18:33). Jesus did not profess guilt or innocence. He just stood there and took it. Pilate had never met anyone who was obviously this innocent, yet really did nothing to speak in his own defense. Pilate was unnerved at Jesus's calmness in the face of his own death.

As Pilate continued to mock and question Jesus, Christ continued to show honesty and humility. He told Pilate, "You are right in saying I am a king. In fact, for this reason I was born, and for this I came into the world, to testify to the truth. Everyone on the side of truth listens to me" (John 18:37).

"What is truth?" Pilate callously responded. Pilate was a pagan man who had no core beliefs other than self-preservation. If Pilate had only opened his heart, he would have realized he was standing before Truth Incarnate. But this jaded Roman governor just wanted this entire fiasco over with. He desperately wanted out of this situation, as many people do when they are confronted with the truth of the gospel.

Maybe you've known people like this. When you start telling them about Jesus, they try to change the subject, leave the room, barrage you with tough questions, and do anything but listen carefully to what you are saying. The Holy Spirit, doing the work of conviction, is the reason for their discomfort. This was the case with Pilate.

PILATE'S PLAN

Suddenly Pilate had an idea. There was a custom among the Jews to release a prisoner at Passover. Barabbas was a wicked man who tried to lead a revolt against Rome. He was tried and convicted of robbery, sedition, and murder. Pilate decided he would offer Barabbas, who was largely hated, and Jesus, who still had his supporters. This clever strategy would surely get Pilate off the hook. It would enable him to release Jesus without defying the will of the Sanhedrin. He could simply argue that he was carrying out the will of the people. It really was a brilliant diplomatic maneuver. Of course the people wouldn't choose the release of a man like Barabbas over someone like Jesus! Or so he thought.

So Pilate posed his question to the religious leaders: "But it is your custom for me to release to you one prisoner at the time of the Passover. Do you want me to release the "king of the Jews"?' They shouted back, 'No, not him! Give us Barabbas!'" (John 18:39–40).

The religious leaders had already infiltrated the fickle crowds and convinced them to demand the release of Barabbas. These were the same crowds who, only days earlier, had cried, "Hosanna! Blessed is he who comes in the name of the Lord!" (John 12:13). There also were, no doubt, those who hated Jesus for what he said and stood for, and some who were simply indifferent. They loved him when he filled their empty stomachs or healed their sick. But once he had served their purposes, they had no use for him.

We like to think we'd be among those begging for the release of Jesus. But would we? Do our lives suggest a commitment to the Lord or a wishy-washy attachment to a belief that comes in handy sometimes? Who is your life pointing to?

80

CROWD CONTROL

The treacherous betray! With treachery the treacherous betray!

Isaiah 24:16

While our focus has been on John's Gospel, the book of Matthew offers an interesting sidebar in the story of Pilate and Jesus. Matthew 27:19 says, "While Pilate was sitting on the judge's seat, his wife sent him this message: 'Don't have anything to do with that innocent man, for I have suffered a great deal today in a dream because of him.'"

This sounded like more than a woman's intuition (although a wise man will learn to listen to his wife). It seems this may have been a God-given dream. It's not clear what the dream was about. But it was troubling enough to convince Pilate's wife that Jesus was both right and innocent.

Undoubtedly Pilate knew what path he should take, but again, this was about career and position and power—all very powerful elements in a man's life. Pilate had worked long and hard to get to this position, and he didn't want to lose it. Still, he had within his power the ability to pardon Jesus:

But the chief priests and the elders persuaded the crowd to ask for Barabbas and to have Jesus executed. "Which of the two do you want me to release to you?" asked the governor. "Barabbas," they answered. "What shall I do, then, with Jesus who is called Christ?" Pilate asked. They all answered, "Crucify him!" "Why? What crime has he committed?" asked Pilate. But they shouted all the louder, "Crucify him!"

Matthew 27:20–23

WHICH JESUS?

The meaning of "Barabbas" is significant: It means "Son of the father." In fact, it's a title, not a name. One or two of the ancient manuscripts gives his name as "Jesus Barabbas," the very name and title of our Lord. Many self-proclaimed messiahs had arisen at this time in history, making messianic claims and calling themselves "Barabbas." Therefore, this Barabbas may have been presenting himself as the Messiah, which makes the crowd's choice all the more appalling.

The way Pilate worded his question suggests that Barabbas's first name was Jesus. Otherwise, why would Pilate ask, "What shall I do, then, with Jesus who is called Christ?" (Matt. 27:22). Pilate was contrasting him with the other Jesus, called Barabbas, essentially saying, "You are choosing Jesus, called Barabbas. What shall I do with Jesus called Christ?" They were required to choose between a man who led a rebellion and committed murder and a man against whom not one charge of violence could be brought.

Behind their choice was a false perception of the kingdom, of a new government that would come by force. Yet as Jesus said to Pilate, "My kingdom is not of this world. If it were, my servants would fight to prevent my arrest by the Jews. But now my kingdom is from another place" (John 18:36). However, these people would have none of it. They screamed for the release of Barabbas and the crucifixion of Jesus.

THE LAST RESORT

The multitude clearly wanted blood, not justice. And even to the hardened, pagan mind of Pilate, their vicious response must have been chilling. So Pilate attempted another compromise, in spite of his failed attempts to turn Jesus over to Herod and to release Jesus. Pilate took water, washed his hands, and declared, "I am innocent of this man's blood. . . . It is your responsibility" (Matt. 27:24).

Pilate could have done the right thing and not allowed this. Instead, he did what was politically expedient and what would advance his career. He took the path of least resistance.

Pilate listened to the wrong voice and made the wrong decision. Tragically, he hardened his heart to the very voice of God. Pilate could see that Jesus was innocent. Deep down inside, he may have even thought Jesus was the Messiah. But then there was his career . . . his position . . . his power.

Judas sold his soul for thirty pieces of silver. Herod traded his for an immoral lifestyle. And Pilate forfeited his for position, power, and prestige. What a story it could have been had he believed in Jesus on the spot. But history tells us that within seven years of this cruel deed, Pontius Pilate, the great Roman governor, was removed from high office by the governor of Syria. He was left broken, destitute, unwanted by Caesar, and all alone. Pilate threw his life away, because he was more concerned with what others thought about him than what God did. His craving for popularity and power cost him everything. And like Judas, he went out into the darkness of night and hung himself.

Choosing Jesus

We all know people like Pilate. Some of them choose their careers over Jesus. It's not that believers aren't allowed to have both, but they will pour themselves into the pursuit of success at the cost of everything else. They are willing to sacrifice their integrity, their standards, their friends, and even their faith for the results they can obtain. That is what Pilate did. And it's sad.

Others will choose people over Jesus. They are more concerned about what's considered cool or acceptable within their social group than what God wants or doesn't want. They avoid standing up for what is right for fear of losing their social position. Pilate did that too. And it's tragic.

Better to succeed in God's eyes and fail in the world's. When Peter pointed out that he and the other disciples had left all they had to follow Jesus, the Lord replied, "I tell you the truth,

. . . no one who has left home or wife or brothers or parents or children for the sake of the kingdom of God will fail to receive many times as much in this age and, in the age to come, eternal life" (Luke 18:29–30).

Make your life's goal to please God, and just watch how he will bless you. You may lose some so-called friends here or a little social status there. But when it's all said and done, you will be glad that you chose to follow God.

81

The Women of the Cross

This child is destined to cause the falling and rising
of many in Israel, and to be a sign that will be
spoken against, so that the thoughts of many hearts
will be revealed. And a sword will pierce your own soul too.

Luke 2:34–35

There are different types of pain. There's the physical pain that comes from a horrible fall or a broken bone. Then there are the kinds of pain that can be worse than physical pain—the pain of rejection, betrayal, or abandonment. It is the kind of pain that comes from a husband saying, "I've been unfaithful to you," or a wife saying, "I want a divorce," or a child saying, "I don't want to live the Christian life." It's the kind of pain that comes when you're betrayed by a friend. It's the kind of pain from which we never fully recover.

The Pain of the Cross

The day of Jesus's crucifixion was all about pain—physical, emotional, and spiritual pain—for Jesus and those who loved him. If I had been one of Jesus's followers on the day he was crucified, I wonder where I would have been. At this point, most of his disciples were in hiding. One had betrayed him, and another had denied him. Only one stood with him—John. A group of women, however, had the boldness to be there. Among them were his mother, Mary; Salome, who was the mother of James and John; and Mary Magdalene. They were present out of devotion, not duty. They simply wanted to be with Jesus. John wrote:

> Near the cross of Jesus stood his mother, his mother's sister, Mary the wife of Clopas, and Mary Magdalene. When Jesus saw his mother there, and the disciple whom he loved standing nearby, he said to his mother, "Dear woman, here is your son."
>
> John 19:25–26

I don't think it's a coincidence that these three women were there. I believe God had something in store for each of them as they watched their Lord die.

WHAT THE WOMEN FOUND

For Mary Magdalene, the cross was a place of redemption. She had been under the power of demons when Jesus came and set her free. Her life was radically transformed that day, and she was never the same. Mary Magdalene had been forgiven of much. She wanted to be close to her Lord, even in death. She would be the first at his tomb on Easter Sunday as well. There at Calvary, she would rejoice in the redemption Jesus had given her.

For Salome, the wife of Zebedee and the mother of James and John, the cross was a place of rebuke. We remember the brash request she brought before the Lord on behalf of her two sons, wanting them to sit at his right and left when he established his kingdom. We can understand a mother's devotion, love, and ambition for her boys, but this was extreme. Jesus responded with a question to James and John, "Can you drink the cup I drink or be baptized with the baptism I am baptized with?" (Mark 10:38).

They both answered, "We can" (verse 39). But little did they—and their mother—realize the cup Jesus spoke of was the cross. Salome must have thought back on that conversation as she gazed sadly upon the beaten, bloodied, traumatized body of Jesus hanging there: *I wanted my sons to have places of honor at his right and left hand, but what I see there are crucified men.*

Thank God he doesn't answer all of our prayers (in the affirmative, at least). As James 4:3 explains, "When you ask, you do not receive, because you ask with wrong motives, that you may spend what you get on your pleasures." Salome must have been ashamed and embarrassed, just as all of us eventually are when we pray selfishly.

A MOTHER'S REWARD

For Mary, the mother of Jesus, the cross was a place of reward. Imagine the anguish she must have felt at this moment. Jesus was her child, the baby she had held in her arms. She knew his utter perfection better than anyone. Yet there she was, watching this wicked crowd of mockers hurl insults at her dear Son. His body was hanging on a Roman cross, and all she could do was watch. No loving mother ever wants to outlive her child, yet here was Jesus, dying in the prime of his life.

The once-tiny forehead she had kissed was now crowned with thorns. The once-tiny hands and feet she'd held had been pierced and nailed to the cross. Those lips she had nursed were now parched and bloodied. His disciples may have forsaken him, but she was by his side until the end.

And she *stood* there. She would not give in to hysterics, running away in horror. She would not faint or crumple to the ground. She would be strong for Jesus and stand there. She was the very model of courage.

Mary had faced difficulties from the very beginning, when God touched her and Jesus was conceived in her womb. Her reputation was questioned. The Pharisees, at one point, told Jesus, "We are not illegitimate children. . . . The only Father we have is God himself" (John 8:41). The scandalous implication was that Mary had conceived Jesus out of wedlock. She made the long, difficult journey to Bethlehem while she was far along in her pregnancy and gave birth to Jesus in a barn. We love to romanticize the Christmas story, but the fact is that it was a long, hard journey and a terribly unsanitary place to give birth. After

Jesus was born, Mary and Joseph had to flee to Egypt because Herod wanted to kill the baby Messiah. Many small children were killed in Bethlehem as the paranoid tyrant searched for the child.

As she stood at the foot of the cross, something profound was happening to Mary. Perhaps as she looked up at Jesus, it all came into focus. Perhaps for the first time, she realized Jesus was not her child, but she was his.

82

The Day the World Went Dark

For the Lord your God is a merciful God; he will
not abandon or destroy you or forget the covenant
with your forefathers, which he confirmed to them by oath.

Deuteronomy 4:31

We have a tendency to grow a bit complacent about the crucifixion. Maybe it's because we know the story so well, or maybe it's because we have a sanitized Hollywood version of the events in our minds. Or maybe it's because we simply cannot comprehend the horror of that day.

As the hours crept by, the earth itself began to mourn the Savior. Without explanation, the mid-afternoon sky turned dark. This would not be the first time we read of in Scripture where God had done something like this. He caused a great darkness to cover the land of Egypt (see Exod. 10:21–22). And some forty years later, God caused the sun to stand still during one of Israel's battles (see Josh. 10:12–14).

This darkness at the crucifixion was probably a sign of God's judgment. Isaiah spoke of "darkness and distress" that would cover the land: "In that day they will roar over it like the roaring of the sea. And if one looks at the land, he will see darkness and distress; even the light will be darkened by the clouds" (Isa. 5:30).

The Creator was dying on the cross and all creation, shrouded in blackness, was in pain.

ABANDONED BY GOD?

The darkness was pierced by the voice of Jesus as he spoke from the cross: "My God, my God, why have you forsaken me?" (Matt. 27:46). These words surprise us, disarm us, and cause us to wonder what Jesus meant. But we may never fully know, because, in many ways, this moment is impossible for human beings to fathom.

No man or woman has ever experienced such loneliness and isolation as Jesus did at this point. In spite of the betrayal and abandonment of his friends, Jesus knew his Father was still with him. He said, "But a time is coming, and has come, when you will be scattered, each to his own home. You will leave me all alone. Yet I am not alone, for my Father is with me" (John 16:32). But at the cross, God the Father turned away his face. Why? Because God, in all his holiness, could not look at sin. The holy Father had to turn away his face and pour his wrath upon his Son.

Jesus felt forsaken of God, because this was the necessary consequence of sin. He experienced this separation from God so that we don't have to. Jesus was forsaken so that we might be forgiven. Jesus entered the darkness so that we might walk in the light. As we read in Isaiah 53:5, "But he was pierced for our transgressions, he was crushed for our iniquities; the punishment that brought us peace was upon him, and by his wounds we are healed."

THE DEEPEST PAIN

The physical pains of crucifixion, horrible as they were, were nothing when compared to the wrath of the Father being poured out upon his Son. This is what caused Jesus's sweat to become like drops of blood in Gethsemane. This is why he looked ahead to the cross with such horror. We can't begin to understand what he was going through at this time. All of our worst fears about the horrors of hell—and more—were realized by Jesus as he received the full impact of our sin.

This indeed was God's most painful moment. This was the greatest sacrifice God could have possibly made on our behalf.

WHEN GOD SEEMS ABSENT

This brings us back to the question Jesus asked (one we ask, too): "Why have you forsaken me?" But for Jesus, this was not a cry *against* the Father, but *to* him.

In times of crisis, many people will cry out *at* God. They're angry with him and want to blame him for their struggles. "I'm mad at God!" they say. Or they doubt God's wisdom in their circumstances. But this wasn't the case with Jesus. His cry was "My *God*, and *my* God."

Job, after his suffering, said, "Though he slay me, yet will I hope in him; I will surely defend my ways to his face" (Job 13:15). And when many of Jesus's followers were turning away, Peter said, "Lord, to whom shall we go? You have the words of eternal life" (John 6:68). When we don't understand what God is doing, we should always fall back on that which we do understand: God loves us and has our best interests in mind. You may have felt abandoned by God, but God has never forsaken you.

Perhaps you feel alone, even forsaken, right now. Maybe it seems as though God has somehow forgotten you. But nothing could be further from the truth. Jesus was forsaken so we might never be forsaken. He experienced terrible loneliness and isolation so we would never be alone. He was misunderstood so we might know the truth and be set free. He died so we might live. God has promised, "Never will I leave you; never will I forsake you" (Heb. 13:5). That's a promise we can trust.

83

WHY JESUS DIED

But this is how God fulfilled what he had foretold
through all the prophets, saying that his Christ would suffer.

Acts 3:18

If you are the kind of person who wears a cross necklace, or hangs a cross in your house, I have a question for you. Do you ever think about what that cross represents? I don't just mean thinking about who it stands for, but thinking about the true meaning of the cross.

The cross is the end and the beginning joined together. It is both death and life, sin and grace. It is where everything was finished and where everything started.

THE BATTLE CRY OF THE CROSS

Right before Jesus died, he spoke again. John wrote, "When he had received the drink, Jesus said, 'It is finished.' With that, he bowed his head and gave up his spirit" (John 19:30). This statement from the cross was not the whimper of a defeated man. It was the triumphant shout of victory of the Son of God.

He didn't say "I am finished." His wasn't the shout of a victim overwhelmed by circumstances. His was the shout of a victor who had overcome all his enemies. In Greek, the statement is one word, consisting of ten letters: *tetelestai*. It means "It *is* finished, it *stands* finished, and it *always will be* finished."

Matthew's Gospel tells us Jesus shouted this with a loud voice (see Matt. 27:50). I call it the battle cry of the cross. It's as if Jesus was saying, "The war is over." These words were

not only heard by those who stood at the foot of the cross—
the soldiers, the group of brave women, and John. They also
reverberated, no doubt, through the forces of heaven and hell.
In the presence of the Father, they were a cry of victory. They
marked the birth of a new covenant relationship between God
and humanity.

A JOB COMPLETED

"It is finished!" or *"Tetelestai!"* was a commonplace term in
the first century. It was used by workers when they had completed a job: *"Tetelestai*—I have finished the work you gave me
to do."* Jesus Christ had completed the job the Father had given
him to do. One day, we all will have to give an account of what
we have done with our lives. Romans 14:12 says, "So then, each
of us will give an account of himself to God." We need to find
the work God has given us to do . . . and then do it.

All of the Old Testament sacrifices were pointing to what
Jesus would do on the cross. John the Baptist said of him, "Look,
the Lamb of God, who takes away the sin of the world!" (John
1:29). When Jesus died, his followers probably felt like *they* were
finished. All their hopes and dreams were dashed as they looked
at their dead leader hanging on that cross. But everything was
proceeding as God had planned it.

The storm had finally passed, the cup Jesus had been given
had been drained, the devil had done his worst, and the Lord
had bruised him. The darkness had ended.

A MEANS TO AN END

As we have looked at what Jesus went through leading up to,
and on, the cross, we may wonder, "*Why* did he have to suffer
and die like that?" Well, there are a number of reasons.

First, he suffered and died to show his love for us. Jesus said,
"For God so loved the world that he gave his one and only Son,
that whoever believes in him shall not perish but have eternal

life" (John 3:16). If ever you're tempted to doubt God's love for you, look at the cross.

He also suffered and died to absorb the wrath of God. If God were not just, there would be no demand for his Son to suffer and die. And if God were not loving, there would be no willingness for his Son to suffer and die. But God is both just and loving. At the cross, God lovingly met his own demand for justice. We have sinned against and have offended God. So that just and loving God sent Jesus as the substitute for us. God's wrath that should have been placed on us was placed on him.

Conventional wisdom says God "grades on the curve." In other words, if our good deeds outweigh our bad deeds, then we're okay. But that's neither biblical nor true. If we are saved from the consequences of our bad deeds, it will not be because they weighed less than our good deeds. Salvation isn't attained by balancing records. It is only acquired by canceling records! This is why Jesus suffered and died for us. Colossians 2:13–14 says, "He forgave us all our sins, having canceled the written code, with its regulations, that was against us and that stood opposed to us; he took it away, nailing it to the cross."

Finally, Jesus suffered and died to provide our forgiveness and justification. "Since we have now been justified by his blood, how much more shall we be saved from God's wrath through him!" (Rom. 5:9). To be justified means to be forgiven of the wrong we have done. But it is also a legal term that means, "Just as if it never happened."

Imagine being in debt for $10 million. You had charged yourself into oblivion, and there was no conceivable way to pay back those debts. In fact, you have exactly $1.34 in your checking account. Now, imagine a complete stranger heard about your situation and said, "I love you so much, I'm going to pay off your debts." And then he pays off your debt of $10 million.

You would say, "Thank you so much! I can't believe I'm debt-free!"

Then he says, "I think you ought to go down and check your account balance." So you go down to your local ATM machine and check your balance. And then you see it: $20 million! Not only did he forgive you of a debt of $10 million and pay it for you, but he put $20 million in your account!

Think about that for a moment. And then think about the fact that what God did for you is infinitely greater. Now that's a lot to be thankful for. And it came as a result of God's most painful moment.

84

A New Beginning

We were therefore buried with him through baptism into
death in order that, just as Christ was raised from the dead
through the glory of the Father, we too may live a new life.

Romans 6:4

American corporations trying to break into international markets
sometimes have a very difficult time communicating uniquely
American ideas and colloquialisms. The problem is that something often gets lost in the translation. In Italy, for example, a
campaign for Schweppes Tonic Water translated the name into
Schweppes Toilet Water.

When Coca-Cola was introduced in China, it was first ren-
dered as "Ke-kou-ke-la." Unfortunately, it wasn't until after
thousands of signs had been printed that the company discovered
the phrase means, "Bite the wax tadpole," or "Female horse
stuffed with wax," depending on the dialect.

In Taiwan, the translation of the Pepsi slogan, "Come alive
with the Pepsi Generation," translated, "Pepsi will bring your
ancestors back from the dead."

When General Motors introduced the Chevy Nova in South
America, the company apparently was unaware that in Spanish,
"No va" means, "It won't go."

Things Aren't Always What They Seem

In the same way, when Jesus spoke to his disciples about his
impending death and resurrection, it seemed to go right over their
heads. They just didn't get it. Jesus spoke in plain and simple

terms, yet his message didn't penetrate their minds or hearts. As they read the Old Testament, they saw the glory but not the suffering. They saw the crown but not the cross.

As Jesus went to his death, they must have thought he had let them down. And for many, perception is often reality. Perhaps you feel that way right now as well. Perhaps you feel as though God has somehow let you down, that he hasn't kept his promises. But Jesus hadn't failed the disciples, they had failed to see what he had come to do. The same is true of us when it seems as though God has failed us. Perhaps we need a new understanding of his ways.

All the disciples could see was that their Master had been killed—and not just killed, but tortured, humiliated, and murdered in cold blood before their very eyes. When he uttered the words "It is finished!" from Calvary, it seemed for them that indeed it was finished.

Two disciples on the road to Emmaus pretty much summed up how everyone felt: "But we had hoped that he was the one who was going to redeem Israel" (Luke 24:21). Prior to the crucifixion, everything seemed to be progressing beautifully. When Jesus rode into Jerusalem, it appeared to the disciples that he was finally ready and willing to establish the kingdom as Israel's long-awaited Messiah.

But then, without warning, everything began to unravel in the upper room. Jesus just didn't sound like himself, speaking as though it were an end to something. Then came the arrest, the trial, the crucifixion, the horror of it all. How could anything good come after this?

What the Resurrection Means

But what a difference a day makes! Jesus rose from the dead as he had promised repeatedly. This would forever change that group of disillusioned, discouraged, and frightened followers into bold and courageous disciples who turned their world upside-down.

Of course, not everyone believes Jesus Christ rose from the dead, and I think there are reasons for that. I don't think people reject Christ's resurrection because they have carefully researched it and have concluded that the evidence for its historicity and reality came up wanting. I think they reject it for the same reason they reject the biblical account of the creation: If God did indeed create the world, then we're not just highly evolved animals. It means we are responsible to our Creator and will have to answer for our actions. And if the resurrection of Jesus is true, then there *is* life after death.

The real reason a person doesn't believe is not intellectual or rational, but moral and spiritual. David wrote, "The fool says in his heart, 'There is no God'" (Ps. 14:1). The fact that the foolishness referred to is moral, and not intellectual, is clear from the rest of the text: "They are corrupt, their deeds are vile; there is no one who does good." Atheism's rejection of God appeals to people who wish to avoid judgment for their sinful lifestyles.

LIFE WITHOUT GOD

If you don't have God at the beginning, then you don't have God at the end. And you don't have God in the middle, either. If you believe you evolved, then you say your life is an accident, maybe even a mistake. You have come from nowhere, you are going nowhere, and your life has no eternal purpose. You don't belong to anyone, and you have no accounting to give to anyone.

But we were created by God, and we will be judged by God: "For he has set a day when he will judge the world with justice by the man he has appointed. He has given proof of this to all men by raising him from the dead" (Acts 17:31). This reminds us, among other things, that God's justice ultimately will prevail. We have all witnessed wrongs committed against others (and ourselves). But it's all going to be settled at the judgment seat of Christ, who rose from the dead and conquered sin, forever.

85

THE DAY THAT CHANGED EVERYTHING

> He was not seen by all the people, but by witnesses whom God had already chosen—by us who ate and drank with him after he rose from the dead.
>
> Acts 10:41

Jesus's friends thought their lives had changed for the worst. What they didn't know was how dramatically their lives were about to shift. Imagine being one of these desolate, grieving friends of Jesus, all your hopes dashed, all your dreams buried in a cave with your Lord. Then imagine this:

> Early on the first day of the week, while it was still dark, Mary Magdalene went to the tomb and saw that the stone had been removed from the entrance. So she came running to Simon Peter and the other disciple, the one Jesus loved, and said, "They have taken the Lord out of the tomb, and we don't know where they have put him!"
>
> John 20:1–2

THE WOMEN ARRIVE

Luke 8:2 simply describes Mary Magdalene as someone "from whom seven demons had come out." She most likely had lived a very wicked life until Jesus came along. From that moment on, she completely turned her back on her previous life. And she became a fervent, devoted follower of Christ.

She probably had a sleepless night and couldn't wait until the break of day. So early the next morning, Mary rose and was joined by another Mary (the wife of Clopas), Salome, and others. All they wanted to do was to anoint Jesus's dead body. This was the first-century equivalent of placing a beautiful bouquet of flowers on a loved one's grave. You just want to do something—anything.

As they made their way to the tomb, they were concerned about how to move the stone so they could get in. They arrived at the tomb and were shocked to find the stone had been rolled away. It didn't even cross the women's minds that Jesus had risen. They thought someone had taken the body. But why? Who? And where?

Where Is Jesus?

The ladies huddled and decided that Peter and John should be told. Mary was either dispatched or she volunteered, and then she made her way to where they were.

Meanwhile, the other women cautiously approached the empty tomb. There they saw angels:

> The angel said to the women, "Do not be afraid, for I know that you are looking for Jesus, who was crucified. He is not here; he has risen, just as he said. Come and see the place where he lay. Then go quickly and tell his disciples: 'He has risen from the dead and is going ahead of you into Galilee. There you will see him.' Now I have told you." So the women hurried away from the tomb, afraid yet filled with joy, and ran to tell his disciples.
>
> Matthew 28:5–8

Meanwhile, Mary found Peter and John, and they both ran back to the tomb, leaving Mary in their dust:

> Both were running, but the other disciple outran Peter and reached the tomb first. He bent over and looked in at the strips of linen lying there but did not go in. Then Simon Peter, who was behind him, arrived and went into the tomb. He saw the strips of

linen lying there, as well as the burial cloth that had been around Jesus's head. The cloth was folded up by itself, separate from the linen. Finally the other disciple, who had reached the tomb first, also went inside. He saw and believed.

John 20:4–8

Notice from verse 4 that John outran Peter. Why do we have this little detail? Was it because John was the "other disciple" mentioned in this verse, and he just wanted us to know that he won? I think there is a more spiritual reason behind it.

Peter's last contact with Jesus was when he had denied him in the firelight of Caiaphas's courtyard. Yes, Peter was running to the tomb, but he probably had mixed emotions, to say the least. And this would also explain the way he looked into the tomb.

TAKING A LOOK

The story tells us how these three people—Mary, Peter, and John—reacted to the empty tomb of Jesus. Their reactions tell us a great deal about what the resurrection would mean for them. John tells us that Mary "looked into the tomb" (John 20:11 NKJV), Peter "saw" (verse 6), and John "saw and believed" (verse 8).

The word used to describe the way Mary looked into the empty tomb simply means she saw—just the ordinary word. The word used to describe Peter's looking is quite different. It means, "He looked carefully and critically." He wasn't sure what to make of it. Luke's Gospel tells us he went home again, "wondering to himself what had happened" (Luke 24:12).

Lastly, we see John's reaction. The word used for his looking into the tomb means, "He perceived and understood." John, the "apostle of love," always seemed to have a unique spiritual perception. At the Sea of Galilee, when a stranger called from shore, "Boys, do you have any fish?" it was John who knew it was Jesus and said, "It's the Lord!" Apparently, all that time leaning on Jesus's chest seemed to help.

It's interesting how several people can see the same thing in different ways. For example, when a husband and wife are out driving and he loses his way, she says, "Let's ask for directions."

But he hears, "You're not a man."

She says, "Can I have the remote control?"

He hears, "Let's watch something that will bore us beyond belief!"

She says, "I would like to redecorate."

He hears, "Let's take our money and flush it down the toilet."

She says, "You need to get in touch with your feelings."

He hears, "Blah, blah, blah."

She says, "Are you listening to me?"

He hears, "Blah, blah, blah."

It all depends on how you look at things.

86

ALONE AT THE TOMB

You will be secure, because there is hope;
you will look about you and take your rest in safety.

Job 11:18

The group at the empty tomb of Jesus quickly dissipated, leaving Mary Magdalene alone. She was confused, abandoned, and unsure what to believe. She was at the breaking point and simply burst into tears.

The angels who were still standing at the entrance to the tomb asked Mary why she was crying. She replied, "They have taken my Lord away, . . . and I don't know where they have put him" (John 20:13). Mary didn't care much about angels. They may have impressed the other women, who bowed before them, but not Mary. All she wanted was Jesus. When she watched him die, she was lost. Now, she had only her own pain, and her heart was once again as empty as the tomb—and just as desolate.

MARY'S SURPRISE

Maybe she thought to herself, *What do I do now? I can't go back to what I used to do. Where will I go, who will I be without Jesus?*

Then a voice spoke, "Woman, . . . why are you crying? Who is it you are looking for?" Thinking it was the gardener speaking, she said, "Sir, if you have carried him away, tell me where you have put him, and I will get him" (John 20:15). Even if Jesus were slight of weight, Mary was offering—without thinking—to carry the weight that would be more than a strong man could carry. But she didn't think of this, because she loved the Lord. How touched Jesus must have been by this statement.

Softly, Jesus said, "Mary."

Suddenly, like a bolt of lightning, Mary recognized this voice. It was Jesus!

"Rabboni!" she cried out, which means "Master," or "Teacher." Then she flew to Jesus and wrapped her arms around him, like a drowning person clutching her rescuer.

Jesus then said, "Do not hold on to me, for I have not yet returned to the Father. Go instead to my brothers and tell them, 'I am returning to my Father and your Father, to my God and your God'" (John 20:17).

"Do Not Hold On to Me"

What did this mean? After all, a few hours later, Jesus would invite Thomas to touch him. And in Matthew's Gospel, we read, "They came to him, clasped his feet and worshiped him" (Matt. 28:9). His words to Mary presented an entirely new command; he had never told anyone to stay away from him. His words to Mary could be translated, "Stop clinging to me." It was as if to say, "Don't cling to me in the old way. Things are different now. This desire to hold on to the physical part of me must change. In the past, I was there for you to reach out and touch. But things are going to change now. They will be even better, because I am going to live in your heart! You never will be separated from me again. So let go and prepare for something more."

Mary couldn't wait to tell the others. I find it interesting that the first person the Lord appeared to was a woman. The first human to preach the resurrection was a woman. It's hard for us to appreciate how significant this was. Among the Jews in that day, the testimony of a woman wasn't held in high regard. The rabbis taught, "It is better that the words of the Law be burned than be delivered to a woman."

By appearing first to Mary, Jesus was essentially saying, "Oh, yeah? Well check this out, boys! I am choosing a woman to be the first to proclaim my message!"

LESSONS FROM THE RESURRECTION

The story of the resurrection reminds us that God loves ordinary, flawed people. They didn't come any more ordinary or flawed than Peter, John, and Mary. This brings hope to all who were the last picked for the team, the ones who didn't break records, win contests, or distinguish themselves from the crowd. These are often the very people God chooses to do extraordinary things.

We also discover that God blesses those who seek him with all their heart. There's no question that Mary's persistent faith and love were richly rewarded. She was the last at the cross and the first at the tomb. She cared little for the social ramifications of being a friend to Jesus, whether it was popular, or even if it meant her life. She loved Jesus, and she wanted the world to know. She made time early in the morning and found the risen Lord.

Mary was weak in her faith but strong in her love for Jesus. She came with what she had, and Jesus met her more than halfway. Perhaps your faith has been weakened. Maybe tragedy has befallen you, a loved one has died, or a marriage has collapsed. Your faith and hope have suffered. Jesus is calling your name, just as he called Mary's. He is standing next to you, ready to restore your hope.

This is the message of the resurrection of Jesus: Death is not the end. Because Jesus died and rose again, we shall be raised like him. Now that's what I call a new beginning.

87

JESUS AND THE SKEPTIC

Be merciful to those who doubt.

Jude 22

All my life, I have always asked lots of questions. It is because of my upbringing, which, in many ways, was really no upbringing at all, due to my mom's alcoholic lifestyle. I was passed off from living with her, to my grandparents, to aunts, to military school, and then back to my mom again. I learned to be self-sufficient and had to develop survival skills to . . . well, survive.

So when I first encountered Christians, it was hard for me to wrap my mind around the concept of faith. I was doubtful God could love someone like me. But at the same time, my desire for something good and right drove me on. So, I took that leap of faith and gave my heart to Jesus Christ.

After my conversion, I had my share of doubts. *Was this real? Was God really going to work in my life? Could God ever have a plan for someone like me? Could I ever actually live this Christian life?*

Some Christians are reluctant to admit they have any questions at all. I think sometimes we have the idea that to question God is an act of spiritual treason, or that doubt is an unpardonable sin. But I am confident that if we're honest, we could all admit to having struggled with doubt at times.

Doubt was certainly on the minds of the disciples as word of the resurrection spread. Mary Magdalene had met the risen Lord near the tomb and had told the others. Jesus then appeared to two discouraged disciples on the road to Emmaus. They came back and told the disciples how Jesus had met them and talked with them. And then . . . guess who came to dinner?

> On the evening of that first day of the week, when the disciples were together, with the doors locked for fear of the Jews, Jesus came and stood among them and said, "Peace be with you!" After he said this, he showed them his hands and side. The disciples were overjoyed when they saw the Lord. Again Jesus said, "Peace be with you! As the Father has sent me, I am sending you." And with that he breathed on them and said, "Receive the Holy Spirit."
>
> John 20:19–22

Now that Christ had died and risen, his work was complete. The Holy Spirit was about to come to the disciples, which Jesus had promised. The same is true when we put our faith in Christ. Ephesians 1:13–14 tells us, "Having believed, you were marked in him with a seal, the promised Holy Spirit, who is a deposit guaranteeing our inheritance until the redemption of those who are God's possession—to the praise of his glory."

The risen Lord personally appeared to the disciples, the Holy Spirit was breathed on them, and a charge was given to represent him. It was quite a meeting—a bad day to miss church. But one of them did: Thomas.

WHY WE NEED EACH OTHER

Like the others, Thomas was devastated by the crucifixion of Jesus. And in his personal pain, he withdrew not only from God, but from others. But when we are hurting, that is the time we should be seeking out the fellowship of God's people. So when the disciples saw Thomas, they probably said, "You should have been there last night!" Thomas had missed out on an appearance of the Lord himself. "Now Thomas (called Didymus), one of the Twelve, was not with the disciples when Jesus came. So the other disciples told him, 'We have seen the Lord!' But he said to them, 'Unless I see the nail marks in his hands and put my finger where the nails were, and put my hand into his side, I will not believe it" (John 20:24–25).

An Honest Request

No one could ever accuse Thomas of failing to think for himself. He certainly was an individual, not willing to simply believe what others said or experienced. And there's nothing wrong with that. How easily Jesus could have ignored Thomas altogether, seeing that he wasn't even present with the disciples when Jesus appeared: "Hey, Buddy, you snooze, you lose! Show up next time!" But Jesus condescended to Thomas's personal doubts and skepticism, and he lovingly offered him personal proof:

> A week later his disciples were in the house again, and Thomas was with them. Though the doors were locked, Jesus came and stood among them and said, "Peace be with you!" Then he said to Thomas, "Put your finger here; see my hands. Reach out your hand and put it into my side. Stop doubting and believe." Thomas said to him, "My Lord and my God!"
>
> John 20:26–28

Jesus does that with countless others, coming to where they are, lovingly offering personal proof of his love for them. When I first came to Christ, I was filled with doubt and skepticism. I said to God, "If you're real, then you need to make yourself real to me!" It wasn't rebellion on my part or even a challenge to God. It was a plea, a cry for God to help a hardened, skeptical, cynical young man. And he did.

Reasonable Doubt

Thomas didn't ask for anything more than what the others had seen. He didn't ask for a special revelation. He simply asked for the same proof. And though we can argue the fact that he wanted to personally see the risen Lord, everyone needs to internalize their own faith—not live off the faith of others.

Upon seeing the risen and living Lord, Thomas's skepticism gave way to belief: "My Lord and my God!" he cried. This is the difference between skepticism and unbelief. Skepticism contains an openness to belief, but unbelief refuses to believe. Skepticism is honesty; unbelief is stubbornness. Skepticism is looking for light, while unbelief is content with darkness. So skeptics of the world, fear not, for God offers all the proof we need.

88

THE GIFT OF GRACE

They will be a garland to grace your head and
a chain to adorn your neck.

Proverbs 1:9

If you've ever wronged someone, then bumped into them on the street or at church before you've had the chance to apologize, then you have some idea of how nervous the disciples must have been when they realized Jesus had returned.

The disciples were gathered together, Thomas was with them, and Jesus appeared, greeting them with the familiar Jewish phrase, "*Shalom*," or "Peace to you!" How easily he could have greeted them with rebuke! He could have reminded them of their unfaithfulness and fear the previous weekend. He could have laid them all off and hired a new set of disciples. But grace is giving us what we don't deserve.

A STEP TOWARD THE SAVIOR

Up to this point, no doubt, Thomas admired Jesus as a tremendous hero, role model, and messenger of God, but John tells us how that changed when Jesus arrived to prove his resurrection to Thomas. "Then he said to Thomas, 'Put your finger here; see my hands. Reach out your hand and put it into my side. Stop doubting and believe.' Thomas said to him, 'My Lord and my God!'" (John 20:27–28). It's not enough to acknowledge Jesus as God. We need to make him *our* God. The Bible tells us that "Even the demons believe that—and shudder" (James 2:19).

Also notice that Jesus accepted this worship from Thomas, saying, "Because you have seen me, you have believed; blessed are those who have not seen and yet have believed" (John 20:29). When God led Peter to bring the gospel to Cornelius, the man fell at Peter's feet. But Peter corrected him: "Stand up, . . . I am only a man myself" (Acts 10:26). Peter would not accept worship or allow someone to bow before him. That was for God alone.

Jesus, however, was God, and therefore rightfully accepted Thomas's worship. So much for those who argue that Jesus never claimed to be God.

A BLESSING FOR US

Jesus's response to Thomas is a special blessing for us as well. It's important for us to know that God loves to bless us. Jesus both began and concluded his earthly ministry with blessing people. When children came to him, he took them in his arms and blessed them. And Luke's Gospel tells us that after his resurrection, "When he had led them out to the vicinity of Bethany, he lifted up his hands and blessed them" (Luke 24:50).

Jesus isn't speaking of a subjective faith, but a satisfied faith. He is speaking of a faith that is content with what God gives rather than one that focuses on what God doesn't give. The Bible is filled with accounts of visions, signs, wonders, and spiritual gifts at work. Perhaps we have longed for a vision of an angel or a miracle in our own lives. That isn't a bad thing, necessarily.

When I first became a Christian, I wanted a miracle-filled life. I wanted a personal word from the Lord (audibly if possible) every day, like an operative on *Mission Impossible*: (Mission Impossible theme playing in the background) "Good morning, Mr. Laurie. Your mission, should you choose to accept it, is . . ." I wanted signs and wonders and emotional experiences. After a time, I discovered the Christian life is a life of faith, not feeling. The Bible says, "The righteous will live by faith" (Rom. 1:17).

Some Christians want these things to the extent that they become a distraction. Consider this: believers should not follow after signs and wonders; signs and wonders should follow after them.

Seeing and experiencing miracles does not guarantee a strong faith. Pharaoh saw many miracles, but his heart only became harder. The children of Israel saw dramatic signs from God, but they rebelled. The church of Corinth was awash in miracles—and also in rampant immorality. I'm not trying to denigrate miracles, signs, and wonders. God can bring them where and when he desires, and when he does, we are to thank him. But we also are to be thankful for what we presently have—and apply it in our lives.

Now, we have not seen Jesus . . . yet. But the day is coming when every eye shall see him. The day is coming when every knee shall bow. Until then, we are to believe.

BELIEF FROM UNBELIEF

Mark's Gospel tells the story of a distraught father who brought his demon-possessed child to Jesus. "If you can do anything, take pity on us and help us," he told Jesus.

Jesus answered, "Everything is possible for him who believes."

So the man prayed an honest prayer: "I do believe; help me overcome my unbelief!" (see Mark 9:22–24).

You might be a skeptic today, like I once was. You may say, like Thomas, "Show me, and I'll believe." But Jesus said, "Call to me and I will answer you and tell you great and unsearchable things you do not know" (Jer. 33:3). Just come to God with your doubts, questions, and even your skepticism, and say, "Lord, come into my life. Forgive me of my sins."

89

BACK IN THE BOAT

And I tell you that you are Peter, and on this rock I will
build my church, and the gates of Hades will not overcome it.

Matthew 16:18

The disciples thought they could live without Jesus. But Jesus
wasn't willing to let them go. He wanted to help his disciples by
teaching them a valuable lesson. So he called to them from the
shore: "Friends, haven't you any fish?" (John 21:5). Of course
Jesus knew the answer. The point was to show the disciples the
futility of living without him.

God did the same thing in the Garden of Eden after Adam
had eaten the forbidden fruit: "Have you eaten from the tree that
I commanded you not to eat from?" (Gen. 3:11). God wanted
acknowledgment and confession from Adam, not excuses. To
Elijah, who had run away in terror after receiving a death threat
from Queen Jezebel, God posed the question, "What are you
doing here, Elijah?" (1 Kings 19:9).

To his disciples out in the boat Jesus was saying, "Well, boys,
are the fish biting?" In other words, had they been successful?
Were they satisfied? Were they willing to admit their failure?
Before we can find God's forgiveness and restoration, we must
first admit our need. That means no excuses, and no blaming
others—just honest confession as we take responsibility for our
own actions.

PROBLEM SOLVED

Jesus would never leave his friends, so he offered them an option. He said, "Throw your net on the right side of the boat and you will find some" (John 21:6). This would have reminded Peter of an earlier encounter with Jesus at the Lake of Gennesaret, when Jesus told him, "Put out into deep water, and let down the nets for a catch" (Luke 5:4). And just as it happened then, it happened again. The net was filled to capacity with fish. John, the spiritually perceptive one, recognized what was happening. "It is the Lord!" he told Peter. So Peter impulsively flung himself into the water and swam toward the shore. By this time, the disciples would have been about three hundred feet out. John tells us,

> The other disciples followed in the boat, towing the net full of fish, for they were not far from shore, about a hundred yards. When they landed, they saw a fire of burning coals there with fish on it, and some bread. Jesus said to them, "Bring some of the fish you have just caught." Simon Peter climbed aboard and dragged the net ashore. . . . Jesus said to them, "Come and have breakfast."
>
> John 21:8–12

Imagine, the Creator of the universe in human form, who had just been crucified and was now resurrected, was serving breakfast to his disciples.

ONE QUESTION, THREE WAYS

Now, we come to the three profound questions Jesus had for Peter: "Simon son of John, do you truly love me more than these?" (John 21:15). Interesting. The way we determine someone's spirituality is by his or her doctrine, or faith, or even personal obedience to the Word of God. These are all very valid, but they are not necessarily the most important. Jesus didn't ask, "Are you doctrinally correct?" or "Do you have faith?"

or "Have you been obedient?" Rather, he asked, "Do you love me?" Why is this question so important? Because if you really love the Lord, you will *want to* be doctrinally correct, studying his Word. If you really love the Lord, you will *want to* grow in faith. If you really love the Lord, you will *want to* obey him. And if these things don't follow your love for God, then it isn't real love. It would be like saying, "I love my wife," but not wanting to spend time with her. That isn't love. So Jesus wanted to put first things first: "Do you love me?"

Peter arrived on shore, dripping wet, filled with excitement to see the risen Lord. At the same time, he was feeling a deep shame for his sins. As they sat around the fire, there was an awkward silence. Peter's thoughts probably flashed back to the glow of another fire where he had denied the Lord. Jesus broke the silence and reached out to Peter.

Jesus proceeded to test Peter three times to see if he had really learned anything from his failure. In the original language, the word "love" Jesus used came from the Greek word *agape.* It is an all-consuming, dedicated, sacrificial love. We get our English word "agony" from it. So Jesus was saying, "Peter, do you *agape* me? Do you have this all-consuming, sacrificial, 100 percent love?"

"Lord, I *phileo* you," Peter responded. In other words, "Lord, I love you with a 60 percent love."

Peter wasn't saying he didn't love Jesus. He simply wasn't boasting of his love for the Lord any longer. And that's a good thing for us to remember. Our love can be fickle and moody at times. But God's love is consistent and unchanging regardless of the circumstances. John wrote, "How great is the love the Father has lavished on us, that we should be called children of God!" (1 John 3:1).

When we sin we are tempted to believe we have no love for Christ. But let this story encourage you. It's impossible for any true lovers of God to pursue an endless course of sin. It is quite possible for us to stumble in sin, although we will be miserable there.

90

Signs of Love

By day the Lord directs his love, at night his song is with me—
a prayer to the God of my life.

Psalm 42:8

Three times Jesus asked Peter the same question. And Jesus is still asking this question today: Do you love me? Most of us would say yes, but let's take a test from Scripture. Here are the signs the Bible points to as the earmarks of a person who truly loves God and is growing in that love: *A person who loves the Lord will long for personal communion with him.* David wrote,

> My soul thirsts for you, my body longs for you, in a dry and weary land where there is no water. I have seen you in the sanctuary and beheld your power and your glory. Because your love is better than life, my lips will glorify you. I will praise you as long as I live, and in your name I will lift up my hands. My soul will be satisfied as with the richest of foods; with singing lips my mouth will praise you. On my bed I remember you; I think of you through the watches of the night.
>
> Psalm 63:1–6

When your heart overflows with love for God, you will delight in worship and praise. When you're really in love with someone, you can't wait to be in his or her presence. When you hear of husbands and wives who are spending less and less time together, spending more time with their friends, and taking separate vacations, this is a warning signal.

LOVING AS GOD LOVES

A person who loves the Lord will in turn love the things he loves. We know what God loves by what he has declared to us in his Word. The psalmist declared, "Oh, how I love your law! I meditate on it all day long" (Ps. 119:97). Do you love the Word of God? Do you love his church? Do you love lost people? God does.

A person who loves the Lord will in turn hate the things he hates. As we grow in our love for the Lord, his nature will become our nature. Psalm 97:10 says, "Let those who love the LORD hate evil, for he guards the lives of his faithful ones and delivers them from the hand of the wicked." God hates sin, and so should we. The Bible tells us, "Hate what is evil; cling to what is good" (Rom. 12:9). The problem is, we are often fascinated by evil. We are drawn to it, first as observers, then as participants. But instead of flirting with evil, we need to run from it.

A person who loves the Lord will long for Christ's return. The apostle Paul rejoiced in what the future had in store: "Now there is in store for me the crown of righteousness, which the Lord, the righteous Judge, will award to me on that day—and not only to me, but also to all who have longed for his appearing" (2 Tim. 4:8).

LIVING FOR GOD

Finally, a person who loves the Lord will keep his commandments. Jesus said, "Whoever has my commands and obeys them, he is the one who loves me. He who loves me will be loved by my Father, and I too will love him and show myself to him" (John 14:21). And he also asked, "Why do you call me 'Lord, Lord,' and do not do what I say?" (Luke 6:46).

Not only was Peter forgiven of his sins, but he was recommissioned for service. Perhaps you have failed recently. Maybe you have done things you're ashamed of. You understand what Peter must have felt like that morning at the Sea of Tiberias, reluctant to look at Jesus. Perhaps you even have been reluctant to go to church—or to pick up this book. But Jesus is asking you today, "Do you love me?" If you do, then get on with the business of walking with and obeying him.

THE CALL OF CHRIST

Just as Jesus called from the shore to the disciples, he is calling you right now. Perhaps you're curious and want to know more about Jesus Christ. If so, he says, "Come and see for yourself!"

Maybe you're tired. Jesus says, "Come and rest."

It could be your life hasn't been what you had hoped it would. If you've been pulling up a lot of empty nets, then it's time to let Jesus come on board.

Come and see.

Come and rest.

Come now.